# The Power of Place

# The Power of Place

# Urban Landscapes as Public History

Dolores Hayden

The MIT Press Cambridge, Massachusetts London, England

First MIT Press paperback edition, 1997


Chapter 6 of this book appeared in *California History*, Fall 1989. Parts of chapters 2 and 10 appeared in the *Journal of Urban History*, August 1994.

This book was set in Melior and Franklin Gothic No. 2 by Asco Trade Typesetting Ltd and was printed and bound in the United States of America.

ISBN 0-262-08237-3 (hc)—ISBN 0-262-58152-3 (pbk);
ISBN-13 978-0-262-08237-2 (hc)—ISBN-13 978-0-262-58152-3 (pbk)

10 9 8

Library of Congress Cataloging-in-Publication Data

Hayden, Dolores.
The power of place : urban landscapes as public history / by Dolores Hayden.
p. cm.
Includes bibliographical references and index.
ISBN 0-262-08237-3 (Hc.), 0-262-58152-3 (Pbk.)

1. Public history—California—Los Angeles. 2. Public spaces—California—Los Angeles. 3. Minorities—California—Los Angeles—History. 4. Women—California—Los Angeles—History. 5. Historic sites—Interpretive programs—California—Los Angeles. 6. Cities and towns—Interpretive programs—California—Los Angeles. 7. Public art—California—Los Angeles. 8. Los Angeles (Calif.)—History. I. Title.
F869.L857H39 1995
304.2—dc20 94-23424
CIP

**The beauty that we see in the vernacular landscape is the image of our common humanity: hard work, stubborn hope, and mutual forbearance striving to be love.**

**John Brinckerhoff Jackson, *Discovering the Vernacular Landscape***

**An aesthetic of urban design must be rooted in the normal processes of nature and living.**

**Anne Whiston Spirn, *The Language of Landscape***

**There is . . . a politics to place construction ranging . . . across material, representational and symbolic activities which find their hallmark in the way individuals invest in places and thereby empower themselves collectively by virtue of that investment.**

**David Harvey, "From Space to Place and Back Again"**

For Laura

## Contents

# Preface

I moved from Cambridge, Massachusetts, to Los Angeles in 1979. "You'll know Los Angeles," residents told me, "after five years or one hundred thousand miles on your car, whichever comes first." Between 1979 and 1984, I struggled to understand Los Angeles, to have some idea of the history of South Central and East Los Angeles as well as the mainly white Westside. As I grappled with my own lack of local background, I began to see how many authors of books on the history and design of American cities have ignored the working women and men of diverse ethnic groups who inhabit the urban landscape. Yet memory endures in certain places. A student introduced me to a group of retired farmworkers who gathered daily in a wooden bungalow behind a Filipino community center to play cards and talk about their working lives. And a young colleague invited me to an annual reunion where hundreds of men, women, and children evicted from Chavez Ravine in the 1950s came together to reminisce decades after their neighborhood had been bulldozed.

Coming to know Los Angeles led me to launch The Power of Place in 1984. It was a small nonprofit corporation, and its purpose was to situate women's history and ethnic history in downtown, in public places, through experimental, collaborative projects by historians, designers, and artists. This book is an extended reflection on the next eight years of experience in both research and practice, an exploration of how the social history of urban space may lead to public history and public art, and may enlarge the practice of urban preservation and the writing of urban history by introducing new perspectives. As Hazel Carby, noted scholar in African American studies, has commented in "The Multicultural Wars," reading about the lives of Americans in diverse communities is only the first step in knowing these same communities as urban places through personal experience.[1] For many of us, recognizing the importance of race and gender to urban history will "escort one to the edge of one's ignorance," as historian Patricia Limerick has put it, and launch "a constant process of disorientation and reorientation, taking part in the pleasures, the discomforts, and the conflicts of discovery."[2]

I am writing for three audiences: students and scholars in the growing, interdisciplinary field of the history of urban space; practitioners who deal with urban space as public historians, preservationists, environmentalists, urban planners, architects, landscape architects, and artists; and the general reader who cares about public places and may be active as a citizen sustaining the quality of a city or town. No two readers will come to this text with the same amount of scholarly, technical, or political background, so I have attempted to summarize basic concepts and to avoid using academic and professional jargon. I cite more specialized works in the endnotes, books that discuss the practice of public history, preservation, and public art, and others that take up the issues raised by processes of collaboration between communities and professionals, or between professionals trained in different areas.

Academic debates concerning the definition of history, the relationship between history and memory, and the difference between personal memory and collective memory promise to flourish for another decade, along with theoretical studies of the manipulation of places by capitalist development. My own purpose is to explore some ways that locating ethnic and women's history in urban space can contribute to what might be called a politics of place construction, redefining the mainstream experience, and making visible some of its forgotten parts. I have also cited current debates about space, postmodernism, and global capitalism in the endnotes, where possible, since my focus is not primarily theoretical, and many of these debates proceed without much concern for issues of gender or race at the urban scale. At the same time, I recognize that what happens at the urban scale is constantly influenced by the global restructuring of capital and production. My concern in this book is not to analyze these processes but to discuss how to identify and preserve significant public places in opposition to them.

Part I, "Claiming Urban Landscapes as Public History," proposes new ways to understand the urban cultural landscape. "Contested Terrain" asks why social and aesthetic perspectives on the historic built environment have traditionally been fragmented. "Urban Landscape History: The Sense of Place and the Politics of Space" proposes a more unified approach to scholarship, combining aesthetics and politics and incorporating ethnic and women's history. "Place Memory and Urban Preservation" connects urban landscape history to memory rooted in places. It suggests how new kinds of professional roles and public processes may broaden the practice of public history, architectural preservation, environmental protection, and commemorative public art, when these are perceived as parts of a wider urban landscape history.

Part II, "Los Angeles: Public Pasts in the Downtown Landscape," reflects on practical work in one city. "Invisible Angelenos" looks at the problem of making visible the history of a city where the majority of residents are women and people of color. "Workers' Landscapes and Livelihoods" sketches the production of space in the urban landscape—the ranches, vineyards, groves, oil fields, and factories of the growing city—and the women, children, and men who formed the labor force of the expanding city between the earliest settlement and World War II. It traces the involvement of many different ethnic groups in building up the city. "The View from Grandma Mason's Place" examines the city's landscape through the perspective of one working woman, Biddy Mason, an African American midwife, a former slave who won her freedom in court and lived in the city from the 1850s through the 1890s.

Introducing the complexities of combining public history with public art, "Rediscovering an African American Homestead" traces the Biddy Mason project where I served as director and historian, working with Donna Graves and three artists—Susan King, Betye Saar, and Sheila Levrant de Bretteville—to mark the midwife's homestead. "Reinterpreting Latina History at Embassy Auditorium" discusses the reinterpretation of a union hall used by Latina and Russian Jewish garment workers—a project directed by Donna Graves, and including artists Rupert Garcia and Celia Muñoz, as well as architect Brenda Levin and historians Vicki L. Ruiz and

George J. Sánchez. "Remembering Little Tokyo on First Street" covers the creation of a historic district of small businesses launched by Japanese American immigrants. It looks at how architectural preservation—proposed by the Los Angeles Conservancy—an ethnic history museum—The Japanese American National Museum—and public art—by artists Sheila Levrant de Bretteville, Sonya Ishii, and Nobuho Nagasawa, sponsored by the Community Redevelopment Agency and originally planned by Susan Sztaray with The Power of Place—all contribute.

These chapters sketch the story of Los Angeles as African American, Latina, and Asian American women and their families have known it, the often overlooked history of the majority of Los Angeles citizens. Each project deals with bitter memories—slavery, repatriation, internment—but shows how citizens survived and persevered to make an urban life for themselves, their families, and communities. "Storytelling with the Shapes of Time" sums up the transformations of roles and expectations that these projects demanded from many of the participants, and explores some of the obstacles to community processes and interdisciplinary work, as well as some of the rewards. The epilogue, "Los Angeles after April 29, 1992," deals with the intensifying problems of Los Angeles after the civil unrest that erupted in South Central LA and illustrates the difficulties of finding common meaning in the devastated urban landscape, as well as the ways work on urban landscape history can contribute to inner-city reconstruction.

Most books deal with theory or practice, but not both, and, as a construction, a book does not easily reflect the iterative process of working with abstract ideas in social contexts, where practice informs theory as much as the other way around. So readers can engage with these parts in any order that seems appropriate, viewing the terrain of urban landscape history and then negotiating the terrain of urban practice, as I have ordered it, or the other way around. Looking down on a city from its highest skyscraper and walking the streets provide different sensations for the mind and the eye, just as considering the intellectual possibilities of the cultural landscape provides a very different sensation from encountering officials at public meetings while trying to plan a project.

The Power of Place worked with collaborative teams of historians, artists, architects, planners, and sometimes with other organizations, to find ways to rebuild public memory in the city around different sites and buildings. I am grateful to many people for their contributions to the projects and the research for this book. The Graduate School of Architecture and Urban Planning at UCLA housed The Power of Place for many years. I am especially mindful of the intellectual and political support offered by Harvey Perloff, founding dean of the school, who understood that The Power of Place was going to be controversial and encouraged me, as a scholar, to learn to live with controversy. I would also like to give special thanks to Sheila de Bretteville, whose early thoughts about "Private Conversations and Public Places" at the Woman's Building in Los Angeles launched a generation of women artists, writers, and designers into the public realm. Her skill and dedication helped make a lasting place out of a small space allocated to Biddy Mason, and her sidewalk for Little Tokyo promises to set a new standard for public participation in public art processes in the city of Los Angeles.

An interdisciplinary, culturally complex public project of any kind means many different things to the people who engage with it, and I can only try to convey the fullness of energy and talent contributed by many people over eight years of urban work. During these years there were many ups and downs, and sometimes a sense of accomplishment was possible only after a good deal of experiment, often with accompanying frustrations. Students from the Graduate School of Architecture and Urban Planning at UCLA worked as interns, researchers, and administrators, while professional artists, designers, and historians were recruited to join collaborative teams for specific projects. Donna Graves, a former art museum curator, served first as my assistant on the Biddy Mason project and then as Executive Director of the organization. She directed the Embassy project, ably assisted by

Nancy Stillger and other students. Margaret Crawford, Drummond Buckley, Catherine Gudis, Daniel Hernandez, Sue Ruddick, Mary Beth Welch, Ronald Brooks, Rudolph Brown, Timothy Sales, Susan Sztaray, Sherry Katz, Gail Dubrow, and Carolyn Flynn all contributed their own special insights and professional expertise, on their way to careers as historians or urban planners. (Donna Graves has edited a book on collaborative processes, *Shared Spaces*, and Gail Dubrow has written a book on *Planning for the Preservation of American Women's History*, both soon forthcoming.) Many more students and interns engaged in the process, and I have tried to thank each one personally when their work is cited. Most of all, people in Los Angeles sustained the project by their enthusiastic response.

Beyond the historians on the project teams, others involved with workshops included Emory Tolbert, William Mason, Knox Mellon, Vicki Ruiz, Albert Camarillo, and Kevin Starr. Members of the board included film maker and preservationist Margaret Bach, artist and designer Sheila Levrant de Bretteville, urban economic development planner Rebecca Morales, activist, lawyer, and black studies teacher Arnett L. Heartsfield, Jr., preservationist and historian Knox Mellon, and historian George J. Sánchez.

Peter Marris, as both colleague and husband, has contributed his wide knowledge of cities around the world and their people, as well as his specific comments on numerous drafts. Martin Wachs, my colleague at UCLA, was a steadfast supporter who never missed a public history workshop, though his own field is transportation. Michelle Isenberg, Robert Chattel, and Richard Rowe, as well as planners at the Los Angeles Community Redevelopment Agency and members of the University of Southern California administration, helped in crucial ways. The manuscript—parts and the whole, in various stages—has benefited from helpful readings by scholars interested in public space and history, including Temma Kaplan, Knox Mellon, Lucy Lippard, Michael Dear, Sam Bass Warner, Jr., Sarah Deutsch, Eric Foner, Jeremy Brecher, Richard Orsi, David Lowenthal, Gwendolyn Wright, and Lynn

Lees. I have also had extended conversations with Setha M. Low about place and with Ronald Lee Fleming, John Kuo Wei Tchen, and Pamela Worden, who have shared their sense of processes and products in public history and public art. The editors of *Passage*, *Places*, *The Public Historian*, *California History*, *The Journal of Architectural Education*, *Design Quarterly*, and *The Journal of Urban History*, as well as of the book *American Architecture: Innovation and Tradition*, published drafts of parts of the book, beginning in 1983, and I appreciate their advice.[3] I am fortunate in the intellectual support I have had from Roger Conover, senior editor at the MIT Press, and in the skills of Matthew Abbate, Mimi Ahmed, Brooke Stevens, and other staff members there.

Fellowships to support this book came from the National Endowment for the Arts, Design Arts Program, and from the American Council of Learned Societies/Ford Foundation. Some of the earliest research was funded by the California Council for the Humanities and by UCLA. The public art and public history projects of The Power of Place were funded by the National Endowment for the Arts, Design Arts Program and Art in Public Places Program, the California Arts Council, the Los Angeles Community Redevelopment Agency, the National State County Partnership, the Los Angeles Cultural Affairs Commission, the National Trust for Historic Preservation, the First African Methodist Episcopal Church of Los Angeles, and various private donors.

At UCLA, the skills of Donna Mukai, Diane Mills, and Vanessa Dingley and the institutional support of Allen Heskin as chair of the Urban Planning Program were invaluable. At Yale, Robin Byrd, Andrew Myers, Frank DeSantis, Cathy Gudis, and Herman Ilaw Hernandez tirelessly obtained photographs and permissions. Robert Frew and Leigh Knopf-Williams untangled my software. My thanks to everyone.

# The Power of Place

# I Claiming Urban Landscapes as Public History

# 1 Contested Terrain

I still remember my first sight of New York. It was really another city when I was born—where I was born. We looked down over the Park Avenue streetcar tracks. It was Park Avenue, but I didn't know what Park Avenue meant downtown. The Park Avenue I grew up on, which is still standing, is dark and dirty. No one would dream of opening up a Tiffany's on that Park Avenue, and when you go downtown you discover that you are literally in the white world. It is rich—or at least it looks rich. It is clean—because they collect the garbage downtown. There are doormen. People walk about as though they owned where they are—and indeed they do. . . . You know—you know instinctively—that none of this is for you. You know this before you are told. And who is it for and who is paying for it? And why isn't it for you?

James Baldwin, "A Talk for Teachers," 1963

In January and February of 1975, Herbert J. Gans and Ada Louise Huxtable debated the public meaning of the built past on the op-ed pages of the *New York Times*. Gans, an urban sociologist, opened the controversy by attacking New York's Landmarks Preservation Commission for what he called rewriting New York's architectural history: "Since it tends to designate the stately mansions of the rich and buildings designed by famous architects, the commission mainly preserves the elite portion of the architectural past. It allows popular architecture to disappear. ... This landmark policy distorts the real past, exaggerates affluence and grandeur, and denigrates the present."[1]

Ada Louise Huxtable, architectural critic, member of the editorial board of the *Times*, and a supporter of preservation, defended the commission's record. She warned: "to stigmatize major architectural monuments as products of the rich, and attention to them as elitist cultural policy, is a perverse and unserviceable distortion of history.... These buildings are a primary and irreplaceable part of civilization. Esthetic singularity is as important as vernacular expression. Money frequently made superb examples of the art of architecture possible, and there were, fortunately, great architects to design and build great buildings."[2] She also argued that, in addition to monumental buildings she judged essential to public culture, the Landmarks Preservation Commission had designated twenty-six historic districts including 11,000 buildings, most of them what she called "vernacular."

Gans countered Huxtable's plea for "great buildings" by great architects in a second article, where he made the case for a broader approach to ordinary buildings as part of public history: "Private citizens are of course entitled to save their own past, but when preservation becomes a public act, supported with public funds, it must attend to everyone's past."[3] He went on to analyze New York's designations in quantitative terms, looking at landmark designations among buildings erected after 1875: 105 of 113 were by major architects, 25 by one firm, McKim, Mead and White. Most of these were not accessible to the public. 91 were located in Manhattan, which left the other boroughs with very few or no historical landmarks. 17 of the 26 historic districts were built as neighborhoods of the affluent. Although these numbers might have won the day, Huxtable nevertheless had the last word. Gans's second article was not published on the op-ed page, but appeared in abbreviated form as a letter to the editor. His arguments about the equitable use of public funds and the neglect of boroughs other than Manhattan never reached a metropolitan audience.

In this exchange from two decades ago, a leading urban sociologist and a distinguished architectural critic were unable (or unwilling) to understand each other's language. When he said "architecture," he meant that all urban buildings, or the built environment. When she said "architecture," she meant buildings designed by professionally trained architects operating with aesthetic intent, or perhaps one percent of the built environment. When he said "vernacular" he was classifying buildings by social use, referring to definitions of social class and accessibility, and implying tenements, sweatshops, saloons, and public bathhouses. When she said "vernacular," she meant that the architect was unknown, and the classification was by architectural style and/or typology, such as Greek Revival side-hall row house, so that, in her terms, there would be many "vernacular" town houses on the wealthy Upper East Side, as well as in more modest areas. When he said "neighborhood" he meant a complex network of social as well as spatial ties, and implied a working-class population, giving examples like Williamsburg and Bushwick. She said "neighborhood" and meant the physical line bounding a historic district such as the Upper East Side or Greenwich Village.

As they argued, their underlying values made the debate more heated. He wanted more social history, she wanted more culture. He wanted taxpayers' money spent equitably in all neighborhoods. She believed aesthetic resources should be ranked in order to buy the best in terms of connoisseurship. She wasn't against designating the occasional public bathhouse or tavern or tenement or philanthropic housing project as a landmark, but her passion was for preserving the aesthetic qualities of great buildings: "Because their restoration and re-use are formidably difficult and costly and their land values usually high, these are the hardest buildings to preserve." She scolded Gans, "So 'elite' them not; they need all the help they can get."[4]

They exasperated each other, because he wasn't interested in aesthetic quality and she didn't want to spend a lot of money on social issues. He believed the past had different meanings for different people, all equally valid in social terms, but he had little interest in design: "whether buildings are beautiful or ugly is a personal judgment that should not be left solely to professional estheticians." She argued that history, expressed in designated landmarks, was socially "inclusive," yet she didn't agree that there could be more than one standard of what was important when it came to aesthetics.

Neither delved into the downside of what they promoted. He did not explore the problems of preserving and interpreting ghetto locations or bitter memories. She did not ask how to justify spending taxpayers' money without giving public access or interpretation. And neither of them tried to identify opportunities to realize both his ideal of urban preservation and her ideal of architectural preservation. For instance, more warehouses, shops, and boardinghouses, the kind of urban vernacular buildings he defended, might have been saved to supply the social and economic context for the row houses she defended. Or the private clubs and mansions she defended could have been interpreted in terms of the masons' and carpenters' skills in constructing them, and the maids' and gardeners' skills in maintaining them, to supply the urban working-class history he desired.

The debate appeared to be a dead end at the time. But from today's perspective, both Gans and Huxtable seem to have shared a common concern that Americans were losing significant public memories when neighborhoods like Boston's Italian American West End were bulldozed or monuments like New York's Penn Station met the wrecking ball. And they shared an inability to predict either the changed social composition of the city's population two decades after their debate, or the worsening economic condition of the American city. As an eminent sociologist, Gans was an outsider to preservation, raising some polemical questions. He thought this debate was primarily about social class in the city. As a distinguished architectural critic, Huxtable emphasized buildings. Neither anticipated that the 1990s would involve major controversies about the definitions of public history and public culture in a democratic society.[5]

Today, debates about the built environment, history, and culture take place in much more contested terrain of race, gender, and class, set against long-term economic and environmental problems, especially in the large cities of the United States. The citizens of New York were still over 75 percent white in the 1970 Census. By 1990, New York had a white population of only 38 percent, outnumbered by African Americans, Latinos, and Asian Americans who comprised 61 percent of the city, including both long-term residents and new immigrants.[6] (Across the nation, the top ten cities show similar changes, from about 70 percent white in 1970 to less than 40 percent in 1990.)[7] Federal support for cities has declined over the past twenty years, while extreme poverty and homelessness have become increasingly concentrated in the inner city. Environmental problems are concentrated there as well—unhealthy air, polluted harbors, abandoned housing units, rusting bridges, broken water mains.

While the urban landscape may be less attractive, there are far more claims being made upon it to furnish resources for public history and public culture. Today, James Baldwin's question "And why isn't it for you?" echoes across the city streets where he felt excluded as a young boy. An African American group seeks support for the protection of the remaining traces of the African Burial Ground near the present City Hall in Manhattan, and its sympathetic interpretation as a site where people of color were buried in the colonial period. "The city has been commemorating other aspects of its history for three hundred years," notes Howard Dobson, head of the Schomburg Center for Research on Black Culture in New York.[8] His indignation is echoed by many other groups across the city and across the country. Centuries of neglect of ethnic history have generated a tide of protest—where are the Native American, African American, Latino, and Asian American landmarks?

Gender involves similar, interconnected questions. Why are so few moments in women's history remembered as part of preservation? Why are so few women represented in commemorative public art? And why are the few women honored almost never women of color? Issues about working-class and poor neighborhoods remain—what, if anything, can public history or preservation projects add to their identity and economic development? How do these issues intersect with the claims for ethnic history and women's history? And what kind of public processes and techniques best represent commitment to social history in public places?

Private nonprofit institutions (such as museums and preservation groups), as well as public agencies (city landmarks commissions and arts councils), are challenged daily to become accountable to the diverse urban public, whose members are both taxpayers and potential audiences. Current census statistics suggest that it is indeed appropriate to find new ways to deploy tax dollars in cultural programs that may range from exhibits to the preservation of historic buildings and landscapes, or the creation of permanent works of public art. While some private institutions and public agencies struggle to address their ways of working, and sponsor various kinds of "cultural planning" in order to become more accountable, many impatient citizens' groups are putting forward their own projects to represent their communities' history and tell their own stories in public space.[9] The politics of identity—however they may be defined around gender or race or neighborhood—are an inescapable and important aspect of dealing with the urban built environment, from the perspectives of public history, urban preservation, and urban design.

Indeed, interest in themes of identity is not limited to the city. Women's history and ethnic history drive many preservation controversies across the country. Recently, the National Trust for Historic Preservation established goals for cultural diversity in preservation.[10] There have been successful efforts in Tennessee, Alabama, and Georgia to preserve buildings associated with the civil rights movement and Martin Luther King. *Historic Preservation News* recently announced the start of an effort to preserve the Woolworth's store in Greensboro, North Carolina, "where four black students staged a historic sit-in at the whites-only lunch counter in 1960."[11] At the same time, the first national conference on Preserving Women's History was held at Bryn Mawr in 1994, coinciding with the publication of a guide to landmarks of women's history across the nation, *Susan B. Anthony Slept Here.*[12] Dozens of other guides to landmarks of ethnic and women's history are becoming available from states and cities around the country, as well as scholarly accounts.[13] Yet both the ethnic and women's landmarks are proposed at a time when some of the large questions Gans and Huxtable debated are still unresolved. Architecture, as a discipline, has not seriously considered social and political issues, while social history has developed without much consideration of space or design. Yet it is the volatile combination of social issues with spatial design, intertwined in these controversies, that makes them so critical to the future of American cities.

Change is not simply a matter of acknowledging diversity or correcting a traditional bias toward the architectural legacy of wealth and power. It is not enough to add on a few African American or Native American projects, or a few women's projects, and assume that preserving urban history is handled well in the United States in the 1990s. Nor is it enough to have a dozen different organizations advocating separate projects. Instead, a larger conceptual framework is required to support urban residents' demands for a far more inclusive "cultural citizenship," as Rina Benmayor and John Kuo Wei Tchen have defined it, "an identity that is formed not out of legal membership but out of a sense of cultural belonging."[14] Benmayor and Tchen argue that public culture needs to acknowledge and respect diversity, while reaching beyond multiple and sometimes conflicting national, ethnic, gender, race, and class identities to encompass larger common themes, such as the migration experience, the breakdown and reformulation of families, or the search for a new sense of identity in an urban setting. They are asking for an extremely subtle evocation of American diversity, which at the same time reinforces our sense of common membership in an American, urban society.

Public space can help to nurture this more profound, subtle, and inclusive sense of what it means to be an American. Identity is intimately tied to memory: both our personal memories (where we have come from and where we have dwelt) and the collective or social memories interconnected with the histories of our families, neighbors, fellow workers, and ethnic communities (figure 1.1). Urban landscapes are storehouses for these social memories, because natural features such as hills or harbors, as well as streets, buildings, and patterns of settlement, frame the lives of many people and often outlast many lifetimes. Decades of "urban renewal" and "redevelopment" of a savage kind have taught many communities that when the urban landscape is battered, important collective memories are obliterated. Yet even totally bulldozed places can be marked to restore some shared public meaning, a recognition of the experience of spatial conflict, or bitterness, or despair. At the same time, in ordinary neighborhoods that have escaped the bulldozer but have never been the object of lavish municipal spending, it is possible to enhance social meaning in public places with modest expenditures for projects that are sensitive to all citizens and their diverse heritage, and developed with public processes that recognize both the cultural and the political importance of place.

The power of place—the power of ordinary urban landscapes to nurture citizens' public memory, to encompass shared time in the form of shared territory—remains untapped for most working people's neighborhoods in most American cities, and for most ethnic history and most women's history. The sense

**1.1 Women and men of all ethnic groups, workers in the Long Beach shipyards during World War II. (UCLA Special Collections.)**

of civic identity that shared history can convey is missing. And even bitter experiences and fights communities have lost need to be remembered—so as not to diminish their importance.

To reverse the neglect of physical resources important to women's history and ethnic history is not a simple process, especially if preservationists are to be true to the insights of a broad, inclusive social history encompassing gender, race, and class. Restoring significant shared meanings for many neglected urban places first involves claiming the entire urban cultural landscape as an important part of American history, not just its architectural monuments. This means emphasizing the building types—such as tenement, factory, union hall, or church—that have housed working people's everyday lives. Second, it involves finding creative ways to interpret modest buildings as part of the flow of contemporary city life. A politically conscious approach to urban preservation must go beyond the techniques of traditional architectural preservation (making preserved structures into museums or attractive commercial real estate) to reach broader audiences. It must emphasize public processes and public memory. This will involve reconsidering strategies for the representation of women's history and ethnic history in public places, as well as for the preservation of places themselves.

Despite the eloquent pleas of a few architects in favor of building and city as "theatres of memory" as much as futuristic "theatres of prophecy,"[15] most consideration of the built past in the United States has dealt with European architectural fashions and their application to American monumental buildings. For many years American cultural landscapes and urban vernacular buildings were ignored. Today the vernacular is subjected to more thoughtful scholarly and professional analysis, but often this is still based on physical form rather than social and political meaning. The same kind of creative work writers and artists have undertaken in claiming American places is yet to be accomplished by American architects, landscape architects, and urban planners, locating ourselves in the cities of the United States in a serious way, coming to terms with the urban landscape as it exists and has existed, connecting the history of struggle over urban space with the poetics of occupying particular places.[16]

This implies a stronger connection between scholarship in urban landscape history and work on cultural identity, as well as firmer links between theory and practice in urban design. In the last decade there has been an explosion of scholarly work on cultural identity. Cultural and political geographers have mapped the tensions as urban communities struggle for terrain; social historians have looked at women's, workers', and ethnic history. Scholars in cultural studies have forged new syntheses of work on feminist, class, and ethnic issues, and emphasized new ways of looking at popular culture. At the same time there has been new interest in studying space as a cultural product. Environmental psychologists and anthropologists have examined people's responses to places. Environmental historians have applied new agendas to urban history. Geographers have put forth "postmodern geographies" with some connection to architecture and literary studies. But all this work is fragmented in separate disciplines, disciplines that are constantly attempting to reconnect aspects of knowledge within themselves, whether social, economic, environmental, or cultural. Also, scholars' fresh insights about urban space are not always available to professionals and community activists struggling to create new kinds of projects. And the activists' or artists' experience does not always reach either professionals or scholars.

A socially inclusive urban landscape history can become the basis for new approaches to public history and urban preservation. This will be different from, but complementary to, the art-historical approach to architecture that has provided a basis for architectural preservation. A more inclusive urban landscape history can also stimulate new approaches to urban design, encouraging designers, artists, and writers, as well as citizens, to contribute to an urban art of creating a heightened sense of place in the city. This would be urban design that recognizes the social diversity of the city as well as the communal uses of space, very different from urban design as monumental architecture governed by form or driven by real estate speculation.

As the debate between Gans and Huxtable demonstrated, saving a public past for any city or town is a political as well as historical and cultural process. Decisions about what to remember and protect involve the grounding of historical scholarship as well as the possibilities of public history, architectural preservation, environmental protection, and commemorative public art. Yet all of these approaches to conserving the past operate in partial and sometimes contradictory ways. The traces of time embedded in the urban landscape of every city offer opportunities for reconnecting fragments of the American urban story.[17] But until historians have more understanding of the intricate relationship between cultural landscape history and place-specific memory, making the whole more than the sum of the parts will be difficult.

George Kubler once described the historian's craft as delineating the "shape of time." The art of the historian, he wrote, resembles that of the painter, "to discover a patterned set of properties that will elicit recognition all while conveying a new perception of the subject."[18] The historian who confronts urban landscapes in the 1990s needs to explore their physical shapes along with their social and political meanings. Learning the social meanings of historic places by discussing them with urban audiences involves the historian in collaboration with the residents themselves as well as with planners and preservationists, designers and artists. It engages social, historical, and aesthetic imagination to locate where narratives of cultural identity, embedded in the historic urban landscape, can be interpreted to project their largest and most enduring meanings for the city as a whole.

# 2 Urban Landscape History:

# The Sense of Place and the Politics of Space

**Authentic knowledge of space must address the question of its production.**

**Henri Lefebvre, *The Production of Space***

Layered with the traces of previous generations' struggles to earn a living, raise children, and participate in community life, the vernacular landscape, as John Brinckerhoff Jackson writes, "is the image of our common humanity—hard work, stubborn hope, and mutual forbearance striving to be love."[1] His definition carries cultural geography and architecture straight toward urban social history. At the intersection of these fields lies the history of the cultural landscape, the production of space, human patterns impressed upon the contours of the natural environment. It is the story of how places are planned, designed, built, inhabited, appropriated, celebrated, despoiled, and discarded. Cultural identity, social history, and urban design are here intertwined.

Indigenous residents as well as colonizers, ditchdiggers as well as architects, migrant workers as well as mayors, housewives as well as housing inspectors, are all active shaping the urban landscape. Change over time can be traced in incremental modifications of space as much as in an original city plan or building plan. This chapter sketches a way to frame the social history of urban space, a scholarly terrain where many fields overlap. It combines an approach to aesthetics (based on work dealing with the sense of place from the humanities, architecture, and landscape traditions in geography and environmental psychology) with an approach to politics (based on work on space in the social sciences and economic geography) and suggests how both apply to the history of urban landscapes.

"Place" is one of the trickiest words in the English language, a suitcase so overfilled one can never shut the lid. It carries the resonance of homestead, location, and open space in the city as well as a position in a social hierarchy. The authors of books on architecture, photography, cultural geography, poetry, and travel rely on "sense of place" as an aesthetic concept but often settle for "the personality of a location" as a way of defining it. Place for such authors may engage patterns in the mellow brick of an eighteenth-century building, the sweep of the Great Plains, the bustle of a small harbor full of sailboats, but such images can easily become cliches of tourist advertising. In the nineteenth century and earlier, place also carried a sense of the right of a person to own a piece of land, or to be a part of a social world, and in this older sense place contains more political history. Phrases like "knowing one's place" or "a woman's place" still imply both spatial and political meanings.

People make attachments to places that are critical to their well-being or distress. An individual's sense of place is both a biological response to the surrounding physical environment and a cultural creation, as geographer Yi-Fu Tuan has argued.[2] From childhood, humans come to know places through engaging all five senses, sight as well as sound, smell, taste, and touch.[3] Extensive research on perception shows the simultaneous engagement of several senses in orientation and wayfinding. Children show an interest in landmarks at three or earlier and by age five or six can read aerial maps with great accuracy and confidence, illustrating the human ability to perceive and remember the landscape.[4]

As social relationships are intertwined with spatial perception, human attachment to places attracts researchers from many fields. Environmental psychologists Setha Low and Irvin Altman define "place attachment" as a psychological process similar to an infant's attachment to parental figures. They also suggest that place attachment can develop social, material, and ideological dimensions, as individuals develop ties to kin and community, own or rent land, and participate in public life as residents of a particular community.[5] (Some earlier sociological studies of the aftermath of urban renewal, those that convey the process of mourning for a lost neighborhood, have utilized attachment theory as well[6] to explain the power of human connections to places that may no longer exist physically.)

Cultural landscape studies, as geographer Carl Sauer developed them, focused on the evolution of places and included the "combination of natural and man-made elements that comprises, at any given time, the essential character of a place."[7] Cultural landscape has much more specific meanings than place. Yet the earliest cultural landscape methods for studying places, and people's shaping of them and attachments to them, were not adequate to convey their political dimensions. Unlike social history, which developed in the 1960s with an urban bias, cultural geography from the 1940s on leaned to the study of rural, preindustrial landscapes, rather than the complicated urban variety, mapping ethnicity along with vernacular house types or patterns of cultivation, considering ecology but avoiding issues of political contestation.[8]

As the productive landscape is more densely inhabited, the economic and social forces are more complex, change is rapid, layers proliferate, and often abrupt spatial discontinuities result that cultural landscape studies seem unable to address adequately. One can't simply turn to economic geography (or any other kind of quantitative analysis) because there the human experience of place is often lost. Rather, the cultural geographer's model of landscape needs to be better anchored in the urban realm, retaining the biological and cultural insights necessary to convey the sense of place while adding more focused analysis of social and economic conflict. This is the project of many politically sensitive geographers today, including Michael Dear, Jennifer Wolch, David Harvey, Neil Smith, Derek Gregory, and Kay Anderson.[9] At the same time, environmental historians like William Cronon are claiming some of this subject matter, with phrases that sound rather like Sauer: "if environmental history is successful in its project, the story of how different peoples have lived and used the natural world will become one of the most basic and fundamental narratives in all of history, without which no understanding of the past could be complete."[10] Yet for many environmental historians, the deployment of land and natural resources has been the central preoccupation, without much concern for the aesthetic and social aspects of the built environment, although the two are intertwined.

At the heart of Carl Sauer's definition of the cultural landscape was "the essential character of a place." It has often proved easier to study either the natural or the built components of a cultural landscape than to wrestle with the combination of the two in the concept of place. In recent decades, as geographers John Agnew and James Duncan have shown, social scientists have frequently avoided "place" as a concept, and thus have sidetracked the sensory, aesthetic, and environmental components of the urbanized world in favor of more quantifiable research with fewer epistemological problems.[11] Some have argued for the importance of an increasingly "placeless world," or a "non-place urban realm," but speaking critically of bad places is more effective than dismissing them as places.[12] The process that transforms places demands analysis. As a field of wildflowers becomes a shopping mall at the edge of a freeway, that paved-over meadow, restructured as freeway lanes, parking lots, and mall, must still be considered a place, if only to register the importance of loss and explain it has been damaged by careless development. Places also suffer from clumsy attempts to market them for commercial purposes: when small towns in Iowa that once seemed to embody everyday life in the Midwest developed "themes" to make them more attractive to tourists, the places became caricatures of themselves.[13]

If place does provide an overload of possible meanings for the researcher, it is place's very same assault on all ways of knowing (sight, sound, smell, touch, and taste) that makes it powerful as a source of memory, as a weave where one strand ties in another. Place needs to be at the heart of urban landscape history, not on the margins, because the aesthetic qualities of the built environment, positive or negative, need to be understood as inseparable from those of the natural environment.[14] Together these two provide the basis for considering the history of the American urban landscape.

## The Production of Space

Henri Lefebvre, the French sociologist who began writing about the "production of space" over two decades ago, provides a framework that can be used to relate the sense of place encountered in cultural landscape studies to the political economy. Lefebvre argues that every society in history has shaped a distinctive social space that meets its intertwined requirements for economic production and social reproduction.[15] In terms of production, Lefebvre would be close to cultural geography in identifying spaces or landscapes shaped for mining, manufacturing, commerce, or real estate speculation. Most original is his analysis of the space of social reproduction, which ranges over different scales, including the space in and around the body (biological reproduction), the space of housing (the reproduction of the labor force), and the public space of the city (the reproduction of social relations). Here he links the physical to the social in decisive ways. (More speculative are his analyses of the role of artists' representations of space, and the role of popular political movements in creating "counter-space" in opposition to existing political structures.) Cultural critic Fredric Jameson, in *Postmodernism*, assessed Lefebvre's importance: he "called for a new kind of spatial imagination capable of confronting the past in a new way and reading its less tangible secrets off the template of its spatial structures—body, cosmos, city. . . ."[16]

Lefebvre suggests that the production of space is essential to the inner workings of the political economy. A small factory on a stream near a waterfall, with a boarding house and a couple of workers' cottages, announces New England in the earliest stages of textile production; a vast aerospace complex next to a suburban tract of ten thousand identical houses exemplifies defense industries and their work force one hundred and fifty years later. But Lefebvre also sees commonalities between the tract houses, the identical suites in corporate skyscrapers, and the identical shops in malls, suggesting that a quality of late capitalist space is the creation of many identical units—similar but not "placeless" places—by the large commercial real estate market that has become, in itself, a distinguishing feature of the economy. And just as analysts begin to count the environmental costs that this production of endless units of salable space may entail, so the cultural costs in terms of identity, history, and meaning can be weighed.[17]

Lefebvre's approach to the production of space can provide a framework for constructing some specific social histories of urban places. Depending on the kinds of arguments historians want to make (and the resources available in oral histories, social histories, and buildings), research might explore working landscapes, territorial histories of groups in the population, or political histories of building types. The first focuses on economic production as it is tied to social reproduction, the others make social reproduction the major theme.

## Working Landscapes

The production of space begins as soon as indigenous residents locate themselves in a particular landscape and begin the search for subsistence. The place may grow into a town, inhabited by new waves of settlers. Many cities begin with farming, mining, fishing, or trading rather than manufacturing. The farm laborers, the miners, the fishermen, or the stall holders in the market, and their families, are the earliest builders of the economic enterprise that eventually becomes a city. Space is shaped for both economic production—barns, or mine shafts, or piers, or a factory—as well as for social reproduction—housing for the workers, managers, and owners, a store, a school, a church. As the town grows, configuring streets and lots formalizes the earliest uses of land and path systems. This leads to infrastructure such as paved roads, bridges, water systems, streetcars, and railroads, all of which have substantial environmental effects.

All of these different kinds of private and public planning activities and public works have a social as well as a technological history.[18] People fight for and against them. People also construct and maintain them (figure 2.1). The ditchdiggers and piledrivers, the streetcar workers and the railroad mechanics, the canal drivers and crane operators represent class, ethnic, and gender history shaping the landscape in ways that have barely been studied. As environmental historian Patricia Nelson Limerick has observed, "Workers, often minority workers, provided the essential labor of envi-

**2.1 Workers' landscapes. Chinese American railroad workers on the tracks, next to an Anglo American supervisor, near Lang, California, 1876. (Security Pacific Collection, Los Angeles Public Library.)**

ronmental change, and members of minority groups often absorbed a disproportionate share of undesirable environmental impacts ... yet environmental history and ethnic history have been very separate enterprises."

The history of the railroad in the nineteenth century offers just one of many possible examples. One can understand the railroad in engineering terms, as the history of trains and tracks, or in architectural terms, as stations and freight yards, or in urban planning terms, as the right and the wrong side of the tracks, without fully capturing its social history as the production of space. Limerick notes that twenty-nine Chinese workers died while building Wrights Tunnel for the South Pacific Coast Railroad through the Santa Cruz Mountains in California in 1879, and dozens more were injured. Other historians have commented that the Chinese "contributed" to

California's economic development. Limerick goes farther: the "'price of progress' had registered in the smell of burnt human flesh."[19] She concludes, "In our times the rediscovery of the landscape hinges on just such recognitions as this one." One could add that coming to terms with ethnic history in the landscape requires engaging with such bitter experiences, as well as the indifference and denial surrounding them.

Like the dwelling, which may be typical of the way millions were sheltered, something as basic as a railroad or streetcar system changes the quality of everyday life in the urban landscape, while marking the terrain.[20] For some it provides jobs in design, or construction, or operation, or maintenance; for others, it makes a journey to work through the city possible; for a few, it may bring profits as an investment. John Stilgoe has shown how to study the clustering of different vernacular building types along railroad lines, and the concept of the space of the railway as a "metropolitan corridor."[21] As Limerick shows, there is also an important underlying story to tell about the work force and the social space of the metropolitan corridor, from the people who blasted the tunnels and drove the trains right down to the workers who kept the cars clean and emptied the trash. From the perspective of social history, it is this story about the work force that can turn an abandoned set of railroad tracks or a decaying freight shed into a potential resource for projects concerned with larger public meanings in the urban landscape.

## Territorial Histories of Cities Based on Race and Gender

Lefebvre emphasized the importance of space for shaping social reproduction. One of the consistent ways to limit the economic and political rights of groups has been to constrain social reproduction by limiting access to space. For women, the body, the home, and the street have all been arenas of conflict. Examining them as political territories—bounded spaces with some form of enforcement of the boundaries—helps us to analyze the spatial dimensions of "woman's sphere" at any given time.[22] And just as gender can be mapped as a struggle over social reproduction that occurs at various scales of space, the same is true of race, class, and many other social issues.

As Michael Dear and Jennifer Wolch have written, the interplay between the social and the spatial is constant: "Social life structures territory ... and territory shapes social life."[23] Ghettos and barrios, internment camps and Indian reservations, plantations under slavery and migrant worker camps should also be looked at as political territories, and the customs and laws governing them seen as enforcement of territory.[24] The territories of the gay and lesbian communities can be mapped. So can those of childhood or old age. The spatial dimensions of class can be illuminated by looking at other boundaries and points of access.[25] Since many of these categories interlock, studying how territories defined by gender, class, race, ethnicity, sexual preference, or age affect people's access to the urban cultural landscape can be frustrating.

How can one find evidence about social groups' experiences of these overlapping territories? Frequently observations about urban space are ignored by historians because the comments appear to be spatial description rather than social analysis, but they can form the basis of a territorial history focusing on access to the public spaces of the city. For example, Loren Miller, Jr., an African American lawyer who grew up in a middle-class family in Los Angeles in the 1940s, didn't see a segregated movie house until he went to Kansas in 1948. He could go to the beach any time on the streetcar. But he observed, "As teen-agers, we knew not to drive into Compton, to Inglewood, not to drive into Glendale 'cause you would just be out, with your hands on top of the car, ... LAPD did the same thing. You got too far south on Western, they would stop you." This man also remembered, as a child, having Japanese American neighbors interned, going to visit them in temporary quarters at the Santa Anita race track, and finding that "soldiers with guns wouldn't let me go on the other side of the table, and they wouldn't let me play with my friends."[26] This is one individual account of spatial barriers about race. Another writer, Lynnell George, comments on this city in the 1940s, "Off-limits for people of color in Los Angeles ran the gamut . . . not West of Main, not Glendale after dusk, never ever Fontana and its dusty flatlands dotted with burning crosses."[27]

Accounts like these begin to make it possible to map spatial segregation for the larger African American community: not only streets and neighborhoods, but schools, hotels, stores, fire stations, swimming pools, and cemeteries would be some of the places to examine. Photographs often convey territorial history as well, documenting both residential segregation and communities' struggles against territorial exclusion (figures 2.2, 2.3).[28] In images of public space from the 1940s, a small cafe has different entrances for "White" and "Colored" labeled over the doors, while a movie theater has a large arrow painted on the side of the building, pointing "Colored" to an exterior stair leading to a balcony. Documentary photography, newspaper photography, commercial photography, and amateur snapshots all reveal different sides of a city. It can be revealing to consider the gender and ethnic background of the photographer as well as the architectural subject selected for the picture.

A territorial history based on limitations of gender in the public spaces of the city would use similar sources and would put buildings or parts of them off limits, rather than whole neighborhoods.[29] In the twentieth century, spatial segregation includes private men's clubs, university faculty clubs, programs in higher education, and numerous other spaces. The segregation need not be absolute—women might be permitted to attend a class, but sit separately, or they might be allowed to enter a club as men's guests, provided they remained in a special room reserved for ladies, and so on. In the nineteenth century the list would be longer, and forbidden activities might include voting, entering a public saloon, or sitting in the main body of an assembly hall rather than the more restricted balcony. To understand the intersecting segregation of race, class, and gender, the spatial dimensions of traditional "woman's sphere" have to be studied in combination

**2.2 Territorial histories. Exclusion of Japanese Americans from a residential neighborhood in Hollywood, California, took the form of signs as well as deed restrictions, 1920s. (Visual Communications.)**

**2.3 Territorial histories. Segregated tract, with African American observer, Los Angeles County, early 1950s. (Southern California Library for Social Studies and Research; the original source is possibly the California *Eagle*, Charlotta Bass Collection.)**

**2.4 Territorial histories. Male and female students sitting separately at a lecture on physics, University of Michigan Medical School, late 1880s. (Bentley Historical Library, University of Michigan.)**

with the spatial limits imposed by race or class. Because white women's clubs, charities, and suffrage organizations were often segregated, African American women sometimes formed their own parallel groups, with their own meeting places, to help working women and girls in their own communities.[30] Or, to take another example, one photograph of a class at a state university open to women in the 1890s shows the men and women sitting separately. It is equally important to ask if there appear to be people of color present, segregated by gender and race, sitting at the very back of each group (figure 2.4).

Political divisions of territory split the urban world into many enclaves experienced from many different perspectives. Cognitive mapping is a tool for discovering fuller territorial information about contemporary populations. Urban planner Kevin Lynch studied mental images of the city by asking people to draw maps or give directions.[31] At the time, in 1960, Lynch suggested that such images could be combined into a composite portrait of a city, useful to urban designers, but not all Bostonians see Boston the same way. Subsequent studies, including some of Lynch's own, explored class, gender, age, and ethnicity. Most striking was a study done in Los Angeles that showed graphically the differences between the residents of an affluent white suburb, an inner-city African American neighborhood, and a mixed neighborhood close to downtown that had long been home to new immigrants working in downtown factories and using a few downtown bus lines.[32] The space of the city, as understood by these different groups, varied greatly in size as well as in its memorable features (figures 2.5, 2.6, 2.7). The maps are striking images of inequality of access to the city.

Lynch's work from the 1960s and 1970s suggests not only that the sprawling, spatially segregated city is difficult for citizens to map, but also that architects and planners, as well as specialists in public history, have an important role to play in making the entire city more coherent in the minds of its citizens. Out of Lynch's work comes what Fredric Jameson has called "an aesthetic of cognitive mapping." Acknowledging

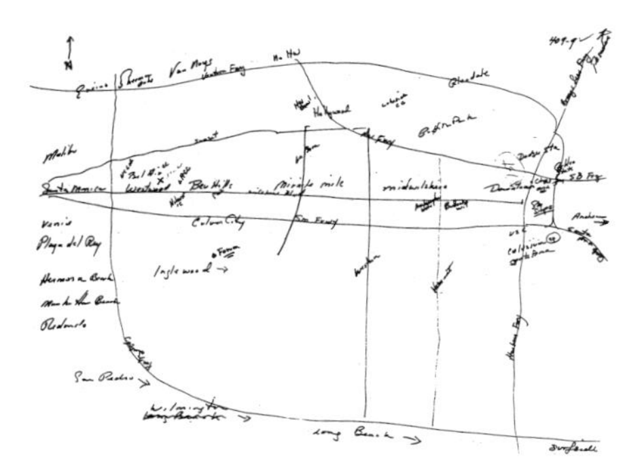


Actual citizen's map: Westwood

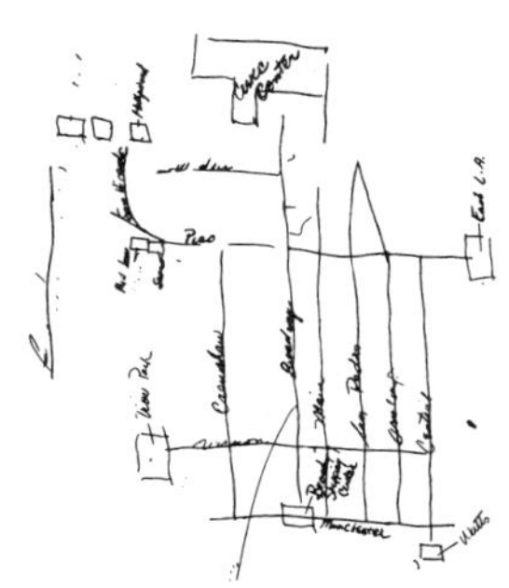


Actual citizen's map: Avalon

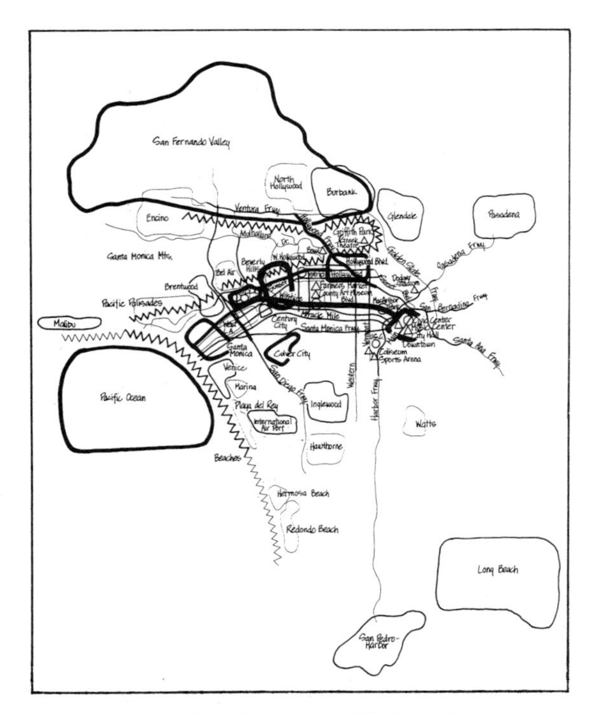


Composite citizen image: Westwood

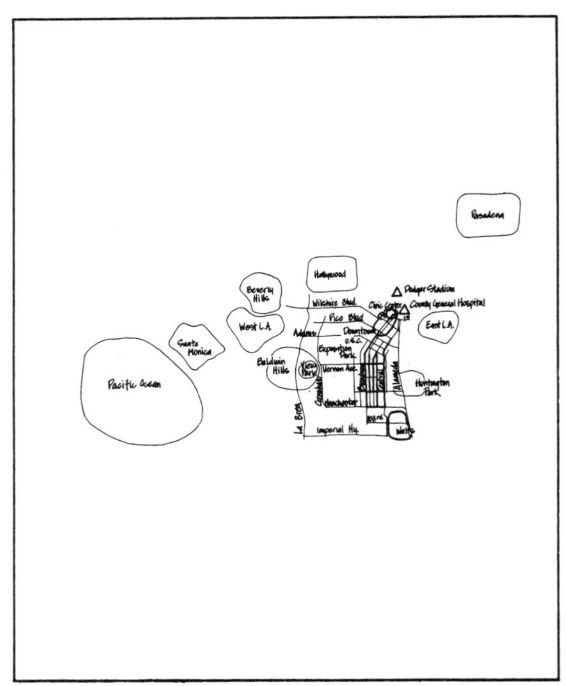


Composite citizen image: Avalon

**2.5, 2.6, 2.7 Cognitive maps of Los Angeles as perceived by predominantly Anglo American residents of Westwood, predominantly African American residents of Avalon, and predominantly Latino residents of Boyle Heights. (*The Visual Environment of Los Angeles*, Los Angeles Department of City Planning, April 1971, pp. 9–10.)**

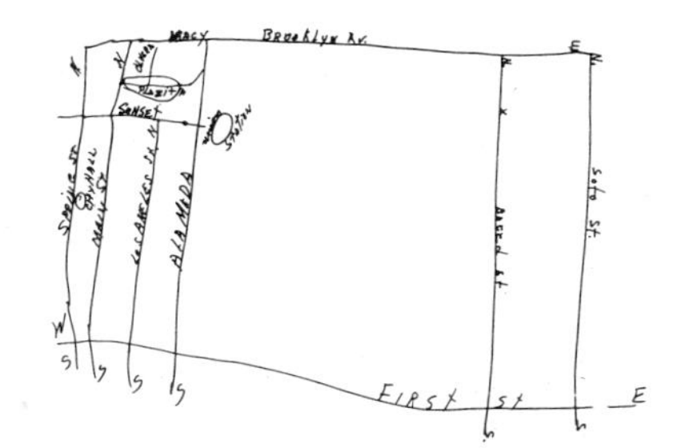


**Actual citizen's map: Boyle Heights**

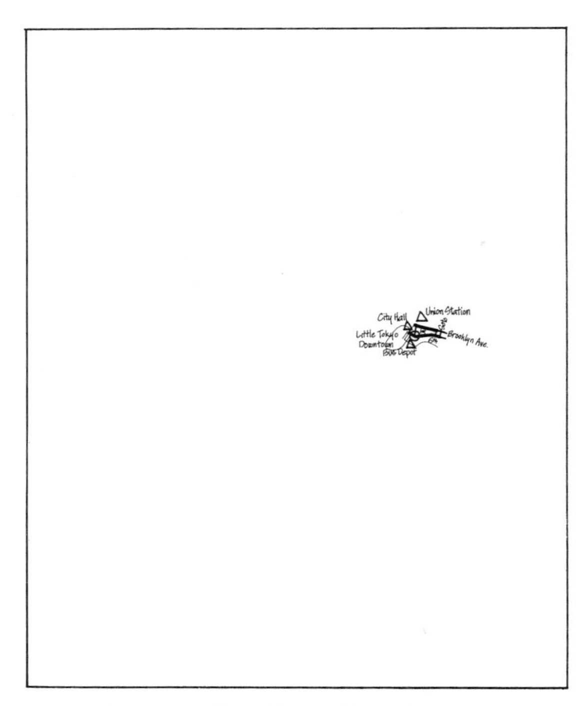


**Composite citizen image: Boyle Heights**

some of the political limits of Lynch's work, Jameson applauds the potential of his insights about how to give individuals a heightened sense of place, and suggests that mapping can raise political consciousness.[33] This is a direction some individual artists are exploring, as well as groups like New York's Chinatown History Museum and London's Common Ground (discussed in the next chapter).

Another way to analyze the production of space historically is to look at power struggles as they appear in the planning, design, construction, use, and demolition of typical buildings, especially dwellings. While architectural history has traditionally been devoted to stylistic analyses of the works of a small group of trained architects, recently more attention has been given to vernacular buildings and urban context.[34] Buildings are rich sources for analyzing the material conditions of urban life.[35] Buildings—tens of millions of them—can be surveyed, identified, and classified according to shape and function, but a larger sense of their political meaning is necessary.[36] Camille Wells, social historian of architecture, puts it this way: "most buildings can be understood in terms of power or authority—as efforts to assume, extend, resist, or accommodate it."[37]

Urban historians, such as Sam Bass Warner, who studied Boston's streetcar suburbs, James Borchert, who looked at Washington's African American alley dwellings, and Elizabeth Blackmar, who looked at the growth of Manhattan's rental housing from colonial times onward, demonstrate how the built world's dimensions illuminate a larger urban economy.[38] These methods have influenced architectural historians interested in the political uses of design. Architectural studies of communitarian settlements and company towns reveal spatial struggles at every turn. In a similar way, Gwendolyn Wright's study of the politics of urban planning and architecture in the cities of French colonies has suggested how power can operate from the top down through the regulation of the built environment.[39]

Like work on the cultural landscape, much scholarship on ordinary (or vernacular) buildings has focused on rural or small town subjects, on agriculture or craft industries. More has been written about farmhouses and barns than urban boardinghouses or saloons, more about rural one-room schools than urban public high schools.[40] (Some scholars would still prefer to define the field this way. For them, the best vernacular building will always be the purest, the best preserved, or the most elaborate example of its physical type.) A simple, rural building, constructed by local people who may also own and occupy it, can illustrate a process of the production of space that is much less difficult to analyze than urban real estate (figure 2.8), although it may still convey some surprises—such as women doing the construction. Yet greater potential lies in using the methods developed with preindustrial material to look at urban types like the tene-

**2.8 Dwellings and social reproduction. Rural vernacular architecture and the building process: house in Chamisal, New Mexico, receiving a new application of adobe by local women, 1940. (Photograph by Russell Lee, Library of Congress.)**

**2.9 Dwellings and social reproduction. A much less romantic vernacular: urban tenements and market on the Lower East Side of New York, ca. 1900. (Library of Congress.)**

ment, the public library, or the office building, to provide broad social interpretations of construction and habitation. Most can be learned from urban building types (figure 2.9) that represent the conditions of thousands or millions of people.[41]

Writing the social history of buildings can begin with material culture theory and method, identifying "mind in matter,"[42] but beyond evaluating an urban building as an artifact it is necessary to probe the complexity of habitation and finance, turning not only to building plans but to all the public records of ownership, taxation, and regulation that may exist. The final results of research for an urban building type can be a complex social history linked to many ordinary buildings.[43] In the city, this social history includes the builder, and also the owner or developer, the zoning and building code writers, the building inspector, and probably a complex series of tenants. The production of space on an urban scale involves them all. The basic arithmetic of how much it cost to buy the land and construct the building is balanced by how much rent was collected from how many tenants over how many years.

In a typical New York tenement at the turn of the century, many people's sordid habitat was one landlord's money machine, generating 25 percent return on investment per year.[44] There were few reasons to diminish profits through maintenance expenses, since legal enforcement of building codes and safety regulations was minimal. What did it mean in terms of the sensory experience of place? The building will be a more evocative source than any written records. One can read about unhealthy living conditions, but standing inside a tenement apartment—perhaps 400 square feet of living space for an entire family, minimal plumbing, only one or two exterior windows—leaves a visitor gasping for air and looking for light. The claustrophobic experiences of immigrants living for decades in crowded, unhealthy space (as part of the reproduction of the labor force) are conveyed by the building in a way that a text or a chart can never match. Environmental history may come in the form of "black spot" charts of tenement residents dying of lung diseases, photographs of filthy communal privies serving hundreds of people, and sidewalks piled a yard high with uncollected garbage, but the building itself is the very best resource for interpreting the experience. Because a tenement was typical of hundreds of thousands of tenements all over the city, its implications for the historic urban landscape are broad. One building tells the story of thousands of developers and millions of tenants. It represents daily life in New York at the turn of the century better than historic houses of refined architectural quality.[45]

## From an Ordinary Dwelling to an Urban Residential Neighborhood

Dwellings are the basic, repeated units in an urban neighborhood. In a nineteenth-century or early twentieth-century American city, dwellings cluster along with related buildings such as public bathhouses, food markets, bakeries, union halls, schools, clubs, nickelodeons, saloons, and settlement houses. All of these begin to form a historic urban working-class neighborhood that can be researched through sources such as fire insurance maps and institutional records of trade unions and settlement houses, as well as information on individual buildings. There are patterns of gender segregation, places such as saloons where no respectable woman could go.[46] And there are patterns of ethnic and racial division, as well as distinctive ethnic building types.

Architectural historian Dell Upton once observed: "Large urban ethnic groups evidently built little that was distinctive but instead expressed their ethnicity through language, food customs, religion and social organizations."[47] However, ethnicity, as well as race, class, and gender, can be uncovered as a shaping force of American urban places, provided one looks at the production of social space carefully. In Eastern European Jewish neighborhoods, distinctive ethnic building types include synagogues; in Chinese American neighborhoods, laundries, herb shops, seamen's boardinghouses; in Japanese American neighborhoods, temples, nurseries, and flower markets. (The researcher needs to be able to use sources in Yiddish, Chinese, and Japanese as well as English.)

There are distinctive design traditions for outdoor spaces associated with different ethnic groups—yards or gardens planted in certain ways identify African American or Portuguese or Chinese or Latino or Italian residents.[48] Stoops and porches, and the ways these are used, also speak about ethnicity and gender. Religious shrines do too, and street games for children. A world of shared meanings builds up, couched in the language of small semiprivate and semipublic territories between the dwelling and the street that support certain kinds of typical public behavior. Architect and planner James Rojas has analyzed the ways such spaces are created and used by residents in East Los Angeles, what he calls "the enacted environment."[49] Larger spatial patterns associated with ethnic groups have been studied in certain cities, such as Asian American patterns of building and ownership in the state of Washington, Chinese American gateways and underground passages in Vancouver, Canada, or Latino public plazas in Los Angeles, African American alley dwellings in Washington, or Puerto Rican *casitas* in New York.[50]

The story of the *casita* in New York City is particularly fascinating, as it is a rural dwelling converted into a public place. The *casita* represents a conscious choice by community organizers to construct the rural, preindustrial *bohio* (an eight-by-ten wooden house with a porch and a front yard) from the island as a new kind of community center in devastated tenement districts such as East Harlem, the South Bronx, and the Lower East Side (figure 2.10). Here rural vernacular architecture was chosen to serve a polemical function, emphasizing the importance of the "enacted environment" as a bridge between built and natural worlds. At the *casitas* community organizers host political meetings, musical events, and classes. They often organize community gardening on vacant lots. Painted in coral, turquoise, or lemon yellow, these dwellings recall the colors of the Caribbean and evoke a

**2.10 Counter-space, as a challenge to the reproduction of social relations. Dilapidated and abandoned tenements in New York City provide the context for a Puerto Rican *casita*, a rural house type built as a political gathering place in an East Harlem neighborhood that includes a vacant lot used for a community garden, 1989. (Photograph by Martha Cooper.)**

memory of the homeland for immigrants who find themselves in Alphabet City or Spanish Harlem.

The *casitas* and their community gardens play against the context of abandoned tenements and litter-strewn lots. The organizers have produced their own public space, setting up a series of oppositions—past/present, inviting/uninviting, private/public. They offer an alternative kind of social reproduction within their space, at the same time that they critique the available space, past and present, for Puerto Rican workers. As they attest the power of one cultural landscape to contradict another, they offer an example of Lefebvre's "counter-space." In this way, they resemble the political murals of East

**2.11, 2.12 Urban neighborhoods host many vernacular arts traditions that enable different ethnic groups to claim public space. In Los Angeles, Latino murals enliven the Estrada Courts housing project: the Virgin of Guadalupe and a more militant woman with a machine gun, 1980. (Photographs by Dolores Hayden.)**

Los Angeles, which also set up a political dialogue with the surrounding city and its traditions of housing for Latino workers (figures 2.11, 2.12).[51]

Ethnic vernacular arts traditions have often operated in a similar way to instill community pride and signal the presence of a particular community in the city. Japanese Americans have created flower decorations for streets. Anglos have made fruit, flower, and vegetable architecture for festivals. Mexican Americans have developed hand-painted signs for both commercial buildings and trucks. Many communities enjoy more than one medium. A study of Italian Americans in South Philadelphia by Dorothy Noyes shows how Italian immigrants and their descendants made their presence felt through masonry, confectionery, window dressing, and street festival design.[52]

Festivals and parades also help to define cultural identity in spatial terms by staking out routes in the urban cultural landscape. Although their presence is temporary they can be highly effective in claiming the symbolic importance of places. They intermix vernacular arts traditions (in their costumes, floats, music, dance, and performance) with spatial history (sites where they begin, march, and end). African American jazz funerals marching through the streets of New Orleans, Chinese New Year parades, saint's day processions in Irish American or Italian American Catholic communities,[53] and graveyard ceremonies for the Day of the Dead in Mexican American communities are just a few examples of ethnic traditions with long histories. Slightly different from the religious parades, political parades have been representing communities and their causes for a long time, from workers with the tools of their trades to suffragettes, as scholars such as Susan Davis and David Glassberg have shown.[54] In the last forty years, civil rights marches in southern cities, women's marches to "Take Back the Night" or win abortion rights, and Gay and Lesbian Pride parades in major cities have also established their participants in public space, as part of campaigns to achieve greater political representation.[55] Historical changes in parades can reveal larger social transformations, such as when a group is or is not too controversial to march, or when an entire parade is overtaken by commercial interests and every float becomes an advertisement.

An ordinary urban neighborhood will also contain the history of activists who have campaigned against spatial injustices. Whether one uses territorial histories, or cognitive mapping, or some combination of the two methods, it is possible to identify historic urban places that have special significance to certain populations fighting spatial segregation of different kinds. Territorial history will point to a church where major civil rights meetings were held, or a local newspaper that crusaded for fair housing, or the first place in a city where women tried to vote, or the first place where new immigrants were allowed to own land, or the first integrated primary school. There are also sites of assassinations, lynchings, massacres, and riots with political histories that should not be forgotten. The motel where Martin Luther King was shot, the Lorraine Motel in Memphis, is now a national civil rights museum, but every city and town has similar landmarks where territorial struggles have been waged. Finding these buildings and interpreting their history is one additional way to fuse the social and political meanings of space with the history of the urban landscape.

## From the Urban Neighborhood to the City and the Region

As one moves from the scale of the neighborhood to that of the city, many works of urban history contribute to the understanding of cultural landscape history. A new American urban social history has begun to be written in the last two decades, a history that takes ethnic diversity as a starting point and recognizes disparate experiences of class and gender as well. For many years, urban history was dominated by a kind of "city biography" that projected a single narrative of how city leaders or "city fathers"—almost always white, upper- and middle-class men—forged the city's spatial and economic structure, making fortunes building downtowns and imposing order on chaotic immigrant populations. This narrative tradition in urban history bore many similarities to the "conquest" histories of the American West.

In contrast, urban histories of the twenty-first century may begin by noting that in 1984 white males became a minority in the paid labor force in the United States.[56] Urban historians discovered workers in the 1960s and women in the 1970s. In the 1980s, as the history of suburban development became an essential part of urban history, spatial issues gained more attention.[57] In the late 1980s and 1990s, historians have been reconstructing the entire city, exploring the whole as seen from African American, Latino, Chinese American, or Japanese American perspectives. While socially oriented studies of ethnicity and race have a long tradition, the new, ethnic urban histories often emphasize the sharpness of spatial as well as cultural distinctions.[58] Soon the United States may have an urban history that encompasses the whole of the population, and the whole of the city, socially and spatially. Previous histories of American cities already seem dated if they focused only on the prosperous, white parts of cities—Manhattan without Harlem or the Bronx, Boston without Roxbury, the Westside of Los Angeles without East or South Central Los Angeles. As Toni Morrison's *Playing in the Dark* suggests, Anglo American literature has often been constructed using the presence of African Americans to help define "whiteness": "Through significant and underscored omissions, startling contradictions, heavily nuanced conflicts, through the way writers peopled their work with the signs and bodies of this presence—one can see that a real or fabricated Africanist presence was crucial to their sense of Americanness."[59] This could be said of some older urban histories as well.

New texts ask, "Who built America?"[60] Not only is the history of different ethnic communities becoming more fully represented, but historians increasingly place women at the center rather than the periphery of economic and social life in the city. In contrast to the older city biographies that focused on city fathers and their conquest of the economic and physical obstacles to economic growth, women's history has brought a new emphasis on city mothers, the half of the city consisting of females of all races and classes, nurturing the rest of the population. Following the lead of scholars who worked on women of color a decade ago,[61] historians studying working women of every ethnic group have led the way to the broadest synthetic accounts of urban life, exploring textile mills and canneries, tenements and courtyards, where women struggled for sustenance for themselves, their families, and their communities.[62] Work in the home and paid work are complementary parts of women's urban economic activity, suggesting that urban history, ethnic history, women's history, and labor history are not separate categories. All of these studies of urban working women contain the outline of a larger urban narrative uniting women, children, and men in the struggle for survival, both in the market economy and in the home.

At the same time that social histories of the city are becoming more inclusive and spatial, environmental historians are showing how the old "city biography" tradition failed to convey the dynamic economic and spatial process of building a city, which depended on natural resources extending beyond the city limits. A city has a hinterland of economically dependent places. For Chicago, the cattle ranges of the West and the wheat fields of the Midwest were the environmental resources harnessed by the owners of railroads, slaughterhouses, grain elevators, and meat-packing plants headquartered in the city. For Los Angeles, the growth of the city required aqueducts reaching up through the Owens Valley and out to the Colorado River. An environmental analysis of both the central city and these far-flung places reveals the economic history of a city far better than a narrower look.[63]

**Space as a Social Product, Local and Global**

"Space is permeated with social relations; it is not only supported by social relations but it is also producing and produced by social relations." So Henri Lefebvre sums up the complex, contradictory nature of space.[64] As the production of built space increases in intensity and scale during the later twentieth century, the politics of space becomes more difficult to map. Freeways connect dispersed locations of workplaces and dwellings, typical of contemporary working landscapes. As interstate freeways carry automobiles speeding at 55 miles per hour, it becomes more difficult to analyze the experience they provide in terms of human perception and memory, but easier to track the production of that American automotive space as the world's largest and most grandiose public works project.[65] "At the same time as a regional dispersion of activities is occurring, the global migration of capital leads to manufacturing processes scattered around parts of the world, while housing and factories lie abandoned in older, industrial inner cities in the United States.

In *The City and the Grassroots*, Manuel Castells has noted, "The new space of a world capitalist system, combining the informational and industrial modes of development, is a space of variable geometry, formed by locations hierarchically ordered in a continuously changing network of flows: flows of capital, labor, elements of production, commodities, information, decisions, and signals." He concludes that "the new tendential urban meaning is the spatial and cultural separation of people from their product and from their history." While suggesting that what "tends to disappear is the meaning of places for people," he finds many social movements mobilized against this loss of meaning in places. In a similar vein, David Harvey describes the process of the "destruction, invasion, and restructuring of places on an unprecedented scale," caused by "changing material practices of production, consumption, information flow, and communication coupled with the radical reorganization of space relations and of time horizons within capitalist development."[66]

These changes affect older central cities with particular architectural impact, and the inhabitants of devastated areas need to understand the complex forces that have led to present configurations. Territorial histories based on race and class and gender can be illuminating, as well as the analysis of worker's livelihoods and landscapes. Today suburban malls and edge cities are proliferating, and many inner-city neighborhoods struggle for economic viability.[67] Both citizens and planners may find that urban landscape history can help to reclaim the identities of deteriorating neighborhoods where generations of working people have spent their lives. As Harvey suggests, paradoxically, "the elaboration of place-bound identities has become more rather than less important in a world of diminishing spatial barriers to exchange, movement and communication."[68] Understanding the history of urban cultural landscapes offers citizens and public officials some basis for making political and spatial choices about the future. It also offers a context for greater social responsibility to practitioners in the design fields.

This chapter has explored some of the ways that social history is embedded in urban landscapes. This subject needs to be grounded in both the aesthetics of experiencing places with all five senses and the politics of experiencing places as contested territory. Much the same can be said for organizations of historians, preservationists, or environmentalists, or of individual artists and designers, who wish to use the social history of places to make more resonant connections to public memory. Places make memories cohere in complex ways. People's experiences of the urban landscape intertwine the sense of place and the politics of space. If people's attachments to places are material, social, and imaginative, then these are necessary dimensions of new projects to extend public history in the urban landscape, as well as new histories of American cultural landscapes and the buildings within them.

# 3 Place Memory and Urban Preservation

**What is contained in place is on its way to being well remembered.**

**Edward Casey, *Remembering***

A look at the fields of public history, architectural preservation, environmental activism, and public art suggests that in the 1990s there is a growing desire to engage urban landscape history as a unifying framework for urban preservation. Many practitioners in these fields are dissatisfied with the old narrative of city building as "conquest." There is broad interest in ethnic history and women's history as part of interpretive projects of all kinds, and a growing sympathy for cultural landscapes in preference to isolated monuments. There is a concern for public processes. But there is not often a sense of how, in practice, the public presentation of historic urban landscapes might become more than the sum of the parts.

Different kinds of organizations may find it difficult to work together on large urban themes. Often, groups simply ignore the other areas of activity. In the worst case, they criticize each other's points of view: social historians are baited as overconcerned with class, race, and gender; architectural preservationists are attacked as being in the grip of real estate developers promoting gentrification; environmentalists are lampooned as idealists defending untouched nature and unimportant species while human needs go unattended; commemorative public art is debated as ugly or irrelevant to social needs. There needs to be, and there can be, a more coherent way of conceptualizing and planning the work each group is able to contribute to the presence of the past in the city. Cultural landscape history can strengthen the links between previously disparate areas of practice that draw on public memory. And conscious effort to draw out public memory suggests new processes for developing projects.

"The relationship between history and memory is peculiarly and perhaps uniquely fractured in contemporary American life," writes public historian Michael Frisch. His colleagues, Jack Tchen and Michael Wallace, observe "historical amnesia" and "historicidal" culture. Urbanist M. Christine Boyer writes of architectural history manipulated for commercial purposes. Geographer David Lowenthal wryly calls the past a "foreign country." Citizens surveyed about history will often speak disparagingly of memorized dates, great men, "boring stuff from school" disconnected from their own lives, families, neighborhoods, and work. And certainly there are many people for whom the past is something they want to escape. Yet every year tens of millions of Americans travel to visit historic sites and museums (including some of doubtful quality), as well as historically oriented theme parks and "theme towns."[1] If Americans were to find their own social history preserved in the public landscapes of their own neighborhoods and cities, then connection to the past might be very different.

## Place Memory

"We all come to know each other by asking for accounts, by giving accounts, and by believing or disbelieving stories about each other's pasts and identities," writes Paul Connerton in *How Societies Remember*.[2] Social memory relies on storytelling, but what specialists call place memory can be used to help trigger social memory through the urban landscape. "Place memory" is philosopher Edward S. Casey's formulation: "It is the stabilizing persistence of place as a container of experiences that contributes so powerfully to its intrinsic memorability. An alert and alive memory connects spontaneously with place, finding in it features that favor and parallel its own activities. We might even say that memory is naturally place-oriented or at least place-supported."[3] Place memory encapsulates the human ability to connect with both the built and natural environments that are entwined in the cultural landscape. It is the key to the power of historic places to help citizens define their public pasts: places trigger memories for insiders, who have shared a common past, and at the same time places often can represent shared pasts to outsiders who might be interested in knowing about them in the present.

Place memory is so strong that many different cultures have used "memory palaces"—sequences of imaginary spaces within an imaginary landscape or building or series of buildings—as mnemonic devices.[4] Many cultures have also attempted to embed public memory in narrative elements of buildings, from imperial monuments in Augustan Rome to doctrinal sculptural programs for Gothic cathedrals. The importance of ordinary buildings for public memory has largely been ignored, although, like monumental architecture, common urban places like union halls, schools, and residences have the power to evoke visual, social memory.

A strategy to foster urban public history should certainly exploit place memory as well as social memory. (For example, place memory might include personal memory of one's arrival in the city and emotional attachments there, cognitive memory of its street names and street layout, and body memory of routine journeys to home and work.) According to Connerton, cognitive memory is understood to be "encoded" according to semantic, verbal, and visual codes, and seems especially place-oriented because images are "much better retained than abstract items because such concrete items undergo a double encoding in terms of visual coding as well as verbal expression."[5]

Because the urban landscape stimulates visual memory, it is an important but underutilized resource for public history. While many museum curators concerned with artifacts have long understood the strength of visual memory, social historians often have not had much visual training and are not always well equipped to evaluate environmental memory's component of visual evidence.[6] For example, one well-known social historian on the Baltimore Neighborhood Heritage Project, Linda Shopes, complained in an account of her experiences that oral history interviewers were always hearing about places, eliciting "descriptions of the area in years gone by." She was looking for abstractions such as "the workings of local institutions or the local political machine, the conditions and social relations of work, immigration and the process of assimilation or non-assimilation into American life."[7] Yet stories about places could convey all these themes, and memories of places would probably trigger more stories. More sense of the possibilities of place memory is conveyed by historian Paul Buhle in his recent plea that labor historians turn their attention to photographic collections, as a way to document vanishing working-class neighborhoods developed in the era of industrial capitalism. This could be the beginning of documenting a three-dimensional urban landscape history with a strong social component.[8]

Body memory is also difficult to convey as part of books or exhibits. It connects into places because the shared experience of dwellings, public spaces, and workplaces, and the paths traveled between home and work, give body memory its social component, modified by the postures of gender, race, and class. The experience of physical labor is also part of body memory. In a dusty vineyard, a crowded sweatshop, or an oil field, people acquire the characteristic postures of certain occupations—picking grapes, sewing dresses, pumping gas. In the sphere of domestic work, one thinks of suckling a baby, sweeping, or kneading bread.[9] Thus, Casey argues that body memory "moves us directly into place, whose very immobility contributes to its distinct potency in matters of memory." He suggests that "what is remembered is well grounded if it is remembered as being in a particular place—a place that may well take precedence over the time of its occurrence."[10]

## Urban Public History

The field of public history embraces many different kinds of efforts to bring history to the public, from blockbuster museum exhibitions to documentary films to community-based projects. Within the field there are many different views of its content and audience, but for urban landscape history, community-based public history is a natural ally. The great strength of this approach to public history is its desire for a "shared authority" (Michael Frisch's phrase) or a "dialogic" history (Jack Tchen's term) that gives power to communities to define their own collective pasts.[11] This approach is based on the understanding that the history of workers, women, ethnic groups, and the poor requires broad source materials, including oral histories, because often people, rather than professors, are the best authorities on their own pasts.[12] In the search for new materials, including oral histories, many professionally trained historians have seen how communities gained from defining their own economic and social histories. Hundreds of projects now pursue this approach across the United States. Some also have an interest in community empowerment, and connect work in public history to other kinds of community organizing.

A city-scale, community oral history, the Brass Workers History Project, begun in 1979, involved labor historian Jeremy Brecher in Waterbury, Connecticut. The team also included a video producer, a community organizer, and a union education director. In 1982 they published an illustrated history, *Brass Valley: The Story of Working People's Lives and Struggles in an American Industrial Region.*[13] The book, according to Brecher, was "taken as a kind of collective family album in a community where almost everyone has a relative who worked in the brass industry. Many, many people told me that they found in it pictures of relatives. One family told me that they spent Christmas together going through it."[14] In 1983 the project released a feature-length color videotape for public television, a portrayal of the history of workers in the brass factories of the city, formerly the brass manufacturing capital of the United States.[15]

*Brass Valley* led to a larger community process, including an ethnic music festival that is now a regular event sponsored by the museum, bringing together dozens of choirs, singing groups, and bands whose music reveals the city's diverse ethnic heritage. Among the participants have been the oldest fife and drum band in the United States, dressed in Revolutionary War style, Irish American women who sing traditional Irish lullabies, and a robed Baptist choir famous for gospel hymns.[16] Local teachers were able to use the rich resources for efforts to incorporate Waterbury's ethnic history and musical culture into the school curriculum. All of this occurred at a time when the brass industry had collapsed and plants were closing, so workers' groups in the Naugatuck Valley also found the history project provided a long-term perspective on their efforts to organize to meet the problems of dying industries in their area.[17]

Another example, at the scale of an urban neighborhood, is the New York Chinatown History Project (now Museum), begun in 1980 by John Kuo Wei Tchen and Charles Lai. As one of their newsletters explained: "We seek to learn about the back-breaking toil of Chinese seamen who shoveled coal into the giant furnaces of ocean steamers; the songs composed by lonely wives living in Toishan and bemoaning their sojourning husbands; the ghost stories about the tormented spirits of dead laundrymen; the thriving street life on lower Mott, Pell, and Doyers Streets; and the high-pressured piece-work of garment factory employees."[18] Tchen's analysis of New York's Chinatown before World War II takes a different tone from that of the project about working-class life in Waterbury because of the bitterness of the history of anti-Chinese racism and the territorial form it took: "New York Chinatown, now the largest in the Western Hemisphere, was not the result of some nationalistic clannishness as the prevailing common sense in the United States presumes. Located in New York's Lower East Side, Chinatown was built in a spatial 'crack' between the Irish Five Points, Little Italy, and 'Jew Town.'" Togetherness for Chinese Americans was balanced by a sense of spatial exclusion: "Residents of New York Chinatown could not cross Canal Street into Little Italy without the risk of being beaten up; laundry men in the scattered boroughs and suburbs illegally lived in the back of their shops because they could not rent apartments. Even PhD's couldn't get jobs besides washing and waitering."[19]

The Chinatown History Project made "The Eight Pound Livelihood" the subject of their first major project—an oral history of the laundrymen and women, an exhibit, and a PBS video program (figures 3.1, 3.2). "We blindly went out to interview active and retired laundry workers.... We experienced much resistance. One laundryman screamed back at us bitterly that 'Laundries have no history! Laundries have no history!'" Eventually, Tchen found "Perhaps the single most satisfying response was from a regular of the senior center who came up

**3.1 The New York Chinatown History Project picked the Chinese laundry and its "eight-pound livelihood" as the subject for their first history project. This is Chin Che Yung from Hong Kong, working at a shirtpress, in Queens, New York. (Photograph by Paul Calhoun.)**

**3.2 Lunch break at the shirtpress. (Photograph by Paul Calhoun.)**

to us and proudly declared, while pointing to the exhibit title, that *she* lived the eight pound livelihood. We felt she had claimed it as her own."[20] After more than ten years, the project has remained a national leader in discussion of questions of ethnicity, representation of ethnic groups, and community dialogue around issues of conservation and interpretation of urban cultural heritage. Its recent programs have included comparisons of Chinese and Italian immigrant students' memories of P.S. 23, as well as Chinese and Eastern European immigrants' memories and cognitive maps of Mott Street. "Creating a Dialogic Museum," a recent article by Tchen, stresses the complexity of working with diverse audiences and keeping the conversation open to recording both individual identity and common memories.[21]

The Brass Workers' History Project and the New York Chinatown History Project are just two examples of how communities can reclaim history and recover memory. Each project transcended the response from some of its potential interviewees and audience members that they would prefer to remember the good and forget the bad, to deny their own and their parents' and grandparents' struggles against poverty and discrimination. Both used oral history as well as more traditional research methods. Both looked for the best medium to reach popular audiences: small publishing projects, feature-length films, exhibits in senior centers as well as major exhibition spaces, scholarly books, community newsletters. Both reached their intended urban audiences.

If there were ways to extend the social portraits of the communities they created into urban public space, it might be possible to make these successful projects even more public and more permanent.[22] Beyond running walking tours, how could they have mapped their new views of these places? Could architectural preservation, or landscape preservation, or possibly public art help to focus the attention of citizens on the social identity of these communities? In seeking ways to establish their presence in public space, it would be essential to retain their central commitment to making projects accountable to the residents. Preserving workers' places such as a union hall, a brass factory, or a laundry could help to underline the importance of spatial history. And shared processes would be a significant methodological advance public historians could offer to many practitioners in related fields, including architectural preservation and environmental protection.

## Architectural Preservation

Architectural preservation is usually less concerned with accountability and more expensive than community-based public history, but it does assert its visual presence in the spaces of the city. Since the mid-nineteenth century in the United States, most preservation groups have directed their efforts toward saving historic buildings as a unifying focus for national pride and patriotism in a nation of immigrants, or as examples of stylistic excellence in architecture. Preservation at the national level (the National Park Service) and state level thus tends to the creation of museums, and as historian John Bodnar has argued, these often come complete with patriotic exhortations about the glories of the national past.[23] Preservation at the local level, in most cities and towns, tends to the adaptive reuse of historic structures by local real estate developers, with little public access or interpretation, and often involves gentrification and displacement for low-income residents. There are some notable efforts to integrate the preservation of vernacular buildings with local economic development, as in the National Trust for Historic Preservation's Main Street Program, or to preserve working people's neighborhoods without gentrification, as in the Mt. Auburn neighborhood of Cincinnati, but it is difficult work.

The state of preservation today is uneven, and, like public history, many groups struggle without adequate funds. Almost two decades after the Gans-Huxtable debate, New York does recognize more of its social history, with a National Park Service Museum of Immigration at Ellis Island and a Lower East Side Tenement Museum at 97 Orchard Street. But the old focus on great buildings dies hard. As Antoinette J.

Lee, historian with the National Park Service, has observed, "disagreement between preservation agencies that prize historical and structural integrity on the one hand and historians interested in vernacular and ethnic history on the other, will likely continue for years to come."[24] Only about five percent of national, state, and local landmark designations reflect women's history, and an even tinier proportion deal with so-called "minority" history.[25] How to preserve is as much debated as what to preserve. Women and people of color need to be making policy. And most social history landmarks cannot be turned into commercial real estate to pay for their physical preservation, nor can they all function as income-producing museums. Yet two projects at the national level suggest how important the sense of place can be in supporting African American or women's history with tangible public forms. These projects show how museums of national importance can extend the resources of an urban neighborhood, although they do not seem to have as much local process behind them as the previous examples.

The National Park Service runs a Black Heritage Trail at the Boston African American National Historic Site on Beacon Hill (figures 3.3, 3.4). There, a ranger in a brown, broad-brimmed hat walks the cobblestoned streets of Beacon Hill, followed by members of a tour group. At the Boston Common he or she will discuss the enlistment of free blacks in the Civil War and trace the contours of their faces on the Robert Gould Shaw and 54th Regiment Memorial by sculptor August Saint-Gaudens, erected in 1897. The ranger then leads the tour group behind the Massachusetts State House and down the alleys to the back of Beacon Hill, a red-brick row house neighborhood that was the site of a thriving community of free blacks in the nineteenth century. Thirteen structures, including two schools, two meeting houses, and several residences, are part of the Black Heritage Trail, a concept originated by historian Sue Bailey Thurman and developed by Byron Rushing and the staff of the Museum of Afro-American History.[26]

Visitors see these structures in the context of the elegant, expensive neighborhoods nearby, such as Louisbourg Square. They learn that in the first federal census of 1790, Massachusetts was the only state that had no slaves. And they can hear about the free black community on Beacon Hill campaigning for housing, education, and an end to slavery. They can also see a house that served as a station on the Underground Railroad, where runaway slaves were sheltered. Visitors come away with a sense of the active presence of African Americans in the city for over two centuries, although more material showing that the free black community included women who made important contributions would be welcome. Visitors also get a sense of urban history, although it could be more resonant if it addressed how black residents interacted with Irish and other European immigrants who were crowded into

**3.3 Map of the Black Heritage Trail, Beacon Hill, Boston African American National Historic Site. (National Park Service.)** ***1*, African Meeting House; *2–6*, Smith Court Residences; *7*, Abiel Smith School; *8*, George Middleton House; *9*, Robert Gould Shaw and 54th Regiment Memorial; *10*, Phillips School; *11*, John J. Smith House; *12*, Charles Street Meeting House; *13*, Lewis Hayden House; *14*, Coburn's Gaming House.**

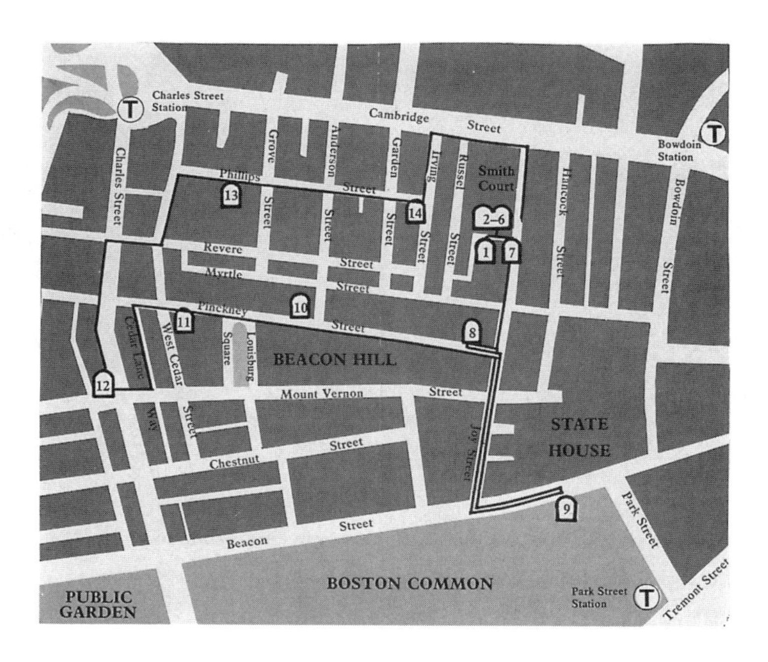

**3.4 The African Meeting House, Boston, late nineteenth century. (Courtesy of The Society for the Preservation of New England Antiquities.)**

tenements at the edges of this area at the end of the nineteenth century. A nationally important struggle for civil rights took place here, yet local participation in the planning and running of the project might widen its potential audience.[27]

The National Park Service is also developing a Women's Rights National Historical Park at Seneca Falls, New York, the site of the first women's rights convention, held July 19–20, 1848, in the Wesleyan Chapel on Fall Street. Here Elizabeth Cady Stanton drafted a "Declaration of Sentiments," modeled on the Declaration of Independence, to demand the vote for women. Both Stanton and Amelia Bloomer, who was editor of *The Lily*, the first American paper devoted to women's rights and owned, edited, and published by a woman, were residents of Seneca Falls and organized women's activities there. Susan B. Anthony was Stanton's frequent visitor and coorganizer.

By 1987, the Wesleyan Chapel had been pretty well battered out of existence, remodeled into a two-story brick and stucco building that had housed various uses including a laundromat. All that remained from the original building of the 1848 era were four wood roof trusses, some roof rafters and purlins, and about forty linear feet of the east and west brick walls.[28] The Park Service held an architectural competition, won by two young women architects, Ann Wills Marshall and Ray Kinoshita, and their design for the preservation of the remains of the chapel is elegant and spare (figures 3.5, 3.6). Unlike many other National Park Service projects, where an expensive restoration freezes a building in time and makes it lifeless, this project will leave the remaining elements visible to visitors, with plenty of room for their own imaginations. Because it is physically integrated with the urban fabric of Seneca Falls, it can engage the life of the town in a way that many larger, more expensive projects do not.

Like the Boston Black Heritage Trail, the Seneca Falls project will emphasize the national history of civil rights leadership over the local history of ordinary people's everyday lives in the nineteenth century, but this doesn't preclude a commit-

**3.5 The Women's Rights National Historic Park, Seneca Falls, New York: the remains of the Wesleyan Chapel, showing the front of the structure remodeled as a laundromat. (National Park Service.)**

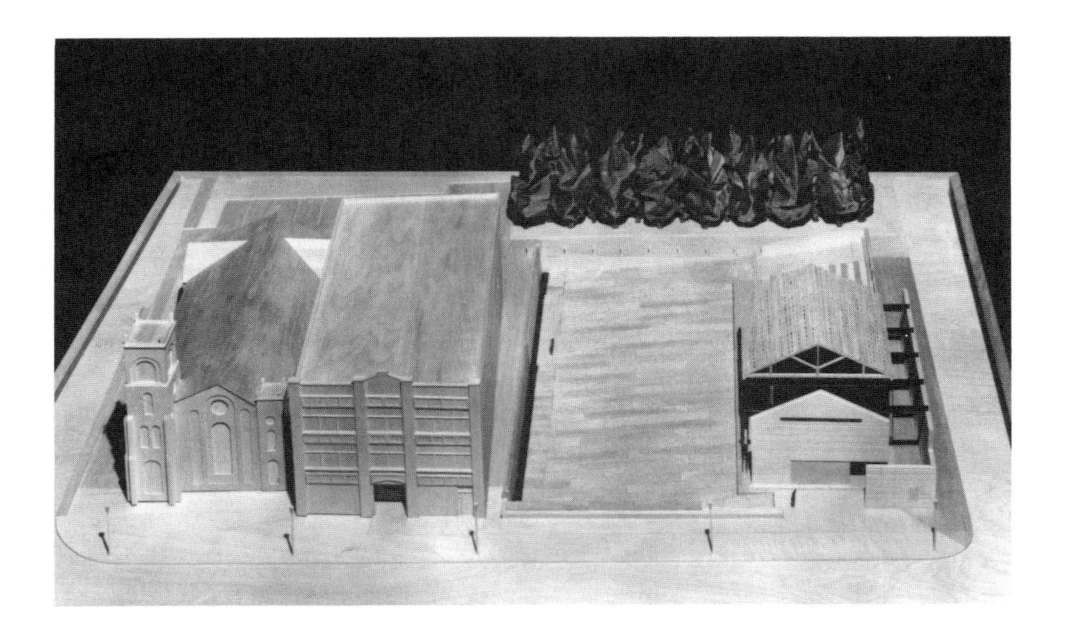

**3.6 Ann Wills Marshall and Ray Kinoshita, architects, model of the winning entry in the competition for the Women's Rights National Historic Park. The remains of the original Wesleyan Chapel are preserved in the design of the pavilion at lower right, adjacent to new open space. (National Park Service.)**

ment to local process. Like the Boston site, Seneca Falls can also encompass broad social issues, such as how limited economic possibilities for women sparked demands for change. In Seneca Falls as well as Beacon Hill, there is an opportunity to show conflict over power as an essential part of history, far more engaging to the public than cheery optimism about progress. Feminism is still controversial. When the site was made a New York State Urban Cultural Park, as well as a National Park Service site, local cynicism was exemplified by the male businessman in Seneca Falls who commented to a reporter that the local merchants "don't give a hoot" about feminism but "they see the money opportunity. I mean, if you've got Old Faithful in your town, you are in favor of geysers."[29]

As the Seneca Falls example shows, a public past tied to mundane, battered, and constantly reused buildings can call on visitors' historical imaginations and be invested with new architectural integrity. But it takes a great deal of research, community involvement, and inventive signing and mapping—as well as restoration—to bring these social meanings forward. When less funding is available, it is still possible to offer significant reinterpretation of existing architectural landmarks' social history or environmental context. A city or town with an extensive array of existing landmarks, selected for their architectural quality, is thus in a fortunate position to reconsider what stories will be told about those buildings.[30] For example, the National Trust for Historic Preservation, owner of many wonderful mansions, could expand its social interpretations. Jay Gould's mansion, Lyndhurst, employed eleven full-time gardeners who maintained the 375-foot-long Victorian greenhouse (figure 3.7), and preservationist Frank Sanchis has suggested designing a tour around their diverse backgrounds and skills, as well as paying closer attention to construction workers and household staff as subjects of other tours.[31] Even when some aspects of social history are already interpreted, as is the history of the work force involved in industrial development at Lowell, Massachusetts, it may be possible to frame the interpretation more broadly. Women workers need to be more visible there (figure 3.8), as they formed the great majority of the work force. At the moment,

**3.7 Reinterpreting the social history of a mansion can mean looking at the lives and work of carpenters, maids, or the grounds workers. Gardeners at Lyndhurst, Tarrytown, New York, photographed ca. 1875–1885. (Lyndhurst Archives, National Trust for Historic Preservation.)**

**3.8 Reinterpreting a preserved industrial site can mean sharpening the focus on different groups of workers. Women weaving room employees at Appleton Mills, Lowell, Massachusetts, and their supervisors, 1913. (Lowell Historical Society.)**

although there is a women's history tour of Lowell given occasionally, and an excellent exhibit in a boardinghouse, a much heavier emphasis is placed on technology. In the same vein, Heather Huyck of the National Park Service has urged her colleagues concerned with the history of the West to go beyond what she calls the "John Wayne view" of the sites they interpret.[32] At Fort Bowie, she pointed to laundresses, soldiers' wives, and soldiers' children who can be represented as part of the life of the community. At Lyndon B. Johnson's boyhood home, she argued that it is important to interpret the room where his mother taught elocution.

Beyond the national level, states are engaged with social history. The efforts of New York State to provide Urban Cultural Parks and similar efforts in Massachusetts, especially at Lowell, provide some suggestions about how to focus on the efforts of working people. California has provided a pathbreaking survey of hundreds of ethnic history sites relevant to its diverse population.[33] These include the Chinese American agricultural workers' town of Locke, Los Angeles's Little Tokyo, and the African American town built by settlers at Allensworth. Although this survey started in 1980, other than Little Tokyo very few of the urban landmarks proposed had been found suitable for architectural preservation by 1993.

This underscores the importance of finding new, community-based ways of working with the physical traces of the past beyond its preservation as museums or adaptive use as real estate. As more states begin to publish resource lists of ethnic architecture or undertake ethnic history context statements,[34] as the United States begins to survey women's history and ethnic history on a national scale, and as the National Trust launches a major campaign to promote "cultural and ethnic diversity in preservation," the need to find processes for simultaneously engaging social and architectural history is pressing. Some public history programs offer models of how to share authority with local residents in deciding what places are most significant, and why. Both social history and architectural preservation have the potential of contributing to neighborhood economic development in the city. It is particularly important as inner cities fall on hard times financially. Surviving urban neighborhoods—such as the Sweet Auburn district of Atlanta, Georgia—can become a greater focus of urban working people's self-respect, if citizens and planners come together to heighten the awareness of past accomplishments of their residents in the face of past hard times. Vernacular buildings—such as a church that launched a civil rights campaign, or the offices of a newspaper that called for fair housing, or the first integrated school in an area—may lie together in a potential historic district to support social memory and embrace the stories that citizens think need to be told. This is one route to forming strategies of urban preservation that ally social historians, and their strategies of dialogic history, with architectural historians concerned with public meaning.

## Environmental Protection and Landscape Preservation

Most American cities and towns host a variety of environmental organizations whose mission is to defend natural landscapes against destruction through carelessness, neglect, toxic substances, or development. There are dozens of different types of environmental groups, some with participatory processes that permit local groups to assess their own sense of what the most important places are to defend, and others that set national agendas (to campaign for the preservation of wetlands as habitations for wildlife, for example). In addition, most cities and states, as well as the federal government, have agencies concerned with regulating treatment of the environment.

While there is much political and scientific activity concerned with protection of the natural environment, there is also a broad cultural and historical debate taking place about the extent to which "nature" and "culture" are intertwined. Urban landscape history shows that simply trying to protect untouched parts of nature has a very limited possibility of success against the constant production of urbanized space. Understanding this interplay suggests that making common cause with other groups concerned with the presence of the past may be a very useful strategy for environmentalists.

Working together with architectural preservationists, landscape architecture historians and landscape architects are increasingly concerned about methods for defining and protecting historic cultural landscapes, although these concerns often seem to focus more on designed landscapes and rural areas than urban landscapes.[35] More promising is the work of some large environmental organizations in protecting rural landscapes with their human activities of gaining a livelihood intact.[36] Most promising of all is work being undertaken in urban regions to protect a variety of natural landscapes interwoven with urban development. At the same time some landscape architects are active in the heart of the city, developing community gardens and educational projects to reach the poorest residents in the most devastated urban areas.[37] Cultural landscape history could become a part of all such ventures to connect efforts to nurture green spaces with a broader understanding of the urban past.

This has been tried with success in England by Common Ground, one of the most popular British environmental organizations, whose founders feel landscape history should form a more prominent part of environmental efforts. They state, "We should be talking more about the conservation of our common cultural heritage and less about science, for example the current emphasis on the preservation of specific rare plants and animals and special 'protected' places."[38] Founded in London in 1983 by environmentalist Angela King and geographer/planner Sue Clifford, Common Ground has entwined the discovery and defense of the natural environment with discussions of places. Its objectives are to "excite people into remembering the richness of the commonplace and the value of the everyday, to savor the symbolisms with which we have endowed nature, to revalue our emotional engagement with places and all they mean to us, and to go on to become actively involved with their care." They elaborate the reasons for a broad organization: "We have chosen to focus attention not singularly upon natural history or architecture or art or

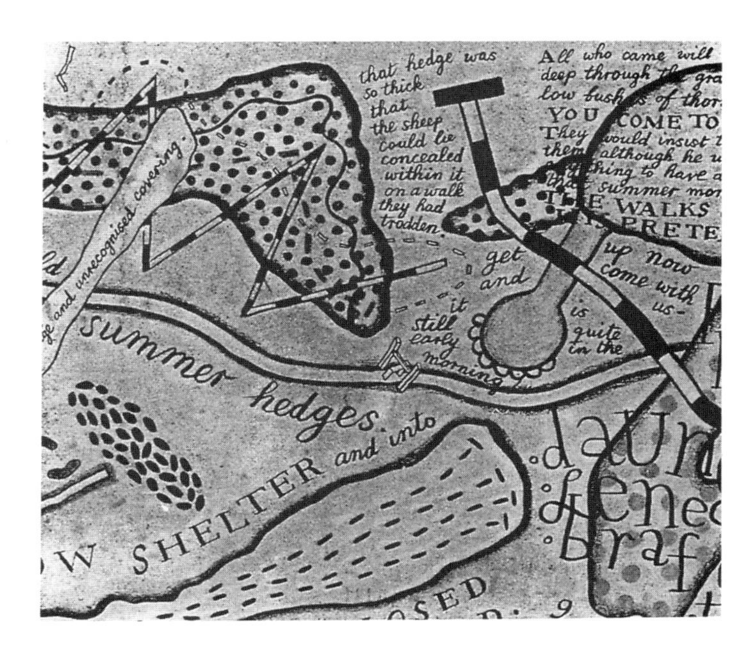


3.9 **Common Ground, Parish Maps project, detail of Simon Lewty's map of Old Milverton, England, 1987. (Common Ground.)**

social history or legend or literature but upon their complex combining which is the reality of people's relationship with their places, and which begins in our hearts but gets mediated by our reason."[39]

The approach of the organization is both to encourage broad, place-based community participation and at the same time to work with recognized artists and writers seeking a fresh look at historic landscapes. One of the first publications was a handbook by the founders, *Holding Your Ground: An Action Guide to Local Conservation*. Accompanying this was the parish (i.e., town) maps project, which involved hundreds of local communities in mapping their towns and defining important features (figure 3.9). Women's groups, school groups, city councils, or conservation groups might sponsor the activity, which could take many forms, from jigsaw puzzles, posters, and quilted wall hangings to a procession "beating

**3.10 Common Ground, The New Milestones project, John Maine, sculptor, *Chiswell Earthworks*, Chiswell, England, 1986–1993. (Common Ground.)**

the bounds" (walking the town boundaries) of Buckland Newton for the first time in the residents' living memory. As one participant from North Yorkshire commented, "The making of the map has been valuable as a shared activity, stimulating conversations, reminiscences and skills. Although the outline design was given, it is not static but constantly changes as people add their contributions, their ideas, and their experience."[40] At the same time, artists made town maps that were exhibited in galleries and museums. Television productions combined the popular public work with the artists' efforts. Both local community groups and artists were participants in these activities, and appreciative audiences for each other's efforts.

Common Ground carried their aesthetic of places into commissioning outdoor sculpture projects such as "Trees, Woods, and the Green Man" and "The New Milestones." Artists like

Andy Goldsworthy, whose *Hand to Earth* conveys a remarkable gift for building a human message in ice, leaves, stems, branches, or stones, rose to individual fame for his work with found materials in natural settings, but other projects involved intense public collaborations.[41] In the town of Chiswell, Common Ground brought sculptor John Maine to work with local residents to create *Chiswell Earthworks*. Sue Clifford describes it as "five terraces to stop the land sliding, held back by dry stone walls, each one built with stone from a different level of the Portland beds, each worked in discrete masonry techniques appropriate to the stone." The objectives were multiple: "At one stroke this would make visible the geology, the long masonry and stone walling traditions and allude to the farming and quarrying history and the dominance of the sea." The project also reintroduced the indigenous grasses of the area. It included about a dozen collaborating organizations, from corporations to youth training schemes to environmentalists (figure 3.10).[42]

Common Ground's 1990 alphabet of "Local Distinctiveness" encouraged poetic possibilities: "*T*ottergrass, twitchel, tor, tarn, tithebarn, tower, Tamworths, thatched walls, towpath, terrace, tump, Tan Hill Fair, red telephone box."[43] Could local distinctiveness also extend to tower block, temple, terraced house, elevated train tracks? The inner city challenges them to try their environmental tactics in tougher, more difficult settings like declining industrial cities (like Waterbury), or inner city enclaves (like Chinatown) and several New Milestones projects are under way in Glasgow. The landscape, as storehouse of culture and history rather than as a scientific problem, seems to be able to rally both individual and social memory in ways that move British citizens to claim places and increase their care for them. But the underlying ideas seem to apply to the United States as well, especially the potential for involving artists. American campaigns for local, community-based history share these British environmentalists' views of the importance of dialogue. Architectural preservationists share their interest in aesthetics and the arts. As Common Ground's "Mayday! Mayday!" poster concludes, "Never forget YOU are an expert in *your* place."[44]

Public historians may conduct interviews, construct territorial histories, chart workers' landscapes, research political histories of housing types or neighborhoods, and document vernacular arts traditions. Many artists, especially those interested in working with urban communities in public places, are attempting similar kinds of tasks, reaching out to history and geography to study the meanings of historic urban landscapes as a way of making more resonant public work.

This couldn't be more different from the conjunction of public history and public art achieved in the nineteenth-century statues that adorn American parks. "It buttered no parsnips that it was raining/ on some statues of older men" runs the opening of John Ashberry's poem "A Call for Papers," summoning our distaste for things stuffy and irrelevant.[45] "Statuomania" preoccupied the capitals of imperial power—London and Washington—at the end of the nineteenth century, as parks and other public places filled up with statues of political leaders and military figures on horseback. It also spread to many small towns, and in every case a political consensus was assumed to support the presence of these statues in public places, although they rarely represented a full range of citizens and often had cliches about white men's conquests as their implicit or explicit narratives, the legacy that artist Judith Baca terms "the cannon in the park."[46] It usually excluded heroic representations of women or members of diverse groups. (As one disgruntled female official remarked in New York after a survey of the civic statuary in Central Park, the only representative of her sex to be found was Mother Goose!)

Today there are many new ways to be an artist: sculptors and painters, muralists and printmakers are joined by environmental artists, performance artists, book artists, and new media artists. For all of them, the key to acquiring an audience is making meaning for people in resonant and original ways. Along with new media come new definitions of public. The older definition of public art is art that is accessible to the public because it is permanently sited in public places. (It is not in galleries or museums or private offices or private homes, but in the streets, the parks, the public realm.) But many artists would agree that a better definition is art that has public content. James Clark says, "Public art is artwork that depends on its context; it is an amalgamation of events—the physical appearance of a site, its history, the socio-economic dimensions of the community, and the artist's intervention."[47] Or as Lucy Lippard, critic and author of the notable book on multicultural art, *Mixed Blessings*, puts it, "Public art is accessible art of any kind that cares about/challenges/ involves and consults the audience for or with whom it is made, respecting community and environment; the other stuff is still private art, no matter how big or exposed or intrusive or hyped it may be."[48]

While these debates continue, two decades of provocative work on urban sites has been done across the country, and artist Suzanne Lacy suggests there is now a convergence of many different artists on a common direction, dealing with identity through connecting art to the history of places, and moving away from a feeling of marginalization toward a sense of centrality in the city.[49] Encouraged by public art planners and curators like Richard Andrews in Seattle, Ronald Fleming and Renata Von Tscharner in Cambridge, Pamela Worden of Urban Arts in Boston, or Mary Jane Jacob in Charleston, artists are undertaking projects that involve complex processes of community engagement, as well as works that claim public places in new ways.[50] Worden has organized the public art on the Orange Line, nine stations leading through the Roxbury and Jamaica Plain areas into downtown Boston. In addition to permanent artworks in the stations, she commissioned works of prose and poetry to be sited in public and organized local history, and photography workshops. Jacob, an independent curator in Chicago, has grouped artists with an interest in history in a series of temporary installations for Charleston, *Places with a Past*.[51]

To take just three examples from the hundreds of artists' projects now emerging that remap urban landscape history. Historians and preservationists will see the polemical impact of the installations of Edgar Heap of Birds, an artist of Cheyenne/Arapaho descent who undertook a project in New York City's parks in 1988. He mounted aluminum signs reading "NEW YORK," in backward letters, followed by "TODAY YOUR HOST IS SHINNECOCK," to force viewers, struggling to read the reversed letters, to remember the original Native American settlements. Different tribes whose land was occupied were the subject of signs in different places: Shinnecock, Seneca, Tuscarora, Mohawk, Werpoe, and Manhattan. He repeated a similar set of signs in Vancouver, British Columbia, using a site outside an old government building with LAND REGISTRY carved on the portal that enhanced the piece. A third project, *Day and Night,* located in Pioneer Square in Seattle, picked up the theme of dispossessed Native Americans in the context of homelessness: "Far Away Brothers and Sisters We Still Remember You." Next to a statue of the chief who gave the city its name, the artist wrote, "Chief Seattle Now The Streets Are Our Home" (in both English and the local Native American language).[52]

*The New Charleston* is a far more exhaustive look at one city and the spatial history of African Americans within it over three centuries (figures 3.11, 3.12). Unlike some of the oral history projects that have slowly drawn out material from a community, here artist Houston Conwill, working in collaboration with Estella Conwill Majozo, a poet, and Joseph De Pace, an architect, jump-started the process with a detailed map of historic places of importance to African Americans—slave markets, the hanging tree, community centers. They painted it on the brown wooden floor of a public room with indigo blue, once grown in Charleston, and white made from local oyster shells. The map serves as the stage for new performances by African American musicians, and opens up the terrain of the city to any interested visitor.

The work of this team is complex because the layering of physical and social history is so intense. There are fourteen places, called "Spiritual Signposts," each marked with a crossroads sign of Congolese origin.[53] Peopling this land-

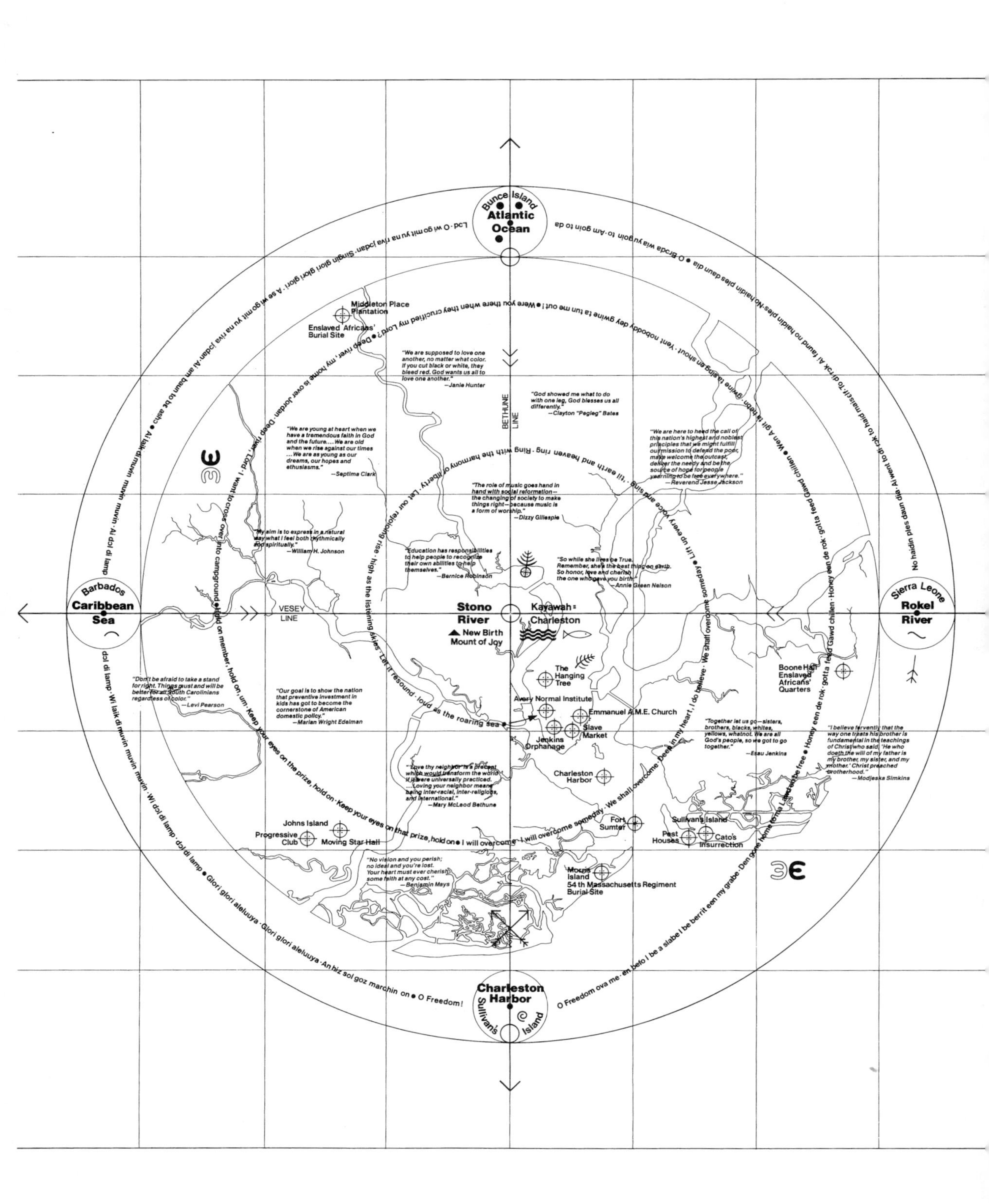
Bunce Island
Atlantic
Ocean
Middleton Place
Plantation
Enslaved Africans'
Burial Site
"We are supposed to love one another, no matter what color. If you cut black or white, they bleed red. God wants us all to love one another."
—Janie Hunter
BETHUNE
LINE
"God showed me what to do with one leg, God blesses us all differently."
—Clayton "Pegleg" Bates
"We are young at heart when we have a tremendous faith in God and the future.... We are old when we rise against our times ... We are as young as our dreams, our hopes and ethusiasms."
—Septima Clark
"We are here to heed the call of this nation's highest and noblest principles that we might fulfill our mission to defend the poor, make welcome the outcast, deliver the needy and be the source of hope for people yearning to be free everywhere."
—Reverend Jesse Jackson
"The role of music goes hand in hand with social reformation—the changing of society to make things right—because music is a form of worship."
—Dizzy Gillespie
"My aim is to express in a natural way what I feel both rhythmically and spiritually."
—William H. Johnson
"Education has responsibilities to help people to recognize their own abilities to help themselves."
—Bernice Robinson
"So while she lives be True. Remember, she's the best thing on earth. So honor, love and cherish the one who gave you birth."
—Annie Green Nelson
Barbados
Caribbean
Sea
VESEY
LINE
Stono
River
New Birth
Mount of Joy
Kayawah =
Charleston
Sierra Leone
Rokel
River
The
Hanging
Tree
Boone Hall
Enslaved
Africans'
Quarters
"Don't be afraid to take a stand for right. Things must and will be better for all South Carolinians regardless of color."
—Levi Pearson
"Our goal is to show the nation that preventive investment in kids has got to become the cornerstone of American domestic policy."
—Marian Wright Edelman
Avery Normal Institute
Emmanuel A.M.E. Church
Slave
Market
Jenkins
Orphanage
"Together let us go—sisters, brothers, blacks, whites, yellows, whatnot. We are all God's people, so we got to go together."
—Esau Jenkins
"I believe fervently that the way one treats his brother is fundamental in the teachings of Christ who said, 'He who doeth the will of my father is my brother, my sister, and my mother.' Christ preached brotherhood."
—Modjeska Simkins
Charleston
Harbor
"'Love thy neighbor' is a precept which would transform the world if it were universally practiced. ...Loving your neighbor means being inter-racial, inter-religious, and international."
—Mary McLeod Bethune
Johns Island
Progressive
Club
Moving Star Hall
Fort
Sumter
Sullivan's Island
Pest
Houses
Cato's
Insurrection
"No vision and you perish; no ideal and you're lost. Your heart must ever cherish some faith at any cost."
—Benjamin Mays
Morris
Island
54 th Massachusetts Regiment
Burial Site
Charleston
Harbor
Sullivan's
Island
Keep your eyes on the prize, hold on · Keep your eyes on that prize, hold on ● I will overcome · I will overcome someday · We shall overcome · We shall overcome · Deep in my heart, I do believe · We shall overcome someday ● Lift up every voice and sing
Glori glori aleluuya · Glori glori aleluuya · An hiz sol goz marchin on ● O Freedom!
O Freedom ova me · en befo I be a slabe I be berrit een my grabe · Den gone home to ma Lawd an be free ● Honey een de rok · gotta feed Gawd chillen · Honey een de rok · gotta feed Gawd chillen ● Wen A git ta hebn · Gwine ta sing en shout · Yent nobody dey gwine ta tun me out ! ● Were you there when they crucified my Lord? ● Deep river, my home is over Jordan · Deep river, Lord · I want to cross over into campground ● Hold on member, hold on, um ·

**3.11** **Houston Conwill, Estella Conwill Majozo, and Joseph De Pace, *The New Charleston*, map of the installation for Avery Research Center of African American History and Culture, 125 Bull Street, Charleston, South Carolina. Part of *Places with a Past*, curated by Mary Jane Jacob, 1991.**

**3.12** ***The New Charleston*, photograph.**

scape, the "Dance Partners: South Carolina Heroic Models" include Mary McLeod Bethune, Benjamin Mays, Septima Clark, William H. Johnson, Janie Hunter, Clayton "Pegleg" Bates, Modjeska Simpkins, Esau Jenkins, Annie Green Nelson, Jesse Jackson, Marian Wright Edelman, Levi Pearson, Bernice Robinson, and Dizzy Gillespie, each of whom is represented by a quotation on the map. What is magical is that, despite the intensive research, the artwork functions not only as a dance floor but also as a cosmogram, a "description of the universe of the African American story," and as an image of a water journey, delineating the waterways that slaves traveled, from the Rokel River in Sierra Leone, across the Atlantic Ocean, through the Caribbean Sea, and into Charleston Harbor.

Drawing visitors onto the dance floor are the spiraling song lines of spirituals (said to originate in Charleston) and freedom songs ("We Shall Overcome" and "Keep Your Eyes on the Prize" originated in Charleston). In the space, spirituals could be heard—sometimes in Gullah—sung by a local group, the Morning Star Hall Singers.[54] The spareness of the space—bare brick walls, uncurtained windows, three wooden columns supporting a wooden roof—makes the floor the dominant element in the room, carrying audiences into the map with its intense indigo outer circle leading to the intriguing, irregular lines of the rivers and creeks. Visitors of all ages and dispositions will find reason to visit and revisit.

The power of public art to engage citizens with urban history also appears in the case of Cincinnati's pigs. In the nineteenth century, Cincinnati was "Porkopolis." Between 1830 and 1870, the first American assembly line was developed there for turning pigs into ham. The landscape suffered while the local economy prospered. The canal ran red with blood from the slaughterhouses; German American immigrant workers came home spattered with blood and smelling of offal.[55] For the celebration of the city's bicentennial in 1989, artist Andrew Leicester proposed a new gateway for Sawyer Point Park that climaxed with a tribute to Porkopolis in the form of four winged pigs atop a suspension bridge. (A collation of images chosen by the artist from local landscape history were also part of the piece, including the Native American Adena culture's serpent mound, smokestacks from old paddle wheel steamers, a canal barge, working locks, and an ark atop a pole showing the flood levels of the Ohio River.)

The citizens erupted in debate about the pigs. Were they a symbol of a smelly industry the city had outgrown? Were they insufficiently genteel? Or did they capture the city's spirit in a witty and wonderful way? The city council heard testimony from both camps. One indignant opponent argued, "We are now poised on entering the twenty-first century as a technologically sophisticated city and pigs are a rural image." He suggested that the pigs represented greed and sloth. Another complained, "I don't think we need the burden of being called the pig city of the world." Proponents claimed, "We've got enough old statues with old bearded men on horses in this town and it's time to have something else." One advocate noted, politely, "I would be pleased to see their porcine presence."[56]

Amid wild applause and loud laughter from partisans, the debate flourished. At least three city council members donned pig snouts before the vote to show their support for the artist, while schoolchildren had their say as well (figures 3.13, 3.14, 3.15). Leicester's winged pigs won, and the piece was constructed. They stand atop the gateway today because Cincinnati's residents chose to remember Porkopolis as an essential part of the city's historic landscape and make it part of a compelling new public history.[57] In this case it was the required review of the art, and the media attention it received, that engaged the public's participation so effectively, but one can find many ways for artists (perhaps in teams with historians) to engage the public at the start.

Metaphorical wit connects private and public, personal and political, the individual and the community, in the most effective public art projects about places that link past and present. Scale and cost are not the defining elements of a public, urban language. Rather, it is metaphorical ingenuity that enables the creators of some projects to summon the res-

**3.13, 3.14, 3.15 Public processes can gather support for controversial history: Cincinnati city council member Arn Bortz, and local children, all wearing pig snouts to show support for artist Andrew Leicester's winged pigs, in *Cincinnati Gateway*, 1988. (Cincinnati Post, Maureen France, Andrew Leicester.)**

onance of urban public life, while others fail and their projects fall flat. Working in the interstices of public history, planning, and preservation to build meaning at the urban scale is complex, but artists' use of the stone walls of Chiswell, the rivers of Charleston, or the pigs of Cincinnati focuses an audience's attention. (Of course, an obnoxious art project draws public criticism fast, as did the city of Dallas's recent attempt to provide itself with a "Wild West" image by commissioning a vast herd of bronze steers driven by three bronze mounted cowboys.) It all comes back to community process. No public art can succeed in enhancing the social meaning of place without a solid base of historical research and community support.

Public history, architectural preservation, environmental protection, and public art can take on a special evocative role in helping to define a city's history if, and only if, they are complemented by a strong community process that establishes the context of social memory. That is not to say that there are simple guidelines for a good public process. This is an emerging area of interdisciplinary work, and in all of these related fields some practitioners are looking for ways to merge their knowledge and concerns with those of residents. There are bound to be conflicts between the outsiders and the insiders, as well as between various individuals, whether members of a project team or residents. Artists, historians, citizens, and planners who come to this kind of work need both historical and spatial imagination to learn to work together to identify and interpret people's history in the urban landscape.

All of the participants in such a process transcend their traditional roles. For the historian, this means leaving the security of the library to listen to the community's evaluation of its own history and the ambiguities this implies. It means working in media—from pamphlets to stone walls—that offer less control and a less predictable audience than academic journals or university presses do. It also means exchanging the well-established roles of academic life for the uncertainties of collaboration with others who may take history for granted as the raw material for their own creativity, rather than a creative work in itself.

For the artist or designer seeking a broader audience in the urban landscape than a single patron or a gallery or museum can provide, it means being willing to engage historical and political material. The kind of public art that truly contributes to a sense of place needs to start with a new kind of relationship to the people whose history is being represented. This means that the artist is involved in an art-making process very different from conventional conceptions of art as the progression of an idiosyncratic, personal style. This kind of process exchanges the established system of shows in galleries or museums for the uncertainties of collaboration with others and community review.

For the public art curator, environmental planner, or urban designer, it means being willing to work for the community, in incremental ways, rather than trying to control grand plans and strategies from the top down. It means understanding that citizens and their grass roots organizations are a source of meaning as legitimate as elected officials and the real estate lobby that often provides the bulk of campaign funding in city politics. It means working alongside—rather than within—the established system of getting things done by phone calls from powerful people in City Hall or the local museum. Funding is always difficult, and the planner on such projects often becomes a nonprofit developer.

For the community member or local resident, it means being willing to engage in a lengthy process of developing priorities for a place, and working through their meanings with a group. This demands patience as insiders educate outsiders and people of different ages, genders, and political views try to agree on what is meaningful and what is creative. Like any other local issue, from parking to street widenings, protection of the public landscape can be exasperating, but it is never unimportant.

While interdisciplinary, community-based projects are not always easy to accomplish, they are not necessarily enormously expensive. They require a labor of love from everyone involved, transcending old roles and expectations, but these are not million-dollar projects. They compare favorably with the funding required to mount a major museum exhibit on city history, or to produce a documentary film for television. And unlike either of these media, public installations in the city refresh the memories of citizens who are passing. A large and diverse audience for urban history exists today in American cities—people who will never go to history museums, attend public humanities programs, or read scholarly journals. Entrepreneurial public historians may be able to reach them occasionally in community centers, churches, or union halls. Successful installations in public places, in all parts of the city, may reach even more people, and, if these are permanent installations, may reach them on a continual basis.

While a single, preserved historic place may trigger potent memories, networks of such places begin to reconnect social memory on an urban scale. Networks of related places, organized in a thematic way, exploit the potential of reaching urban audiences more fully and with more complex histories. There is "a politics to place construction," David Harvey has observed, including "material, representational and symbolic activities which find their hallmark in the way in which individuals invest in places and thereby empower themselves collectively."[58] People invest places with social and cultural meaning, and urban landscape history can provide a framework for connecting those meanings into contemporary urban life.

# II Los Angeles: Public Pasts in the Downtown Landscape

# 4 Invisible Angelenos

**I am invisible, understand, simply because people refuse to see me. Like the bodiless heads you see sometimes in circus side-shows, it is as though I have been surrounded by mirrors of hard, distorting glass. When they approach me they see only my surroundings, themselves, or figments of their imagination—indeed, everything and anything except me.**

**Ralph Ellison, *Invisible Man***

Los Angeles embodies the racially and culturally diverse American metropolis (figure 4.1). The second largest city in the United States, within its limits the 1990 census counted 3,485,398 people: just under 40 percent Hispanic (any race); about 37 percent white (not Hispanic); 13 percent black (not Hispanic); just under 10 percent Asian American or Pacific Islander; and 0.5 percent Native American (representing hundreds of tribal groups from all over the country).[1] Los Angeles County totals almost nine million; the larger LA metropolitan area (SMSA) stretches across five counties, with an area of 34,000 square miles and a population of almost thirteen and a half million. Almost as soon as any demographic figures are totaled they are subject to debate as to their accuracy (illegal aliens and the homeless are undercounted) or simply out of date. And of course many Angelenos have complex ethnic backgrounds that include more than one census category.

Until Los Angeles's citizens are able to forge a coherent account of their own past and their historic urban landscape, it will be difficult to orient either long-term residents or new immigrants to the place. A large number of Los Angeles's residents are foreign born: 37.9 percent of the city, and 32.7 percent of the county.[2] According to Zena Pearlstone, author of *Ethnic L.A.*, "Los Angeles is the second largest Mexican, Armenian, Filipino, Salvadoran, and Guatemalan city in the world, the third largest Canadian city, and has the largest Japanese, Iranian, Cambodian, and Gypsy communities in the United States."[3] Predictably this creates great diversity for public education. The Los Angeles Unified School District enrolls children who speak 96 different native languages. Hollywood High School alone houses students who speak 35 native languages, including "Armenian, Rumanian, Farsi, Tagalog, Khmer, Lao, Samoan, Vietnamese, Thai, Afghan, Dari, Urdu, Cantonese, Portuguese, Russian, Hebrew, French, Bengali, Korean, Hungarian, Arabic, Hindi, Visayan, Formosan, Gujarati, Mandarin, Greek, Mandingo, Swedish, Polish, and Tahitian" as well as English and Spanish.[4]

The mix of cultures projects itself onto the urban landscape quickly. One mini-mall Pearlstone observed at Vermont and

**4.1 Downtown Los Angeles, 1991. (West Light.)**

First streets included "a Filipino beauty salon, a Saudi Arabian-run butcher shop, a Cambodian doughnut shop, and a Vietnamese-run gift store, as well as a Filipino from Hong Kong renting videos and a Hispanic managing the pizza parlor."[5] These overlapping groups produce an energetic, chaotic street scene, full of surprises. Jewish restaurants offer kosher burritos; a restaurant in Little Tokyo displays a plastic pepperoni pizza in the front window as if it were sushi. As artist Guillermo Gómez-Peña has noted, "Cities like Tijuana and Los Angeles, once socio-urban aberrations, are becoming models of a new hybrid culture, full of uncertainty and vitality.... In this context, concepts like 'high culture,' 'ethnic purity,' 'cultural identity,' 'beauty,' and 'fine arts' are absurdities and anachronisms. Like it or not, we are attending the funeral of modernity and the birth of a new culture."[6]

Vernacular architecture changes almost as fast as costume, menus, or slang. An Anglo supermarket becomes a Korean American Christian church, with a billboard advertising grace instead of cantaloupes. An African American home for young working women becomes a shelter for homeless Central American refugees. An Anglo American apartment complex in the San Fernando Valley is taken over by one thousand Cambodian residents, who reorganize it as if it were a traditional village. Laundry is shared and residents tend herb and vegetable gardens in the main courtyard.[7] A Chinese American entrepreneur resists a traffic rerouting plan because it would bring customers to his restaurant by a different door, and *feng shui* suggests "closing off ... one door would be analogous to cutting off one of the heads of the five-headed dragon."[8]

Los Angeles's population has always been diverse, from the day that the Gabrieleño Indians watched forty-four settlers of mixed Spanish, Native American, and African heritage found a new pueblo near the Gabrieleño village of Yang-Na in 1781. Yet city biographies and the official landmark process have favored the history of a small minority of white, male landholders, bankers, business and political leaders, and their architects. In 1986, when Gail Dubrow counted the city of Los

Angeles's designated cultural-historic landmarks, she found that 97.7 percent were Anglo American. Only 2.3 percent celebrated Native American, African American, Latino, or Asian American history, despite the fact that these so-called "minority" groups now comprise about 60 percent of the population. Only 4 percent of the official landmarks were associated with any aspect of women's history, including Anglo American women's history.[9] So three-quarters of the current population must find its public, collective past in a small fraction of the city's monuments, or live with someone else's choices about the city's history. The major ethnic groups that have always been part of the city have been dispossessed. And the new immigrants have every reason to be confused.

Because Los Angeles's history encompasses different ethnic groups, many influential writers have been unable to perceive the importance of the city's nonwhite population, unable to recognize that people of color occupy any significant part of the urban landscape. Such writers may go downtown, but never or rarely to East LA or South Central. The focus of their landscape analysis becomes houses, swimming pools, cars, and pop culture. Charles W. Moore, noted architect and critic, came to Los Angeles in 1964 to review California architecture and urbanism but remained puzzled: "it is not at all clear what the public realm consists of, or even, for the time being, who needs it." Moore found downtown lacking in interest and concluded breezily, "Disneyland must be regarded as the most important single piece of construction in the West in the past several decades . . . it is engaged in replacing many of those elements of the public realm which have vanished in the featureless private floating world of Southern California, whose only edge is the ocean, and whose center is otherwise undiscoverable (unless . . . it turns out to be on Manhattan Island.)"[10]

Following Moore, architectural historian Reyner Banham from England solidified the cult of the LA vernacular. His *Los Angeles: The Architecture of Four Ecologies* in 1971 featured the pop culture "Surfurbia," and "Foothills," and "Autopia," and dismissed "The Plains of Id," Central LA from downtown to Watts (which, despite the 1965 riots, he passed over as a trouble spot lacking transportation). He joked that "like earlier generations of English intellectuals who taught themselves Italian in order to read Dante in the original, I learned to drive in order to read Los Angeles in the original."[11] It never occurred to him that Spanish, Chinese, and Japanese might unlock parts of the city, or that South Central, East LA, Chinatown, and Little Tokyo might demonstrate cultural differences expressed in urban form. The 1972 BBC TV show *Reyner Banham Loves Los Angeles* reiterated the joys of driving and is still notable for some heavy ogling of LA women.

Cliches about Los Angeles take off from the Moore/Banham pop culture view of the urban landscape, where Disneyland, swimming pools, and freeways are icons and people of color are invisible. These ideas still pervade journalism, films, and the casual comments of the cultural elite. Richard Koshalek, director of the Museum of Contemporary Art (MOCA), told *New Yorker* writer Adam Gopnik that moneyed Angelenos seemed to care little for the landmarks of their own city, and do little to defend them. When asked to name a couple of places, he mentioned the demolished Brown Derby (a fashionable Wilshire Boulevard restaurant in the shape of a brown stucco hat) and a La Cienega hot dog stand built in the shape of a hot dog.[12]

Perhaps inability to comprehend ethnic diversity, and the related invisibility of large parts of the cultural landscape, can be remedied. The city's terrain reflects social history and physical forms many professionals are not yet adept at reading. James Rojas, an MIT-trained architect and urban planner who grew up in East Los Angeles and feels at home in the Mexican American streetscape, has a lot to say: "Architects have missed the role of people in creating a 'place' because they are trained to look at people as users of space.... People are both users and creators of a place.... People activate settings merely by their presence. Their bodies, faces and movements create an energy that is almost a metaphysical aesthetic, because the central core of the enacted environment is motion." At another point he comments, "East Los Angeles is not Mexico and the front yards in East Los Angeles combine both the 'plaza' and the 'courtyards' of Mexico into one form that is expressed by the use of the residents. This defines the identity of the place."[13]

No one has yet been able to write a definitive social history of Los Angeles's multiethnic population, a definitive economic history of the city's industries and multiethnic labor force, or a complete account of its historic cultural landscape. An excellent treatment of Los Angeles's past by Carey McWilliams in the 1940s called attention to ethnic diversity. Urban historian Robert Fogelson, writing in the 1960s, also recognized the ethnic complexity of the place, as part of urban expansion. He was discouraged at how the growing city had fragmented between 1850 to 1930, when, as he saw it, "Los Angeles was divided between an overwhelming native white majority and a sizable colored minority. Nowhere on the Pacific coast, not even in cosmopolitan San Francisco, was there so diverse a mixture of racial groups, so visible a contrast and so pronounced a separation among people, as in Los Angeles."[14]

By the 1980s, a fuller, more focused ethnic history was emerging, carrying the topic into the second half of the twentieth century and chronicling far more spirited and engaged ethnic communities than Fogelson had imagined. Scholars including Lucie Cheng, Sucheng Chan, Rodolfo Acuña, Richard Griswold del Castillo, Mario García, Albert Camarillo, Ricardo Romo, Vicki Ruiz, Lonnie Bunch, Ronald Takaki and Noritaka Yagasaki created rich ethnic histories of Latinos, African Americans, and Asian Americans that suggested the larger outline the urban story of Los Angeles must fill. George Sánchez, Timothy Fong, and Valerie Matsumoto are among dozens of authors adding to these ethnic histories in the 1990s.[15]

Any account of the place must begin with the Gabrieleño Indians, whose forty villages dotted the region before the first Mexican settlers ever arrived. One of the largest and most

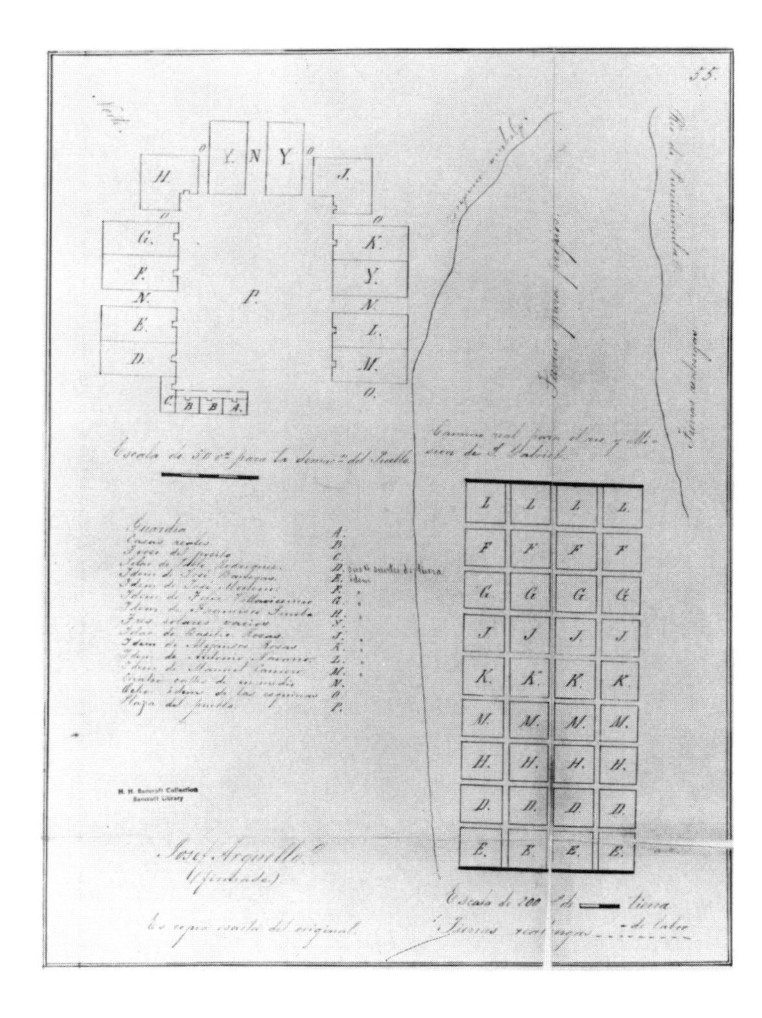

**4.2 Plan of the pueblo of Los Angeles, 1781. (Bancroft Library, University of California, Berkeley.)**

prosperous of these, Yang-Na, drew the admiration of early missionaries and explorers. As a result the Mexican colonizing party of 1781 was directed near the Yang-Na site to found their pueblo of Los Angeles (figure 4.2). Eventually the Gabrieleños' labor was drawn upon for efforts to build ranching and wine-growing operations.[16]

The *pobladores* who came from Mexico to found the town in 1781 included people of Spanish, Native American, African American, and mestizo descent. After California's statehood,

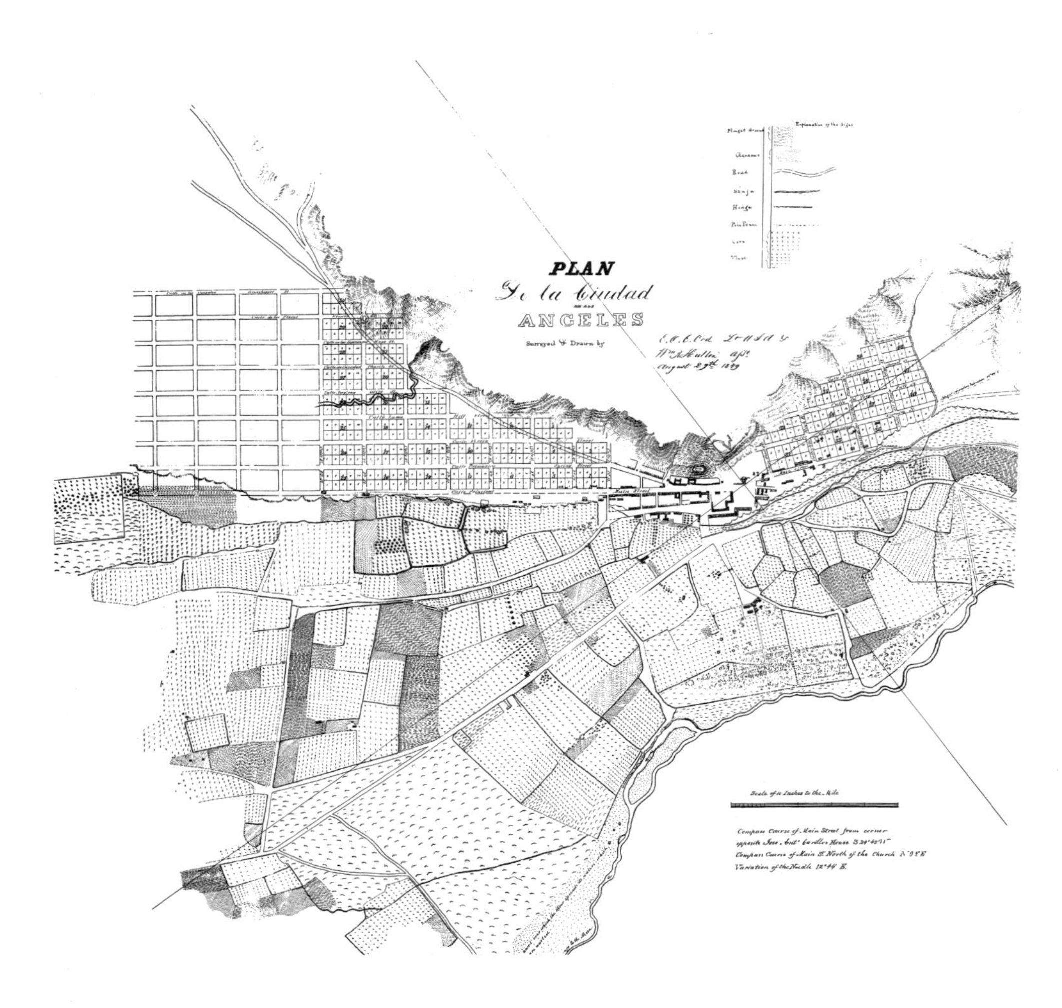


**4.3 Plan of the city of Los Angeles, Ord Survey, 1849. (UCLA Special Collections.)**

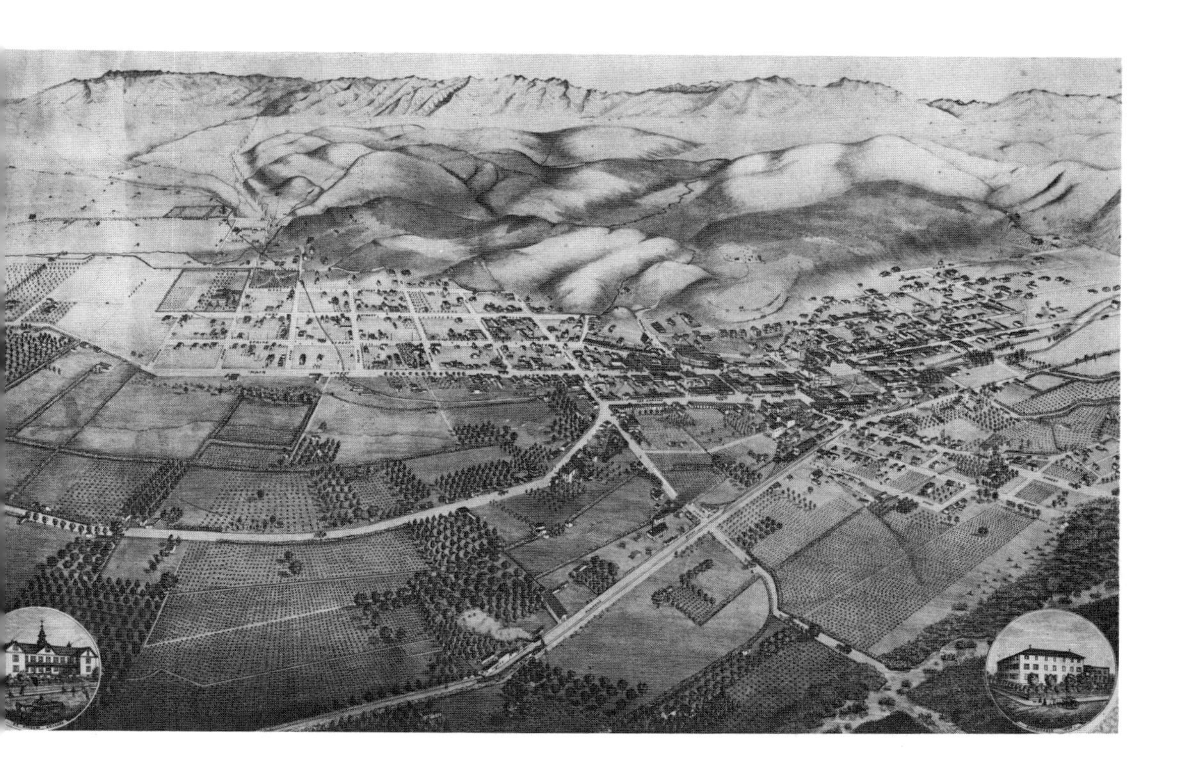

**4.4 View of the city of Los Angeles, 1871, Britton and Rey. (UCLA Special Collections.)**

Lieutenant Ord redrew the town plan to show a new commercial grid, with streets labeled in both Spanish and English (figure 4.3), and the number of persons of Mexican heritage began declining steadily. Still, before the connection was built to the transcontinental railroad in 1876, Los Angeles remained what Antonio Rios-Bustamante has called a "predominantly Mexican town" (figure 4.4).[17] The original Spanish speakers were almost completely absorbed by the Anglo Americans who arrived daily by the trainload after 1876, but at the beginning of this century the Mexican presence increased again with large-scale migration to jobs in railroad and streetcar line construction, migratory agricultural work, the citrus industry, brick, tile, and cement plants, and general manual labor everywhere. Persons of Mexican heritage were the largest minority in the city by 1930.[18] Attempts by Anglo American officials to repatriate residents of Mexican heritage in the Depression had short-term results, but this group continued to grow, joined by immigrants from many other parts of Latin America.

Like Mexican immigrants, African Americans contributed to the founding of Los Angeles. Among the forty-four original settlers in 1781, more than half had some African ancestry. The next wave of migration came with the land boom of the 1880s, when, like other American-born migrants, African Americans were drawn to southern California by the possibilities of jobs in service and industry and a comfortable climate.[19] By 1900, almost three thousand African Americans resided in the Los Angeles area, making it "the largest black settlement on the Pacific Coast."[20] The proportion of African Americans in the total population remained at about 2 to 3 percent until the World War II period, when racial discrimination in war employment was forbidden and migrants seeking jobs in defense plants began to increase steadily.[21]

**4.5 View of the city of Los Angeles, 1890. (UCLA Special Collections.)**

Asians were also a visible minority in the city by 1900. The Chinese came to California originally to mine gold and later to build railroads and aqueducts.[22] They settled in Los Angeles's Chinatown in large numbers between 1880 and 1900, numbering over two thousand in the urban area at the turn of the century. Many ran market gardens and produce operations.[23] Some worked in the vineyards and citrus groves and ran laundries and restaurants. A labor shortage arose from federal restrictions on Chinese immigration during this period, causing an increase in Japanese immigration concentrated in the citrus industry, flower farming, agriculture, and fishing.[24] A large number of Japanese moved to Los Angeles from San Francisco following the 1906 earthquake. By 1908 over six thousand Japanese lived in the urban area.[25] San Pedro was the largest fishing port in the United States, and included a substantial colony of Japanese Americans so that one woman remarked, "When I first came here, I never thought that I was in America. Everything was the same as in my small home in Japan. All our neighbors were Japanese. We [all] knew each other."[26]

Anglo American settlers did not arrive in Los Angeles in substantial numbers until after 1848. At the end of the Mexican War, some saw an opportunity to win land on the ranchos away from their owners through complicated legal challenges to their Mexican land titles. With the completion of the Southern Pacific and Santa Fe Railroads, settlers from the East and Midwest began to arrive, some to retire in the sun, others to engage in extensive real estate speculation. Streetcar lines expanded in all directions. Towns were platted everywhere, but some did not thrive (figure 4.5). Boom and bust followed one another. The discovery of oil in the 1890s proved a stable source of income and led to the development of manufacturing of various kinds, with furniture, sportswear, and prefabricated houses well established before 1930. Film and music developed before World War II. Then the defense industries grew to support the war in the Pacific and remained strong through wars in Korea, Vietnam, and the Persian Gulf.

As the old Anglo American history is rewritten, it is clear that Los Angeles has many ethnic pasts, as well as workers' pasts and women's pasts. These are difficult to synthesize. In addition to the Los Angeles Museum of Natural History, the Southwest Museum, which addresses Native American culture, the California Afro-American Museum, and the Japanese American National Museum are active, and Chinese American and Latino museums are emerging. But as the city approaches the twenty-first century, it seems especially important to sketch the urban whole as more than the sum of the parts, to try to emphasize an inclusive perspective as the framework for a new public history that can be shared by all citizens.[27]

Every ethnic group struggled against the Anglo American community's dominance after the middle of the nineteenth century. With the exception of the Native Americans, whose numbers shrank rapidly in the colonial period, many groups were contending for jobs and housing in Los Angeles at the end of the nineteenth century as the city grew. All were striving to find ways to nurture community and family ties.

While some lived in neighborhoods dominated by a single ethnic group, such as Little Tokyo, many of them shared the spaces of ethnically mixed neighborhoods like Boyle Heights in East Los Angeles, home in the 1890s to immigrants from Japan, Mexico, Russia, and Eastern Europe. Because the city functioned as more than a series of enclaves, the largest story of Los Angeles is one of the migration experience, job opportunities, bachelor life or family life, neighborhood supports and difficulties, with each group's unique experience contributing to a larger set of common urban themes. This is still true today.

The city's different ethnic groups have all had to deal with women's economic roles and civil rights. They have all had to develop attitudes to upward mobility and assimilation, as well as to occupational segregation, economic hardship, and racial prejudice. A resonant public history in Los Angeles will sketch these common themes while accounting for cultural differences. Both individuals and communities need to find ways to connect to the larger urban narrative. Individual lives are unique and resist stereotyping, but pasts are woven together in the making of the cultural landscape and community spirit of an urban center.

The largest theme each group has had to deal with, a constantly recurring theme, is loss of territory, or the threat of losing the right to live in the city, but this comes in different forms at different times. Native Americans struggle to survive against exploitation first by colonizers from Mexico and then by their Anglo American successors. For African Americans in the early days of Los Angeles, the threat is slavery and being returned to slave states. For the Mexican Americans, it is repatriation to Mexico during the hard times of the Depression, and for the militant organizers, political deportation in the late 1940s. For Chinese Americans, a massacre takes place in the 1870s and in the 1880s exclusion laws restrict their arrival. For Japanese Americans, Executive Order 9066 forces their relocation to internment camps during the Second World War; citizens lose homes and businesses. The constant threat of being dispossessed makes each community's attachment to the urban landscape particularly poignant. Heroic efforts were often needed to maintain a livelihood in an ordinary neighborhood.

An inclusive public history, rooted in the struggles over the urban landscape, must attempt to deal in a serious way with issues like slavery, internment, deportation, and economic exploitation, as well as prosperity. While dealing with the specifics of Native American, African American, Japanese American, Chinese American, and Latino history, as well as Anglo American history, it is important not to suggest that each group is the only audience for its own story. This is also a reason not to burden every ethnic group within the city with the exclusive responsibility for preserving and interpreting its own history. When small groups within diverse urban communities attempt to recover their own lost pasts, they may compose compensatory histories. The narratives will often be similar—this is how our grandfathers fought for our share as new immigrants, this is how they succeeded, this is how a few unusual people even amassed wealth and influence. (Perhaps the very same unusual people have funded the exhibition or publication.)

The underlying, sometimes unstated experiences will be less hopeful—confinement to a ghetto or barrio, segregation in housing, schooling, and work opportunities, legal discrimination, competition with other ethnic groups, suppression of women and children by the male competition. Compensatory histories may nurture ethnic pride, but they also breed divisions between ethnic groups, and between men and women, as well as individual bitterness among those who didn't fare as well as the exceptional individuals.

The larger picture of how groups survived, or didn't survive, is more important than how a few members of a group succeeded. Diverse audiences in American cities today know that stories of bitterness and difficult times have to be told as part of their urban history. It is the controversial history Americans need to reclaim as our own, in order to give meaning to the contradictory urban landscapes of cities today, where wealth and neglect, success and frustration, often appear side by side.

# 5 Workers' Landscapes and Livelihoods

**We met in spinach, fell in love in peaches, and married in tomatoes.**

**March, August, and October according to a cannery worker**

Together, the natural and the built environments form the cultural landscape of a city, its diversity and unity. In Los Angeles, the natural landscape within the urban area includes the dry creeks, sycamores, live oaks, and dusty plains of summer drought, as well as the flooded creeks, intense green grasses, sprouting wildflowers, and sharp scent of eucalyptus after the winter rains. The built world is equally vivid. In East LA fresh-cut fruit stands, painted trucks, political murals, and statues of the Virgin of Guadalupe mark the streets. In Little Tokyo, silk kimonos, paper fans, and slow-moving floats form and reform the patterns of the annual street parades. In South Central, one long note wails from a saxophone played by a high school student; rockers creak on the porches of a street of wooden bungalows on a hot summer night.

Contrast historic inner-city neighborhoods shaped by distinct ethnic cultures with the increasing sameness of contemporary American urbanization: freeways, parking lots, office towers, malls, suburban tracts. In the past half-century three federal programs—urban renewal, interstate highway building, and home ownership supported by mortgage subsidies—have obscured large sections of the natural landscape and blotted out the cultural landscape of varied human activities in many American urban places. These projects use taxpayers' dollars to muffle history, pave geography, standardize social relationships. Behind these urban policies lies some mistaken notion about the desirability of assimilation to a suburban world that might be Anglo American if it were not so impoverished in its meanings.

As a nation, Americans are increasingly attuned to rescuing the natural qualities of places—the creeks and the live oaks. But we need to nurture the social characteristics of places too if we are to retain social history in the urban landscape, and learn to design with memory rather than against it. Row houses and bungalow courts, orange groves and factories reflect the varied occupations and family lives of working people through patterns in built space. Without interpretation, the fragile traces of urban neighborhoods constructed by earlier generations of Americans may be too vulnerable to survive economically and physically, given the scale of contemporary real estate development. But they offer the potential of places set against the flow of time, places to recollect the meaning of working lives for the individual, the family, the community, and the city. Rescued and interpreted, modest dwellings, union halls, and small workshops can tell current residents about the texture and pace of life in the city as previous generations experienced it, men, women, and children of every ethnic group.

Tying landscape history to social history, it is possible to portray the creation of Los Angeles as both a spatial and a social process between its earliest settlement and World War II. This emphasizes the making of the place as an activity of ordinary working people as well as business elites, politicians, and designers. At the center of this process is the skill and energy workers have expended to feed, clothe, and house the population. These workers have been men, women, and children of every ethnic group employed in vineyards, citrus groves, flower fields, oil fields, and manufacturing enterprises of many different kinds.

The sequence of historic urban landscapes associated with these productive activities encapsulates the story of how the city evolved from ranching and agriculture to oil, manufacturing, and real estate. Raymond Williams has defined nuanced environmental thinking: "avoid a crude contrast between 'nature' and 'production', . . . seek the practical terms of the idea which should supersede both: the idea of 'livelihood,' within, and yet active within, a better understood physical world and all truly necessary physical processes."[1] Within the idea of livelihood, it is essential to locate women's unpaid labor in the household and community, as well as women's, men's, and children's involvement in the paid labor force, in order to understand the growth of a small Native American village into a world city.

Recently there has been a good deal written about late twentieth-century Los Angeles as a fragmented, "postmodern" space where luxury hotels are juxtaposed with junked cars, and the towers of multinational corporations coexist with homeless shelters. Edward Soja's fascinating *Postmodern Geographies* portrays Los Angeles as the product of the spatial machinations of international capital, decipherable only by a new kind of Marxist analysis that stresses the regional and global structure of economic power and emphasizes space (geography) rather than time (history).[2] Yet the new geography to decode contemporary LA is often abstruse: "The reassertion of space in critical social theory—and in critical political praxis—will depend upon a continued deconstruction of a still occlusive historicism and many additional voyages of exploration into the heterotopias of contemporary postmodern geographies."[3]

Mike Davis's absorbing *City of Quartz* also provides an extensive analysis of the white, male power structure, its police force and prisons, as well as its cultural apparatus and spatial aggressiveness. Missing in both *Postmodern Geographies* and *City of Quartz* are sympathetic accounts of women and ethnic communities, situated historically as well as spatially. The old conquest histories of the city relied on an outworn ideal of a universal, white male citzen, and relegated women and people of color—workers who should be at the center of any city's story—to the fringes. For a new spatial analysis to be balanced, the active roles of diverse workers searching for a livelihood in the city need to be discussed as fully as the decisions of banks, corporations, police, and the military.[4] But Soja writes: "The centre has thus also become the periphery, as the corporate citadel of multinational capital rests with consummate agility upon a broadening base of alien populations." In context, these "alien" populations seem to be new immigrants, but Soja has little interest in distinguishing them from people of color who have lived and worked in the city for a long time. He conflates them all, and women, in another description of the labor force: "the reserve army of migrant and minority workers (augmented by a massive entry of women into the workforce) has grown to unprecedented levels."[5]

In contrast, political philosopher Iris Marion Young suggests that "social justice in the city requires the realization of a politics of difference ... institutional and ideological means for recognizing and affirming diverse social groups by giving political representation to these groups, and celebrating their distinctive characteristics and cultures." There is an underlying spatial and social logic to Los Angeles that diverse citizens can readily understand, if workers' own landscapes and livelihoods are central to public history. Fredric Jameson has intuited "the need for maps," because political culture "will necessarily have to raise spatial issues." His goal, "an aesthetic of cognitive mapping," suggests that politically conscious mapping would enable citizens to situate themselves in relation to both spatial and social forces.[6]

A remapping of downtown Los Angeles can reclaim some parts of its spatial history, by sketching a sequence of working landscapes from the earliest times to about 1940. It can suggest ways to tie the social to the spatial, to develop a method for investigating a city's urban landscapes, based on fragments of knowledge about its social and physical history. One could use this as the framework for a more extended social and environmental history of Los Angeles that would explore ethnic and gender issues in detail; here my focus is on locating men,

**5.1 The Power of Place, locations of historic sites in downtown Los Angeles (* indicates standing structure): Area of Wolfskill Grove, between Third and Sixth, San Pedro and Alameda. *City Market, Ninth to Twelfth, San Julian to San Pedro. *Flower Market, 755 Wall Street. Area of City Oil Field, bounded by Figueroa, Beverly, Belmont, Temple (*some derricks visible). Pacific Ready-Cut Homes, 1330 South Hill Street. *Fire Station 30, 1401 South Central Avenue. Biddy Mason's homestead, now Broadway Spring Center, 333 South Spring Street, *site of public art by Betye Saar and Sheila de Bretteville with The Power of Place. *Embassy Auditorium, 843 South Grand Street, site of Power of Place workshop and subject of art by Rupert Garcia and Celia Muñoz. *First Street Little Tokyo Historic District, north side of First Street between North Central and San Pedro.**

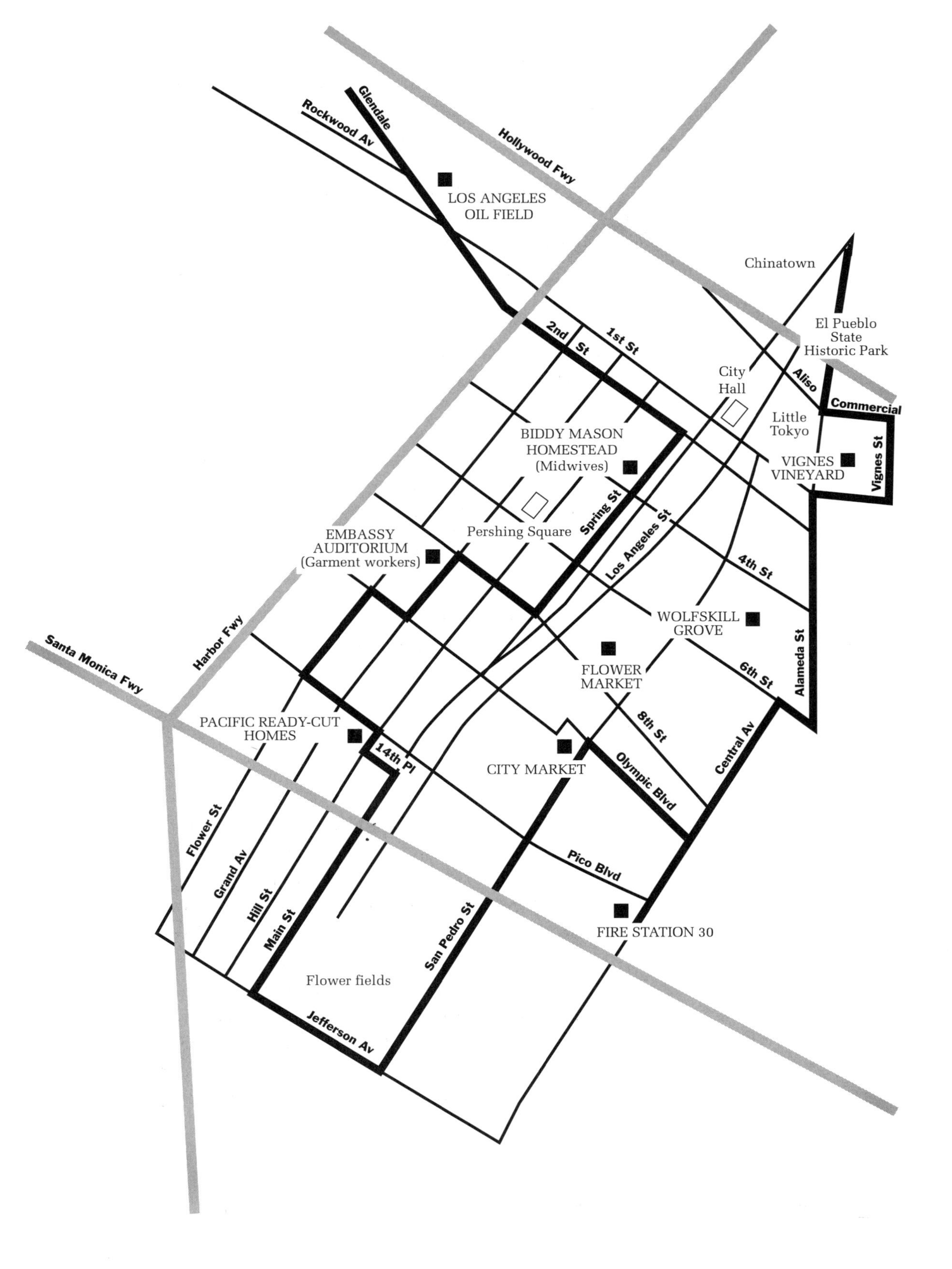
Hollywood Fwy
Glendale
Rockwood Av
LOS ANGELES
OIL FIELD
Chinatown
El Pueblo
State
Historic Park
2nd
St
1st St
City
Hall
Aliso
Commercial
Little
Tokyo
BIDDY MASON
HOMESTEAD
(Midwives)
VIGNES
VINEYARD
Vignes St
Pershing Square
Spring St
Los Angeles St
EMBASSY
AUDITORIUM
(Garment workers)
4th St
WOLFSKILL
GROVE
Alameda St
Harbor Fwy
Santa Monica Fwy
FLOWER
MARKET
6th St
PACIFIC READY-CUT
HOMES
8th St
14th Pl
CITY MARKET
Olympic Blvd
Central Av
Flower St
Grand Av
Hill St
Main St
Pico Blvd
San Pedro St
FIRE STATION 30
Flower fields
Jefferson Av

women, and children in the historic working landscapes of downtown, in order to create some new public history projects. (These interpretive projects by historians, artists, and designers follow in the next few chapters.)

Each shift in the economic development of Los Angeles brought about some change in the work force, and in the landscape. These transformations continue. Today the vineyards and groves have moved to the edge of the county. Oil wells are fast disappearing. The factories endure as new generations of workers struggle for a living in the city. This brief chapter cannot encompass an account of the entire city's spatial development, or the region's. All the spaces mapped here connect into a narrative path that follows economic development up to about 1940 in downtown.[7] It is a selective look at some significant historic landscapes whose traces remain (figure 5.1). Three kinds of resources are noted: buildings with status as designated city landmarks needing broader social interpretation; buildings important to social history that are not now designated as landmarks but should be; and vacant sites of historic importance where no structures remain but where new public art or open space designs might be possible to commemorate their significance.

### Native American Landscapes, from Hunting, Fishing, and Gathering to the Missions, the Pueblo, and the Ranchos

Gabrieleño Indians, a Shoshonean people, the first inhabitants of southern California, lived in as many as forty villages between Laguna Beach and Malibu. Yang-Na was sited north of the location of the first pueblo, on the banks of the Los Angeles River. (It was near the North Main Street Bridge.) The Gabrieleño way of life depended on sustenance from the land itself. The women foraged for acorns from live oak trees, ground them into meal, boiled it into porridge, and seasoned it with herbs they gathered, wild grapes, and berries. The men fished the Los Angeles River, trapped and hunted rabbits, deer, and antelope. From willow branches growing near the river they built frames for round huts covered with tules. The riverbank's oak and sycamore groves, cottonwoods, alders, sagebrush, and wild grapevines offered shelter to elk, antelope, deer, wildcats, and bears. Birds were abundant.

A colonizing party from Mexico admired the fertile location of Yang-Na and decided to site the pueblo of Los Angeles nearby in 1781. The nearest Franciscan mission, established in 1771 at San Gabriel, gave its own name to the indigenous residents who inhabited their territory. The Gabrileños were recruited both to the missions and to the sheep and cattle ranching operations of the Spanish colonial era (figures 5.2, 5.3). They provided the labor for the cultivation of oranges, grapes, and wheat, as well as for the sheep and cattle trade, whose products were wool, hides, and tallow exported by sea.[8] Soon these indigenous workers were joined by laborers drawn from the colonists of mixed Spanish, Native American, and African American heritage.

Yang-Na decreased in size and influence but existed side by side with the pueblo until 1836, when residents of Yang-Na were forcibly relocated to an area close to Commercial and Alameda streets at the southeastern edge of the plaza. (Some others who worked at the winery were housed in an Indian village near the river, close to the Vignes vineyard.) In 1845 police established a site called Pueblito on the hills above the river but demolished it in 1847. A market for Indian labor was also run by the local police, who picked up Gabrieleños for drunkenness and sold their labor to the highest bidder to pay their fines. After a spell of work, often the workers were paid in *aguardiente* (a local brandy) and the cycle of drunkenness, arrest, and labor to pay the fine began again.[9]

A small plaque in Doheny Park marks Yang-Na, but physical traces of the Native American landscape are very hard to find anywhere near downtown. One approach to commemorating the Gabrieleño era would be to focus on features of the natural landscape that were important to their culture, such as the river, the hills, and the indigenous plants (including the foodstuffs and the house-building materials), as well as to highlight the location of Yang-Na.

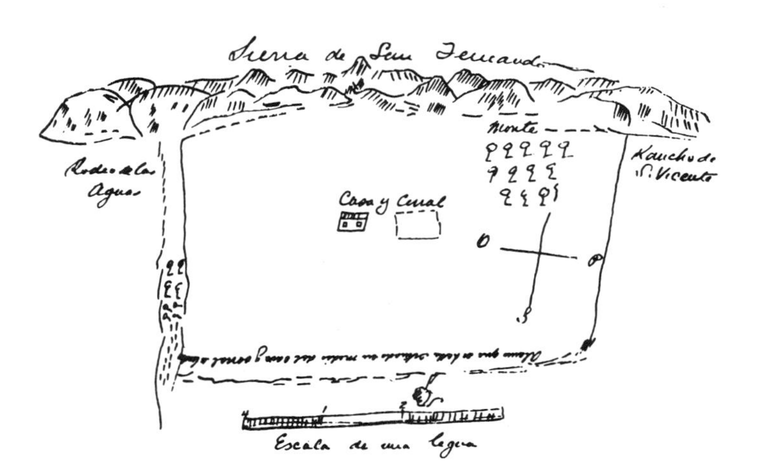

**5.2 Map of Rancho de Buenos Ayres, located in the Westwood area of Los Angeles County, one of many ranchos granted to a soldier who accompanied the party of settlers in 1781. (From W. W. Robinson, *Land in California*, University of California Press.)**

**5.3 Native American sheep shearers. (Security Pacific Collection, Los Angeles Public Library.)**

In "The City of the Angels and the City of the Saints," Captain Edward O. C. Ord's account of a trip to Los Angeles and San Bernardino in 1856, he commented on "a nice hot ride with black dust covering us from ears to toes," a ride by stagecoach across "arid brown steppes" grazed by great herds of cattle, to reach the settlement that first appeared as "a thin line of green some fifteen miles off."[10] That thin line of green, corn fields, vineyards, and citrus groves, patterned the Los Angeles landscape after the 1830s as grapes, oranges, and lemons, first grown in the region by Franciscans and their Native American workers at the San Fernando and San Gabriel missions, became important commercial products.

Ord, in the 1850s, observed the Native American workers with the eyes of an Army officer who had been assigned to subdue indigeneous people in many different settings, from Seminole Florida to Oregon: "Through these vines and behind the hedges low huts peeped out, open sheds or corridors before them, whereunder squatted sundry brown dames in red petticoats, with maybe two of three bare brown babies sprawling about amongst lots of dogs, & perhaps a hairy headed native composed of cigarito, sombrero, serape and spurs, lazily chatting with the dames as he sits on his steed. Maybe a half clad Indian or two are somewhere in the corn or among the vines, making believe to work."[11] In fact, Native Americans provided essential labor for both vineyards and groves.

Joseph Chapman began commercial grape production in 1824 with cuttings from the missions.[12] Jean Louis Vignes came from Bordeaux, France, by way of Honolulu, Hawaii, and established a vineyard in 1831 with imported cuttings on about one hundred acres south of Aliso Street and east of Alameda. His enthusiastic letters lured as many as thirty other wine growers to Los Angeles.[13] At about the same time the citrus industry got started, drawing upon the same Native American labor force as the vineyards. William Wolfskill planted a commercial citrus grove and a vineyard in 1838

**5.4 View of William Wolfskill's groves, Los Angeles. (Security Pacific Collection, Los Angeles Public Library.)**

**5.5 Men, women, and children picking oranges. The woman at left seems to be a tourist. (The Power of Place.)**

between San Pedro and Alameda, Third and Sixth streets (figures 5.4, 5.5).[14] By 1850 Wolfskill's oranges and lemons stretched across seventy downtown acres.[15] His son exploited the possibilities of the transcontinental rail link and sent a trainload of oranges east by rail in 1877, expanding the local marketing by promoting California oranges as breakfast food.

Along with Native Americans toiled nomadic farm laborers of Anglo background, usually settlers who had failed to establish a homestead, nicknamed "blanket men."[16] When Chinese workers arrived in the 1870s, the citrus industry profited from Chinese techniques, many centuries old, of budding and grafting.[17] Chinese workers were also common in the wine-making industry.[18] Around the turn of the century, Japanese immigrants became more numerous, while Italian Americans who came to work in the wine industry created their own community spaces close to the plaza area. Some Mexican immigrants had always worked in the groves. They succeeded the Chinese and Japanese, becoming a majority of citrus workers by the 1940s.[19] As the groves and vineyards developed, not all the work force was in the field, since sorting, packing, and shipping became more complex, and women often held sorting and packing jobs.

Oranges formed the heart of agricultural development in southern California. The dream of owning a small citrus grove drew both investors and retirees to Los Angeles. Carey McWilliams understood the allure: "The orange tree is the living symbol of richness, luxury and elegance. With its rich, black-green shade, its evergreen foliage, and its romantic fragrance, it is the millionaire of all the trees of America.... The aristocrat of the orchards, it has, by natural affinity, drawn to it the rich and the well-born, creating a unique type of a rural-urban aristocracy." McWilliams also noted that conditions for workers in the groves included shanty housing, poor sanitation, and segregated schools.[20]

The city seal of Los Angeles after midcentury carried grapes and vines as a testament to the industry's importance (figure 5.6). Los Angeles residents who did not work in the vineyards and groves enjoyed looking at them nearby, as did tourists, who might be photographed among the workers, picking fresh oranges off the trees, savoring the smell and taste of the ripe fruit. "Orange architecture" at fairs included temples or pyramids of fruit (figure 5.7), creating a unique sense of place to complement what was already outdoors, grapefruit, orange, and lemon groves backed by snow-capped mountains, and shady arbors in the downtown vineyards.

By the mid-1880s, groves and vineyards were being relocated so that centrally located land could bear a new crop of com-

**5.6 Official seal of Los Angeles with grapes and grape leaves, 1854. (Archives of the City of Los Angeles.)**

**5.7 Orange and walnut architecture at the Citrus Fair, Hazard Pavilion, Fifth Street between Olive and Hill, Los Angeles, 1891. (UCLA Special Collections.)**

mercial buildings and a new railroad station (Central Station, predecessor to Union Station). Vignes's home, El Aliso, with a grape arbor ten feet wide and a quarter of a mile long, was the site of city festivals and political rallies from the 1830s on, but his arbor, his magnificent sycamore tree, and Wolfskill's adobe all were demolished in the boom of new construction. The citrus industry relocated itself farther out, in other parts of southern California where the beauty of the groves continues and the accommodations for workers are not much improved.

One tall, slender grapefruit tree, of the variety Wolfskill cultivated, has been preserved, planted in the courtyard of the Japanese-American Cultural and Community Center, 244 South San Pedro Street (figure 5.8). Beyond this tree, some names survive: Aliso Street, Vignes Street, and a mini-mall called Vignes Place. The San Antonio Winery, the last

**5.8 Grapefruit tree now preserved at the Japanese-American Cultural and Community Center. (Photograph by Dolores Hayden.)**

remaining winemaking operation in Los Angeles, still operates just north of the Los Angeles River, but the grapes are grown elsewhere. There remains a shady arbor there, and a modern restaurant for sipping wine. Remembering the vineyards and groves, and perhaps the *zanjas* or irrigation ditches that watered them, would depend on new landscape designs for public space drawing on these traditional plantings, projecting that thin line of green forward in time.

## The Landscape of Truck Gardens and Produce Markets

In the early years of the pueblo, settlers grew food on garden plots allocated to them near the center, but as the town grew, truck gardens and produce markets developed. Chinese immigrants came to Los Angeles in the 1870s to cultivate Chinese vegetables for the workers building the rail link to San Francisco. Many chose to stay on as market gardeners, leasing land southwest of the city along what are now West Pico, Adams, and Washington boulevards.

By 1880 fifty Chinese Americans formed the Wai Leong Hong (Good People's Protective Association) and hawked their vegetables door to door with horses and carts.[21] The first public market was started about 1890 at the Old Plaza (figure 5.9). It moved to Third and Central, and moved again to Sixth and Alameda. The Chinese American produce merchant Louie Gwan promoted the City Market at Ninth and San Pedro in 1909, uniting Japanese, Russian, Italian, and Chinese immigrant farmers.[22] The area around the new City Market developed as a Chinese American neighborhood,[23] but "the original management of the City Market, like its shareholders, was multi-ethnic"[24] (figures 5.10, 5.11).

Farmers running truck gardens often had their entire families working in the fields with them and perhaps also hired hands (figures 5.12, 5.13, 5.14). Some sold their produce directly, but others had brokers sell it for them because "when you're running a farm, you can't be selling at the same time."[25] Kenichi Onishi, a Japanese American who worked in the

**5.9 Produce market at the Old Plaza (La Placita), 1895. (Chinese Historical Society of Southern California.)**

**5.10 Los Angeles City Market, 1930s. (Visual Communications, courtesy Mr. Rikimaru.)**

fields with his parents and sisters before World War I, grew row crops such as cauliflower, beets, turnips, and parsley in West Los Angeles near Culver Boulevard. That area was also known for excellent celery. A Chinese American explained what it took to set up a produce company in the 1920s: "Those days, you could start a business for $150 to $200. I started in the produce business single-handed with a stall and a $170 used truck."[26] The Chino family, renowned today for the exquisite vegetables it cultivates for Alice Waters, Wolfgang Puck, and other chefs specializing in California cuisine, got its start on a thirty-acre leased farm in Venice in the 1930s, selling vegetables to the wholesale market. But first the Chino men did a stint as migrant pickers, to gather capital for their own business.[27]

The City Market still thrives with a multiethnic ownership.[28] Both Japanese American and Chinese American firms remain.[29] The general manager, Peter Fleming, is the son of Walter

**5.11 Louie Produce Company at the City Market, 1934, with three generations of men in the family. (Dr. Dan Louie, Jr.)**

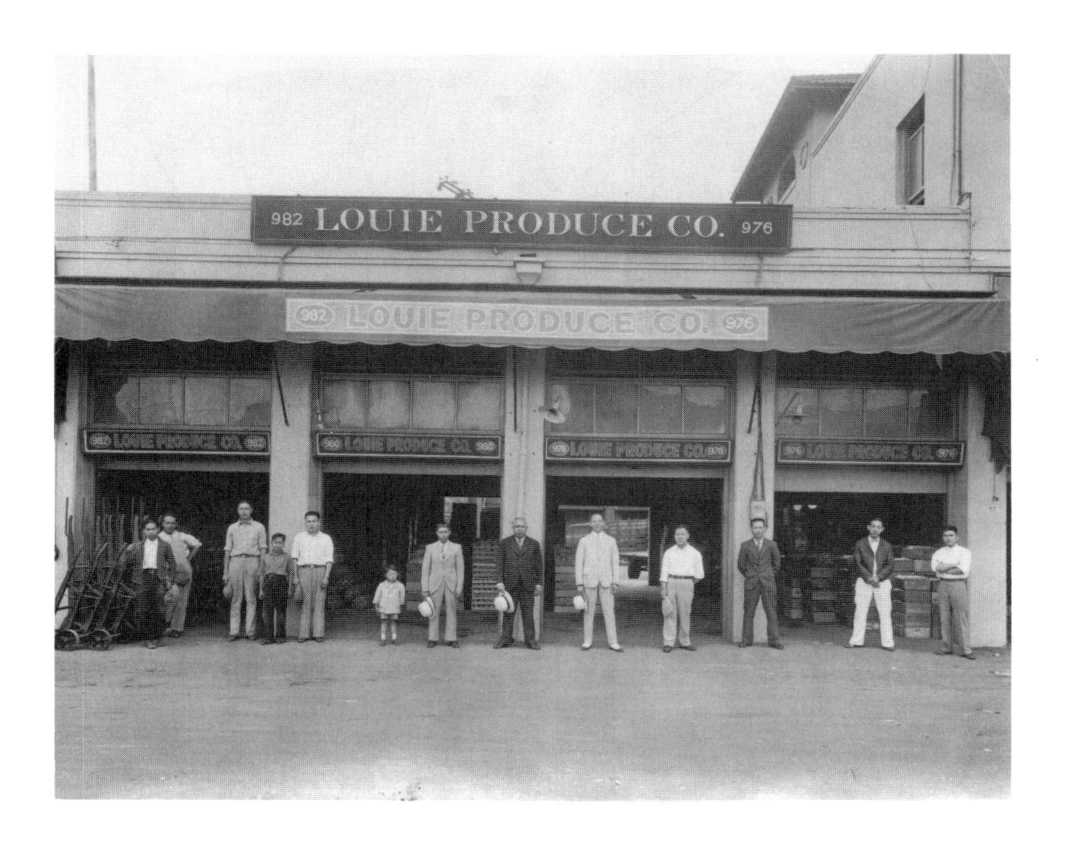

**5.12 Boy on a truck farm, 1939. (Los Angeles Public Library.)**

**5.13 Strawberry pickers, Tropico, Glendale, California, undated photograph. (California Historical Society/Ticor Title Insurance.)**

**5.14 Chinese American field hands, undated photograph. (California Historical Society/Ticor Title Insurance.)**

Fleming, a former general manager, and the grandnephew of Edward J. Fleming, one of the market's original investors. Family ties go back to the founders in every ethnic group, but the market has also provided jobs for successive generations of new immigrants and entrepreneurs, including at least one woman-owned firm specializing in unusual types of vegetables for restaurants serving nouvelle cuisine.

City Market animates ten acres today between Ninth and Twelfth streets, San Pedro and San Julian, spilling out of the 1909 building designed by architects Morgan and Walls,[30] a Spanish mission style structure with towers and gables partially enclosing a courtyard crowded with more growers and wholesalers. The Southern Pacific Railroad built Terminal Market in 1918 at Seventh and Central, a larger but architecturally less attractive structure than the City Market. In 1986 the Community Redevelopment Agency renovated this structure as the Los Angeles Wholesale Produce Market, the world's largest wholesale produce market under one roof. With murals of fruits and vegetables by Thomas Suriya, facilities for big rigs, including "high dock" stalls, and cold storage, this project won some tenants away from the City Market. Designed for the days of horse and wagon, or $170 pickup trucks, City Market is a physical reminder of another era in the history of feeding the city. The historic role of the truck farmers, peddlers, and wholesalers of earlier times is expressed on the small scale and in the neighborhood context of older Chinese residences (houses, apartments, and a single-room occupancy hotel), restaurants, a Chinese grocery store, a noodle factory, and a Chinese Congregational Church. It is a potential historic district of a far more authentic, less showy kind than the tourist-oriented Chinatown near Union Station, built in the 1930s when an existing Chinatown was razed for the station.[31] However, the present shareholders of the market have expressed reservations about any designation of their structure as a city landmark if it would hinder their economic options.[32]

Meanwhile, the Grand Central Public Market, built in 1897 between Broadway and Hill streets and recently renovated, remains the liveliest retail food hall in downtown, bustling with Latino shoppers, a good place to visit for a snack or a week's groceries. Its renovation aimed to make it even more attractive to tourists and residents as a marketplace for diverse ethnic foods. To find the fields where the produce is grown today, one must travel to the far reaches of Los Angeles County in the hills behind Malibu or to adjoining Ventura or San Diego counties to see the rows of lettuces or carrots stretching in the sun. The Chinos have a large farm today near Rancho Santa Fe, in San Diego County, and perhaps their elegant beets, carrots, turnips, radishes, fennel, and endive are the most beautiful monument to what the landscape can produce with the right kind of human effort. ("The crop is the monument," said writer Richard Rodriguez of the cultural landscape in agribusiness's Central Valley, where he grew up.) But those glorious fruits and vegetables are found in such expensive restaurants that the city of Los Angeles should give hard thought to finding the economic and social incentives to make a historic district around what survives near the City Market today.

At dawn in Los Angeles, the Southern California Flower Market animates Wall Street between Seventh and Eighth, filling the air with "the flavor of flowers."[33] Established in 1913, the Flower Market, along with the Southern California Floral Association and the American Florists Exchange, conducts the wholesale flower business in the city. It all began when a Japanese American farmer, Sotaro Endo, leased two lots near downtown at the intersection of South Main and West Jefferson to grow field carnations in 1892, planting a neighborhood as well as an industry.[34] Jinnosuke Kobata joined Endo the next year, and seeing that land was tight near the city center, they leased a couple of acres closer to the coast to grow violets, chrysanthemums, garden plants, and roses. Endo didn't stay, but Kobata prospered and became the first president of the Southern California Flower Market (figure 5.15).

Unlike the Asian American workers in the citrus groves, the Japanese immigrants in market gardening or floriculture often were also entrepreneurs. Starting with leased land, a rough hut of lumber and canvas, a kerosene stove for cooking, and

**5.15 Jinnosuke Kobata in his chrysanthemum field, 1893. (*The Bloomin' News*, June 1962.)**

silkworm shelves for beds, the small grower often had his entire family laboring with him. Later he hired help if he could afford it. When a crop was picked, the farmer packed it into a large wicker trunk called a *yanagi-kori*, covered it with cloth, and carried it on his shoulder to the streetcar stop, in order to peddle flowers on the streets downtown.

The huge trunks of spicy carnations or fragrant roses, and the muddy farmers, crowded and offended the streetcar riders, and streetcar companies prohibited the *kori*. In 1909, a non-profit, cooperative market was proposed by Japanese Americans to provide "the basis for mutual support and self-help."[35] In 1913, the Southern California Flower Market was started, moving to its current address at 753 South Wall Street in 1923, where the organization sold flowers, did research, organized cooperative purchase of supplies, ran social events, and offered insurance. The group marked its presence on Wall Street by creating street decorations with flowers for an annual festival (figures 5.16, 5.17).

As the growers organized, the Japanese American florists and the nurserymen soon followed, but anti-Japanese sentiment increased in 1919, with campaigns attacking them for using female field hands and for working on Sundays. In 1922, a city zoning ordinance forbade the establishment of new nurseries in residential districts. Other flower markets, run by growers of Anglo descent, caused tension until the early 1930s, when coexistence became more peaceful,[36] and then in World War II much of the Japanese American business was destroyed. Frank Kuwahara, manager of Golden State Wholesale Florist, an association of ten Nisei growers, traveled throughout the United States by bus in 1948 to seek new customers for Japanese American flowers from Los Angeles.[37] Despite the danger that this journey represented for someone of his ethnic background, traveling alone so soon after the war, he persevered and was successful.

Today the cultivation of flowers has shifted to the fringes of the region (figure 5.18). Some growers sold their flower farms for housing tracts. Others invested in greenhouses, but then

**5.16 Southern California Flower Market, 753 Wall Street, 1930s. (History of the Flower Industry in Southern California, Japanese-American Cultural and Community Center Library.)**

**5.17 Street decorations, flowers, and banners, Wall Street, Los Angeles, October 1934. (Japanese-American Cultural and Community Center Library.)**

were under pressure to produce cash crops. Kuwahara noted, "Growing a great many types of flowers in a limited space, as many Issei typically did prior to the war, combining business and hobby, is no longer economically feasible."[38] The street decorations became too expensive and were abandoned. The skill remained. Older styles of floral decoration led to newer themes, such as the design of an extravagant floral freeway headdress in 1962, its multiple curving ramps filled with tiny colored toy cars (figure 5.19).

Today the Flower Market, like the City Market, is squeezed for space, debating its future, thinking of relocating. Like the shareholders of the City Market, the flower growers perceive landmark status as something that would limit their real estate options. The old flower fields have become industrial areas and today commercial flowers are grown at the edge of Ventura and San Diego counties, spectacular bands of color striping vast fields, a potential tourist attraction in themselves, but not places anyone ever sets out to see or smell. The elaborate garden created by the Japanese American Nurserymen's Association at 244 South San Pedro Street, behind the cultural center, provides public proof of Japanese American

**5.18 Flower fields, southern California, 1991. (Dolores Hayden.)**

**5.19 Floral headdress, "Freeway U.S.A.," 1962, by Burdick-Shearer Flowers, Los Angeles. (*The Bloomin' News*, June 1962.)**

horticultural skills, as a flowing stream commemorates the Issei, steadily improving their lives through nurturing the southern California landscape. Yet downtown could benefit from more explicit identification of the flower industry's long presence in the landscape. The spicy scent of carnations could be reintroduced in a small public garden, if not a field.

### The Landscape of Wildcatters and the City Oil Field

In 1892 Edward L. Doheny and Charles A. Canfield struck oil just west of downtown in a residential area plotted in small lots and filled with Victorian wooden houses. Wildcatting transformed the landscape: "With such fortunes to be made, a forest of wooden derricks invaded the handsome residential district. Gardens were trampled by teams, lawns flooded with oil, cottages hauled away to make room for wells . . . more than five hundred wells were chugging and wheezing through the night, making sleep almost impossible."[39] The district generated an early homeowners' association, formed to protest drilling. (It did not prevail.)

Two years later eighty wells were pumping in the twenty block area centered on Figueroa, Beverly, Belmont, and Temple Streets, the Los Angeles City Oil Field.[40] In 1895, over three hundred wells in the field were owned by one hundred different wildcatters, and "wells were as thick as holes in a pepper box."[41] By 1897, the number of wells had tripled. Horse-drawn oil wagons were a familiar sight in a landscape that sprouted so many tall wooden derricks the hills seemed to be forested (figure 5.20).[42]

The *Los Angeles Times* commented in 1895: "The view presented at night is a striking one. Mingled with the heavy churning and creaking of the ponderous walking beams, the hoarse, unceasing roll of the machinery belting, and the continuous roar of the blazing petroleum in the furnaces is the seemingly never-ending hissing of escaping steam, while in all directions the whole area is lit up by lurid flames from the burning oil, darting their forked tongues into the darkness of the night. Here and there can be seen workmen moving about . . . while away in the distance on the one side can be discerned the long San Gabriel Mountain chain, on the other the city wrapt in quiet slumber."[43] The oil landscape smelled of petroleum. Oil gushed into the streets and leaked from wooden storage tanks.[44] In 1907, so much had spilled into Echo Park Lake that the lake caught fire, a spectacle both night and day until the crude oil burned off (figure 5.21).[45]

Availability of cheap oil spurred new economic activity, especially manufacturing, with oil-burning engines and machines. Doheny tirelessly promoted new uses of oil in

**5.20 Los Angeles Oil Field, First and Belmont, derricks on the skyline. (Western History Collection, Los Angeles County Museum of Natural History.)**

**5.21 Oil derricks by Echo Park Lake. (Henry E. Huntington Library and Art Gallery, San Marino, California.)**

transportation and business. Oil heated downtown buildings, while asphalt, a petroleum by-product (known in its natural state since the earliest days of the pueblo when *brea* waterproofed adobe dwellings), was used to improve paved roads. The Los Angeles Stock Exchange began trading oil stocks in 1899.

The wildcatters hired small crews, often of English, Canadian, Irish, or Scottish extraction. After a twelve-hour shift they returned to a rowdy shantytown located near Santa Monica Boulevard and Vermont Avenue, where prostitutes in tents and gamblers in shacks crowded around twenty-four-hour saloons.[46] Early drillers used the "spring pole" method, which consisted of dropping a sharp, heavy cutting tool into their oil well and then pulling it out by hand. They then moved to steam engine pumps, and eventually to electric ones.

The most remarkable wildcatter was Emma Summers, a piano teacher with a degree from the New England Conservatory of Music, who lived at 417 Sand Street (figure 5.22). Supporting herself by giving music lessons at night, Summers drilled hole after hole, "overseeing the work herself, . . . keeping her own books, hiring and firing the crewmen."[47] According to a 1912 profile in *Sunset* magazine, "She was expert in testing oil, hired all her men, brought all her tools and supplies, looked after her forty horses and ten wagons, and built her own blacksmith shop."[48] By the turn of the century, her wells and her activities in refining and distribution gave her control of half of the field's production.

Over time oil was found in many other areas around the region, so the original field declined in importance. Today the last trickle of oil is running out, although at least one company was active in 1988, at 1504 Rockwood (a one-story frame Victorian house close to the site of the first strike in 1892). It was owned by The Manley Oil Company, a family-run, fourth-generation oil company that maintained a working oil well in the front yard. Among the fifteen wells they operated was one held over from the early days, run by an old wooden pump

**5.22 Emma Summers, leading wildcatter, inspecting one of her wells. (Drummond Buckley.)**

**5.23 Oil derrick counterbalanced by stones in wooden crate, Manley Oil Company, still working in 1985. (Dolores Hayden.)**

counterbalanced with an orange crate loaded with stones (figure 5.23).[49] Most of Manley's workers have been Latino, now the predominant residential population in the area.

Currently there is a redevelopment project under way in the Temple-Beaudry area (Central City West).[50] High-rise buildings are spreading from downtown into this adjacent area. Under the leadership of Gloria Molina (formerly a city councilwoman, now a county supervisor), Latino residents have engaged in intensive negotiations with developers of commercial real estate and city administrators to secure community benefits. The colorful history of the area could add to the character of the neighborhood if the redevelopment project also aims to interpret the physical remains of the historic landscape. "Someday you will own a horseless carriage," claimed the ads on oil tank wagons run by producers at the turn of the century. Next to the Harbor Freeway filled with thousands of cars and the looming Arco Towers of an oil conglomerate of the 1990s, the beginnings of the industry in the 1890s should be remembered. The wildcatters are gone but traces of the Los Angeles Oil Field remain, able to introduce some historic scale into the landscape today.

## The Landscape of Prefabricated Houses

As Los Angeles experienced a series of real estate booms beginning in the late nineteenth century, subdivisions were platted everywhere. Land auctions were common, where potential customers enjoyed barbecued food while motorcyclists sped new buyers' checks to the bank to make sure they wouldn't bounce. The putting up of houses was a slower business usually undertaken by the new lot owners, until prefabrication began to add speed and flash.

Pacific Ready-Cut Homes, founded in 1909, created houses, schools, bunkhouses, and company stores from a factory at 1330 South Hill Street. The company's catalogues document the range of vernacular buildings that were precut as a kit of parts in the factory and then shipped by railroad to boom towns all over the West (figures 5.24, 5.25). Pacific also sold 25,000 bungalows in Los Angeles during the 1920s for about $2,750 apiece, lining the streets with so many houses erected so fast that they boasted "a complete home every twenty minutes."[51] Their bungalows represent a domestic architecture of assimilation, yet many of the workers and the homeowners were from diverse backgrounds, similar to the workers drawn to furniture factories, garment work, and other industries nearby.

**5.24 Pacific Ready-Cut truck with prefabricated parts of houses. (Carolyn Flynn.)**

With some competition from mail order producers such as Sears or Aladdin, Pacific Ready-Cut homes thrived in the period between the two wars by looking for ways to replace skilled carpenters and small builders with less skilled factory workers. Pacific purchased lumber directly from forest cutters. In a twenty-four-acre mill at Slauson and Boyle avenues, workers precut it by machine in twenty minutes to fit particular specifications. Carpenters on site could then nail a precut house together in four days and finish the interior in less than a month (figure 5.26).[52]

Customers could pick their house style and perhaps some interior fittings from a catalogue, or could visit the exhibition

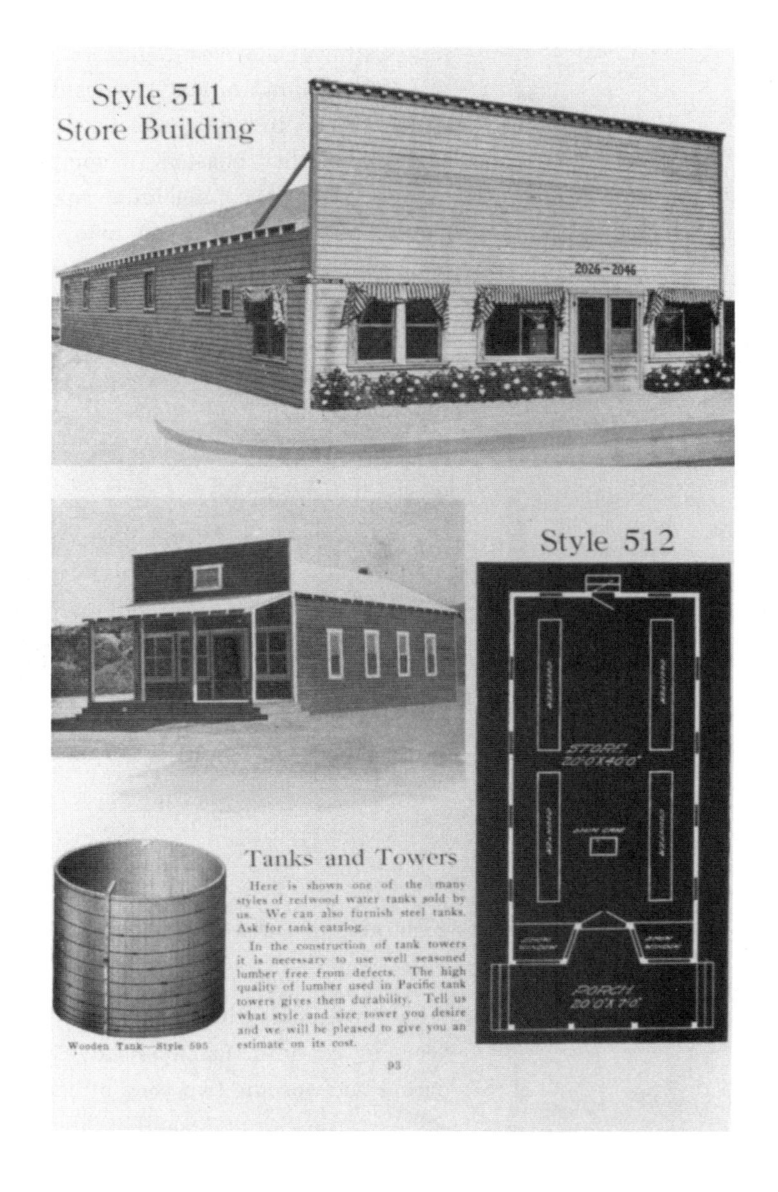
Style 511
Store Building

2026–2046

Style 512

STORE
20'0"X40'0"

PORCH
20'0"X7'0"

Tanks and Towers

Here is shown one of the many styles of redwood water tanks sold by us. We can also furnish steel tanks. Ask for tank catalog.

In the construction of tank towers it is necessary to use well seasoned lumber free from defects. The high quality of lumber used in Pacific tank towers gives them durability. Tell us what style and size tower you desire and we will be pleased to give you an estimate on its cost.

Wooden Tank—Style 595

93

**5.25 Pacific Ready-Cut false-front wooden store of the kind shipped to boom towns all over the West. (Carolyn Flynn.)**

# Pacific Homes are Quickly Constructed

**Here is interesting photolog of a typical Pacific Home. Erection completed in 28 days.**

**Starting**

*The cement foundation has been completed and carpenters are removing forms and are ready to begin construction work.*

**3½ Hours Later**

*A crew of four carpenters has completed and braced the underpinning, placed the floor joists and is laying sub-floor.*

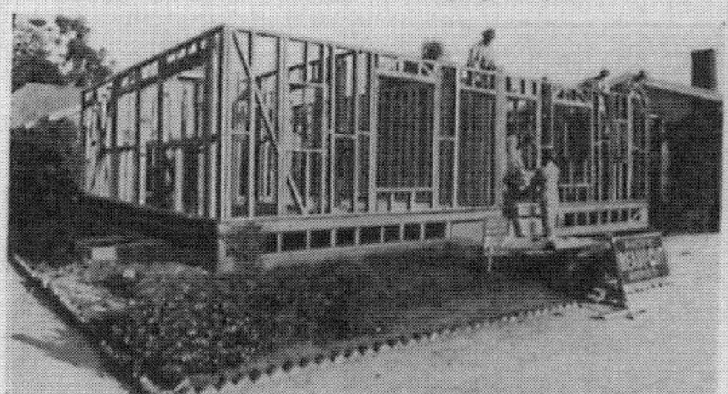

**End of the First Day**

*All walls and partitions are in place, plumbed and braced.*

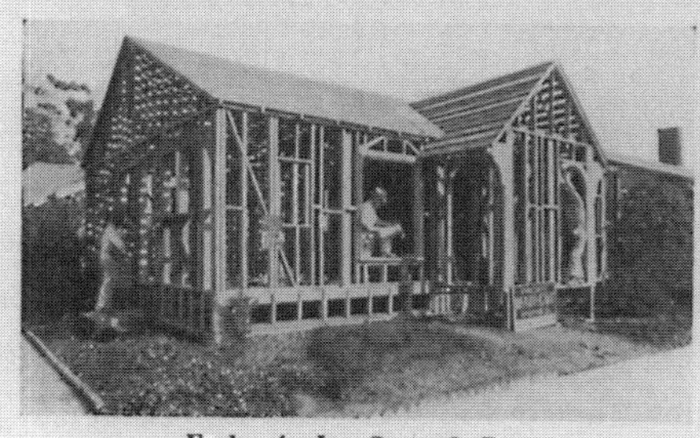

**End of the Second Day**

*By 10:30 A. M. on the second day the ceiling joists and rafters are up. By evening the roof sheathing has been laid and most of the window frames set. The third day, plumbing and wiring are roughed in, valleys and windows flashed.*

**The Fourth Day**

*The roof is shingled and exterior lathed, ready for stucco; interior ready for plaster.*

**The Eighth Day**

*Plastering has been completed and has thoroughly dried. Exterior has received first two coats ready for color coat. House is ready for cabinet work and other interior finish.*

**28 Days After Starting**

*Here is pictured the home complete, ready for occupancy—less than one month's work for average crews working under normal conditions. This is a double house, complete with plumbing, wiring, built-in features, hardwood floors, painting and decorating. It may be inspected on our Los Angeles Exhibition Grounds. The plan is shown on page 66—Style 236.*

18

**5.26 Pacific Ready-Cut Homes, house erected in 28 days, 1925 advertisement. (UCLA Special Collections.)**

grounds on Hill Street which included ten models. One hundred thousand people visited these model homes annually in the 1920s, according to the company. Labor-saving devices were glorified as aids to both the builders and the housewives who would be maintaining the homes.[53]

Pacific's bungalows can still be seen[54] filling areas such as Carson Road north of Wilshire Boulevard in Beverly Hills, and 81st Street between Main and Figueroa. After World War II, small hand tools made on-site building more attractive again, and the Levitts on Long Island pioneered other approaches to prefabrication of parts of the house.[55] Today Pacific's main showroom building survives, moved to Vernon. While the home-building industry has changed, visiting model homes is still a favorite pastime all over southern California. If the efforts at creating low-cost houses for urban consumers could be remembered in downtown, along with the innovations that made these bungalows popular with housewives, the 1920s model of urban real estate development, tied to dreams of better living, might give every commuter with an hour's ride to the remote subdivisions of the San Gabriel Valley a piece of environmental history to ponder on the way home.

## The Landscape of Firefighters

Fire Station No. 30 stands on Central Avenue at Fourteenth Street, in an area that was the hub of African American activities in Los Angeles in the 1920s and 1930s. Two blocks away, at Twelfth and Central, was the "U-car corner," a lively commercial center for black businesses, and the main streetcar stop for passengers heading to South Central Los Angeles. As one resident commented, "If you stood there long enough you'd meet every Black in Los Angeles and greet all those who had just arrived from the south."[56]

From the station, fireman Arnett L. Heartsfield, Jr., and a group of African American firefighters called The Stentorians led the fight for integration in the Fire Department in the

**5.27 Hose Company No. 4, built in 1892 at Belmont Avenue near West First Street, received George Bright, the city's first black fireman, in 1897, and became an all-black station under his command in 1903. (Arnett L. Hartsfield, Jr.)**

1940s and 1950s, a struggle that had begun in 1897 when George Bright became Los Angeles's first African American fireman.[57] Bright worked out of Hose Company No. 4 (figure 5.27), until he was promoted. Having passed civil service exams and provided extra letters of endorsement from his minister and the congregation at the Second Baptist Church, Lieutenant Bright then found himself heading an all-black crew at the city's first segregated station.

From about 1910 to 1955, segregated stations were the rule. In the mid-1920s, the crew at Station No. 30 at 1401 South Central Avenue (figure 5.28) enjoyed the respect of the African American community, but limited opportunities existed for recruitment, training, and promotion of new firefighters. After World War II, Heartsfield, a firefighter who had earned a law

**5.28 Engine Company No. 30, 1401 South Central Avenue, 1925. (Miriam Matthews.)**

degree at the University of Southern California, used his new legal expertise to help achieve a decree from Mayor Norris Poulson in 1955 integrating all civil service employment.

James Backus, the architect who designed Fire Station No. 30, served as Superintendent of Building for the City of Los Angeles from 1905 to 1936. His craftsman design of 1913 (figure 5.29) included stepped parapets and a small crenelated tower, as well as an enormous hose tower that was never built. The station was considered too small for current fire-fighting equipment and became vacant in the mid-1980s. A Cultural Heritage Board Landmark since 1985,[58] the station stands across from the moderne Coca-Cola building and needs renovation.

Central Avenue also includes the Dunbar Hotel, a successful preservation project that is now low-cost housing, originally

**5.29 James Backus's elevation for Fire Station No. 30, 1913. (Redrawn by Daniel Hernandez for The Power of Place.)**

the first hotel where blacks could stay in Los Angeles, site of many civil rights meetings. Memories of Central Avenue, including the history of its jazz clubs, have been celebrated in KCET's "Ode to Central Avenue," part of this public television station's Los Angeles History Project.[59] A greater appreciation of its political history might support the economic development badly needed in this area, since the thriving U-car corner of the 1920s is long gone. The Stentorians who worked for change still meet in another fire station in South Central Los Angeles, but downtown would be enriched by a place where this group's remarkable accomplishments are remembered. Firefighters also need to be reminded of the need for greater diversity, as women who have sought to join the ranks in the 1980s and 1990s attest. It is not easy to be a female rookie these days, despite all the changes that have occurred since 1897.

This sketch of some of the working landscapes created in downtown Los Angeles between the late eighteenth century and the early twentieth century just begins to suggest the sights, sounds, and smells of the places where Angelenos of every ethnic group struggled to earn a living. There are many more possible highlights: the labor market at the Plaza where migrant workers—usually of Mexican or Filipino descent—were hired to travel to work in the San Fernando Valley or the Central Valley; Talley's Electric Theatre, where the first movies were shown continuously in downtown, starting in 1902; the tracks and tunnels associated with the construction of a twelve-hundred-mile-long regional streetcar system; the primitive *zanjas* or irrigation ditches that developed into the gigantic aqueducts of the water system. And, looking beyond downtown, the twentieth century has carved out expansive urban landscapes including those of the motion picture and music industries. The backlots of Hollywood employed hundreds of skilled seamstresses and designers as costumers. At Gower Gulch cowboys gathered with their horses, looking for a day's pay as extras in Westerns. One could also examine defense industries and the military as they generated landscapes of high-tech weaponry,[60] or look at the fishing industry in Santa Monica and Long Beach and the growth of the port. In a more somber tone, the presence of thousands of homeless has created "landscapes of despair" across Los Angeles, tent encampments, neighborhoods of cartons and boxes.[61]

Pierre Nora has defined places of memory as *lieux de mémoire*, "where memory crystallizes and secretes itself." In his essay "Between Memory and History," he observes his own research occurring "at a particular historical moment, a turning point where consciousness of a break with the past is bound up with the sense that memory has been torn—but torn in such a way as to pose the problem of the embodiment of memory in certain sites where a sense of historical continuity persists."[62] So it is for downtown Los Angeles and its fast-vanishing workers' landscapes.

The sites chosen for this particular downtown itinerary represent the greatest concentration of workers of different ethnic groups in a single place. Later industries branched out across the larger metropolitan area, but downtown was where many economic ventures first started and where many groups first began to establish themselves in the city. Many unique neighborhoods with intriguing economic and ethnic histories exist in and around downtown, and each could have its own itinerary of historic resources, similar to this one. The next chapters focus in more detail on a few specific examples of how Angelenos have struggled to earn a living in the changing landscape of the growing city. They explore how typical citizens—often working women—managed to balance paid work and family work, and to nurture community and civic identity. They investigate many paths to public memory in downtown, including conversational, archival, artistic, and architectural strategies.

# 6 The View from Grandma Mason's Place

**Greet the world with an open hand.**

**Biddy Mason**

One pioneer's life cannot tell the whole story of building a city. Yet the record of a single citizen's struggle to raise a family, earn a living, and contribute to a city's professional, social, and religious activities is intertwined with the story of how a city develops over time. This is especially true if the person is Biddy Mason (figure 6.1). Her experiences as a citizen of Los Angeles were typical—as a family head, homeowner, and churchgoer. Yet they were also unusual, since gender, race, and status as a slave increased her burdens. She arrived in southern California in 1851 as the lifelong slave of a master from Mississippi and won freedom for herself and thirteen others in court in 1856. Her case gave Los Angeles's Judge Hayes a chance to make a decision against slavery, in favor of California's new constitution. When Biddy Mason won her case and chose to settle in Los Angeles as part of the small African American community there, her special medical skills, learned as a slave midwife and nurse, provided entry for her into many households, rich and poor, of every race and ethnicity.[1] She established a homestead for her family and worked in the city until her death on January 15, 1891, when her grandsons were forced to turn away from her front door lines of fellow citizens who were awaiting her aid.[2]

**6.1 Biddy Mason. (UCLA Special Collections.)**

Historians have noted that published work on African American women in the West is "sparse," partly because there were so few in the West, especially in the nineteenth century.[3] Many brief accounts of Biddy Mason's life exist, including some anecdotal ones, privately published in the community, that dwell on her role as a pious "good woman" or as a woman who accumulated valuable real estate as the city grew.[4] But no one has attempted a detailed interpretation of her life, including her pioneering travels on foot from Mississippi to Los Angeles, her legal battles, her practice as a midwife, and her success in establishing a homestead as a resource for her family and for a set of community organizations she helped to build, including the Los Angeles branch of the First African Methodist Episcopal Church. In 1988 the FAME Church honored Mason with a celebration, and the California Afro-American Museum included her in their *Black Angelenos* exhibit. Now, a century after her death, a detailed history of this Angelena and her era is long overdue.

When Biddy Mason arrived in California in 1851, the city of Los Angeles housed about sixteen hundred people, half of them under twenty years old. About a dozen were African Americans.[5] Some accounts portray Los Angeles just after midcentury as a tough cow town, a violent place with sixty-two saloons by 1872 and a bad record for rough justice, shooting, lynching, and tarring and feathering.[6] Yet by the 1880s it was a place that increasingly attracted immigrants who wanted to settle down as homeowners and churchgoing Protestants. And by the 1890s, Los Angeles was a city of over fifty thousand, including more than twelve hundred African Americans, with a thriving oil field, a growing financial center, and expanding industries.[7] In most accounts of these decades, one reads of railroads and land booms, of white male Anglo immigrants from the East and the Midwest creating a new urban prosperity. There were other pioneers, including men and women of color, and this chapter traces urban life as created by, and experienced by, Biddy Mason and people like her. Between 1856 and 1891 she changed Los Angeles as she became one of its leading citizens, and at the same time the city changed around her, achieving urbanity, diversity, and density that earlier residents had barely imagined. While Biddy Mason's own recorded words are few, legal history, medical history, and the history of the built environment can give glimpses of the urban world she struggled to create.

### From Mississippi to California: A Black Pioneer Slave

On August 15, 1818, a female slave was born in the deep South, probably in Georgia.[8] Most of her life people called her Biddy. (Mason came later.) She was forbidden to learn to read or write, as most slaves were, but she managed to gain a good knowledge of livestock, herbal medicine, nursing, and midwifery, skills that were useful to her owners and ones that would later enable her to earn her living. Biddy became the property of Robert Marion Smith and his wife, Rebecca Crosby Smith, owners of a plantation in Mississippi. The Smiths had six children, whose births she probably attended, and Rebecca Crosby Smith often needed nursing care, which Biddy later told relatives and friends she provided.[9] It is likely that she was also required to do heavier work in the cotton fields and with livestock. In addition, she added to her master's wealth by bearing children who became slaves. Her first, Ellen, was born October 15, 1838, when she was twenty, her second, Ann, about six years later, and her third, Harriet, four years later.[10]

By 1847, Robert M. Smith, who had become a convert to the Mormon religion, wanted to migrate to the Utah Territory to help to build up the Kingdom of the Saints in Salt Lake City. Brigham Young founded his colony of Deseret there in 1847 after the downfall of the Mormon town of Nauvoo, Illinois, in 1846, and the dispersion of the Illinois Mormons.[11] So on March 10, 1848, Smith joined a party of Mississippi Mormons who gathered with ox teams in Fulton, in the northeastern part of the state, and headed north and west to the Salt Lake Basin, traveling by wagon and riverboat. Smith's party included nine white persons and ten slaves, in three wagons, plus two yoke of oxen, eight mules, seven milch cows, and one horse. There were fifty-six whites and thirty-four slaves in the larger Mississippi party, according to John Brown, a Mormon guide whose autobiography detailed the arduous trip.[12] In rain, hurricane, and drought, Brown led the pioneers north through Lexington and Paris, Tennessee; Fort Mayfield and Paducah, Kentucky. Catching the National Road they journeyed west to St. Louis, Warrenton, Keytesville, and Plattsburgh, Missouri; to Council Bluffs, Iowa; Grand Island, Nebraska, then on to Fort Laramie, Fort Bridger, and finally into Deseret (Salt Lake), where they arrived in late 1848 (figure 6.2). The party rushed to complete log shelters so they could move into them as December snows began to fall.

On this journey, Biddy was in charge of herding the livestock behind the wagons. With a ten-year-old daughter, four-year-old daughter, and baby daughter on the breast, she walked

**6.2 Map of the Overland Trail, 1841–1869. From Fulton, Mississippi, Mason traveled as far as Salt Lake on her first journey. She went from Salt Lake down through what became Utah and Nevada to San Bernardino, California, on her second. (Drawn by Christopher Lukinbeal for *California History*.)**

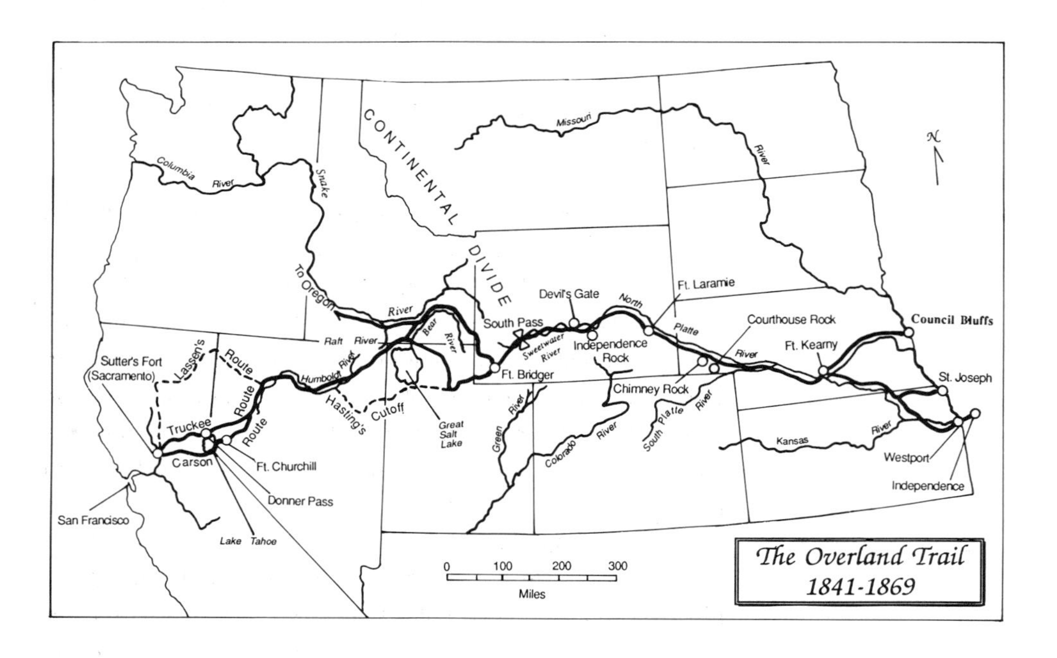

these thousands of miles in about seven months. Her family demands and the demands of the livestock may have been supplemented by calls for her services as a midwife. Another slave in Smith's household, a woman named Hannah four years younger than Biddy, was pregnant about the time the journey took place.[13] Three white women in Biddy's party also gave birth to sons on the journey, according to John Brown, and there may have been daughters and births to the slaves that he did not record.

Brown's accounts of the deliveries convey the atmosphere a competent midwife would have struggled against: "[The boat] ... ran aground and stuck fast and the river was falling ... they finally threw some 12 of the animals overboard, after which the boat floated ... John Bankhead's wife [gave] ... birth to a fine son on board the boat." Or "we reached the Black Hills, where we found little or no feed, and our cattle began to die. Within a few miles of the La Prela River my ox-wagon broke down, where it remained all night. Next morning, August 29th, my wife gave birth to a fine son."[14] Whether or not Biddy was in attendance as a midwife at these births on this journey, her trip surely ranks as one of the most demanding a pioneer could be asked to make, since she was a single parent, a nursing mother, and a slave expected to work for her keep and walk behind the animals when others rode.

Between 1848 and 1851, Smith's household, including his slaves, settled in Utah in the Salt Lake Basin. According to one historian some of the Mississippi Mormon slaves were freed, and some received salaries, land of their own, and recognition from the Mormon church.[15] If this is true, surely only male slaves who had converted to Mormonism would have been so recognized. The Mormons were generally outspoken on their belief in the inferiority of blacks and women. Biddy and Hannah were not recognized as independent family heads, but remained with Smith's household. Given the Mormon practice of polygamy, not only is it likely that the black women's status as slaves or indentured servants of a southern master remained low, but also there was now a religious justification for any sexual exploitation a master wished to enforce.[16]

Fortunately for Biddy and her family, the Salt Lake Basin was not Smith's final stopping place. Three years after their arrival, a Mormon wagon train of 150 wagons left Utah to establish a new outpost in California at San Bernardino. This settlement was intended to become a way station for Mormons coming by ship around the Horn to San Pedro and then journeying overland to Salt Lake.[17] Robert Smith joined the San Bernardino pioneers, along with his slaves, who now included Biddy, Hannah, and their eight children.[18] Again she herded livestock behind the wagons.

## Freedom

During their time in the San Bernardino area, Biddy got to know not only Mormons but also a number of free blacks who had settled there after California was admitted to the Union, among them Elizabeth Flake Rowan and her husband, Charles H. Rowan, who were also in the caravan from Salt Lake arriving in June 1851.[19] The status of the slaves in Smith's household—by 1855, Hannah and Biddy, their ten children, and one grandchild of Hannah's—must have been discussed with the free blacks, since the slaves' legal position was much strengthened by California's statehood. After the Mexican War, a California constitution was drafted in 1849 forbidding slavery. The next two years passed with endless bickering in Congress between pro-slavery and anti-slavery factions until California was admitted to the Union as a free state in September 1850. The passage of the Fugitive Slave Act in the same year was a concession to southern slaveowners. Thus, the years when Biddy trekked across the continent, 1848 to 1851, were years of transition from Mexican rule, to military rule, to statehood in California, and all three types of law were administered simultaneously in confusion. Courts were generally more sympathetic to whites than to people of color, and more to slaveholders than to slaves.[20]

Although California's state constitution prohibited slavery after September 1850, slaveowners who had arrived before that date were permitted to keep their slaves as indentured servants. Other slaveowners simply remained unchallenged, or won their cases in court.[21] Because the Fugitive Slave Act made it easy for masters to recapture escaped slaves, bounty hunters seeking runaway slaves advertised openly in local papers such as the Los Angeles *Star* through the 1850s. Former slaves who had been freed by their masters were also subject to harassment, according to the *Alta Californian*, April 20, 1853: "A person by the name of Brown attempted to have a Negro girl arrested in our town a few days since as a fugitive slave, but was taken all a-back by the girl's lawyer, F. W. Thomas, producing her Freedom Papers. Brown's father set the girl at liberty in 1851, and it is thought by many that the son knew the fact, and thought to catch the girl without her Freedom Papers but fortunately for her he did not."[22]

Despite the legal and administrative confusion, sentiment in California against slavery grew after 1850. Robert Smith became concerned, and late in 1855 he began to make preparations to depart for Texas, a slave state, taking Biddy and the rest of her family. Hannah, large with child, was about to deliver her eighth baby. Most of the members of Smith's household camped in a canyon in the Santa Monica Mountains, readying themselves for the trip, waiting until Hannah was able to travel. Possibly Smith was hiding from those who wished to stop him.

Two free black men of Los Angeles, Charles Owens and Manuel Pepper, wanted to prevent Smith's departure because Charles was in love with Biddy's seventeen-year-old daughter, Ellen, and Manuel was in love with Hannah's seventeen-year-old daughter, Ann.[23] Biddy Mason had confided to Charles Owens that she was extremely worried about Smith's plans to take them to Texas, and Charles told his father, a formidable character who decided to intervene. Bob Owens was a trader in horses and mules who had crossed from Texas by ox team in 1850. He ran a flourishing corral on San Pedro Street, where he and the ten *vaqueros* who worked for him broke wild animals, supplied by ranchos near San Diego, and sold them to new settlers. (According to his grandson, "Many a mule half-broken to the saddle returned to the ranch after dumping its rider," perhaps to be resold to the next newcomer disembarking from the San Francisco steamer *Orizaba*, looking for a place to buy an outfit.)[24] Bob Owens was also the owner of real estate, and in him Biddy found a respected ally, a businessman who was also a cowboy not afraid of a good fight.

Between them, Bob Owens and Elizabeth Rowan were able to get the law in both Los Angeles County and San Bernardino County interested in the case. One or two sheriffs, plus Bob Owens and his *vaqueros*, swooped down on the camp in the mountains and challenged Smith's right to take his slaves out of California. The challenge took the form of a petition for a writ of *habeas corpus* by Biddy and her family. Most of the members of Biddy's family were put "under charge of the Sheriff of this county for their protection" in Los Angeles (figures 6.3, 6.4).[25]

Biddy and her family were stationed at the county jail, under the eye of "Turnkey" Frank Carpenter, who later gave evidence at the trial of their fear of their master.[26] The court, like the jail, was an adobe building with a roof that leaked in the winter rains, and the assembled group opened their umbrellas indoors. Benjamin Hayes, Judge of District Court of the First Judicial District, State of California, County of Los Angeles, presided over the case from January 19 to January 21, 1856, and summarized the issues in his disposition of the case, quoted in an article for the Los Angeles *Star*: "The said Robert Smith is persuading and enticing and seducing said persons of color to go out of the State of California."[27] He noted that none of the slaves could read or write, and that all were ignorant of the differences between the laws of California and of Texas. While slaves in California were free by law, it was impossible to be free and black in Texas, since Texas law forbade the importation of free blacks into the state, and Texans would have regarded them as slaves.[28]

The petitioners stated that they were free. The defendant, Robert Smith, represented in court by Alonzo Thomas, argued that the petitioners were members of his family, that they "left

**6.3 Los Angeles, drawn by Kuchel and Dresel, published by Hellman and Bro., San Francisco, 1857. (California Pioneer Society.)**

**6.4 City Hall and Jail, about 1880, northwest corner of Spring and Franklin streets. (Huntington Library.)**

Mississippi with their own consent, rather than remain there, and he has supported them ever since, subjecting them to no greater control than his own children, and not holding them as slaves; it is his intention to remove to Texas and take them with him." Furthermore, he argued that "Hannah and her children are well disposed to remain with him, and the petition was filed without their knowledge and consent." He added, "It is understood, between said Smith and said persons that they will return to said State of Texas with him voluntarily, as a portion of his family."[29]

Judge Hayes knew that the law of California was perfectly clear: "Neither slavery nor involuntary servitude, unless for the punishment of crimes, shall ever be tolerated in this State." Hayes noted, "Although, then there ought to be no difficulty in the matter in hand, it is not to be disguised that, in some vague manner, a sort of right is claimed over, at least, a portion of these petitioners. It is styled a guardianship, likened to 'patriarchal' rule, and by a few strenuously insisted upon:—so much so, as to incommode and obstruct a public officer in the discharge of his duty."[30] This refers to Smith's claims to legal guardianship, as well as the attempts of one Hartwell Cottrell, a member of Smith's party, perhaps his overseer, to get two of the slave children to go to Texas during the court proceedings. Described as "unscrupulous" by the judge, who saw him as a kidnapper, Cottrell took off for Texas one step ahead of the law.[31]

There seems to be a hint of Mormonism in Smith's advocacy of patriarchal guardianship, and possibly a use of the concept of plural wives from Utah to justify Smith's position. The Los Angeles *Star* described Hannah as Biddy's sister and also as "a woman nearly white, whose children are all nearly so, one of whose daughters (of eight years) cannot easily be distinguished from the white race."[32] In addition to being Smith's slaves, some of Hannah's children may indeed have been his own offspring, or perhaps Cottrell's. The judge observed: "the said Robert Smith from his past relation to them as members of his family does possess and exercise over them an undue influence in respect to the matter of their said removal insofar that they have been in duress and not in possession and exercise of their free will so as to give a binding consent to any engagement or arrangement with him."[33]

To understand Biddy Mason's courage in going to court against her master, it is first necessary to think of her lifetime in Mississippi, her complete immersion in the culture of the southern plantation, where physical torments such as whipping and being hosed down in brine would have been common for both male and female slaves' minor infractions. Even pregnant slaves were routinely whipped, but in special pits to protect the fetus.[34] Any slave's loved ones could be put on the block—husband, wife, child, sold and never seen again. In this context, all slaves' courage in risking a public test of white men's justice is striking. After 1850, California law prohibited blacks, mulattos, and Native Americans from testifying against white persons in either criminal or civil cases. They were present in court as petitioners, but had to remain silent.[35]

Biddy Mason served as head of the extended family throughout the trial. Although she could not speak in court, when questioned by the judge in his private chambers, with Abel Stearns and Dr. J. B. Winston present as two disinterested "gentlemen witnesses," she said, "I have always done what I have been told to do; I always feared this trip to Texas, since I first heard of it. Mr. Smith told me I would be just as free in Texas as here." Hannah's daughter Ann, questioned apart from the others, also asked the judge, "Will I be as free in Texas as here?," a question the legal experts found a poignant response to Smith's bluster that all would travel willingly. "No man of any experience in life will believe that it was ever true, or ever intended to be realized—this pleasant prospect of freedom in Texas," the judge concluded. He observed that Smith had only "$500 and an outfit," that he had "his own white family to take care of," and seemed to have no reason to transport fourteen slaves so far—unless he intended to sell them.[36]

The biggest mistake Smith and his lawyer made was bribing the lawyer for Biddy and the other petitioners, offering him $100 to quit the case on the second morning of the trial without telling his clients. Possibly threats were uttered as well. The lawyer (unnamed in the *Star* article) slipped a note to Judge Hayes and to the opposing counsel saying he was off the case. Biddy and the children, abandoned in the courtroom without any idea of what was going on, roused the sympathy of the judge: "I was pained by an occurrence not to be passed by unnoticed. There was a motion to dismiss the proceedings, based on a note from the petitioners' attorney to the attorney on the opposite side, in these words: 'I, as attorney for the petitioners, being no longer authorized to prosecute the writ, and being discharged by the same and the partner who are responsible to me, decline further to prosecute the matter.' "[37] The judge then subpoenaed and examined the attorney, and denounced his lack of legal propriety.

Accounts of the trial suggest that Smith probably threatened both Biddy and Hannah as well as their lawyer. Judge Hayes tried to establish whether or not any of the slaves consented to Smith's wish to go to Texas. Ultimately he decided that the "*speaking silence* of the petitioners" must be listened to, and that Hannah, in particular, had probably been the subject of threats. "Nothing else—except force—can account rationally for a favorable disposition in Hannah, if she has had any."[38]

The judge decided "as to the immediate cause of her hesitance—not her silence (for her very hesitation spoke a volume)—she is entitled to be listened to when, breathing freer, she declares she never wished to leave, and prays for protection." The judge saw Biddy as the leader of the group and noted: "It is remarkable that the defendant does not pretend that Biddy and her three children are 'well-disposed' to remain with him."[39] Hayes believed that Biddy had Hannah's consent from the beginning in seeking freedom for the whole group. Ultimately the judge decided that "all of the said persons of color are entitled to their freedom and are free forever."[40]

Court costs were to be paid by Robert Smith, who, on Monday, January 21, 1856, failed to appear, and this concluded the legal side of the proceedings. Smith could have appealed this local verdict to the California Supreme Court, where it is likely he would have won the support of conservative justices, such as Hugh C. Murray. However, presumably because of his bribery of the opposing counsel and Cottrell's attempted kidnapping of the children, Smith left town. Biddy Mason and her family were delivered from slavery, unlike other slaves in this decade who struggled with the courts and lost.

This escape was based on Judge Hayes's straightforward interpretation of the California constitution in 1856, a year before the U.S. Supreme Court would have invalidated Biddy's right to protest in court at all. In 1857, in the Dred Scott decision, the U.S. Supreme Court ruled that a slave was not a person but property, and that a slave's residence in free territory did not make that slave free.[41] So Biddy Mason and her thirteen family members won a timely escape from bondage. At the end of their trial, what remained was, in the words of the Judge Hayes, for the "petitioners to become settled and go to work for themselves—in peace and without fear."[42]

## "In Demand as a Midwife"

Once her freedom was secure, Biddy accepted Robert Owens's invitation to remain in Los Angeles and stay with his family (figure 6.5). She became known as Biddy Mason—a name that may have been chosen in homage to the trailfinder, Amasa Mason Lyman, who had led the Mormon wagons to Deseret and later to San Bernardino.[43] A friend of Owens, Dr. John Strother Griffin, offered her employment as a midwife and nurse. As Laurel Ulrich has noted, "caring for the sick was a universal female role, yet several women in every community stood out from the others for the breadth and depth of their commitment. They went farther, stayed longer, and did more than their neighbors." Midwives earned the most of

**6.5 Women of the Owens and Mason families on the porch of the Owens house, Los Angeles, early 1870s. (UCLA Special Collections.)**

all female healers because "they encompassed more skills, broader experience, longer memory."[44]

Soon Biddy Mason earned a local reputation as a medical practitioner of outstanding skills. Griffin's office as a physician and surgeon was located on Main Street, and he was also appointed as official doctor for the county jail and county hospital in 1859.[45] Working for Griffin, Biddy Mason tended the sick in both those places. The county jail would have had a special meaning for her as the place where she was held for her own protection during the trial, a place where she and Hannah prayed for their deliverance. Revisiting the jail again and again, she distinguished herself among the prisoners as a kindly woman. She became known for her courage after nursing many through a smallpox epidemic in the early 1860s, at the risk of her own life.[46]

Most important, she became famous as a midwife. Between 1856 and 1891 she delivered hundreds of babies, children of Los Angeles's leading families as well as children of the impoverished. Ludwig Salvator, in *Los Angeles in the Sunny Seventies*, recalled: "She was in demand as a midwife and as such brought into the world many of the children of the early pioneer families."[47] Her work would have taken her into all kinds of dwellings in Los Angeles, from the spacious old adobes of the wealthy *californios* near the Plaza, to the smaller, painted wooden structures of more recent Anglo immigrants, and the crowded shacks of Native American laborers in the wineries and citrus groves.

Biddy Mason's medical knowledge was no doubt the result of training by older midwives and slave doctors on the plantations where she grew up. While some planters did not provide medical care for their slaves, the extensive medical knowledge other planters encouraged slave doctors to acquire is documented by medical historian Martia Graham Goodson, who quotes a Mississippi planter in 1851: "I have a large and comfortable hospital provided for my negroes when they are sick; to this is attached a nurse's room, and when a negro complains of being too unwell to work, he is at once sent to the hospital and put under the charge of a very experienced and careful negro woman, who administers the medicine and attends to his diet and where they remain until they are able to work again."[48]

Many slave doctors knew African, Caribbean, and southern American herbal medicines. Goodson quotes two slave doctors, Easter Wells and Liza Smith, who explained that they always made their own medicines, using herbs and roots, and that when a slave got sick, the master would send out for the plants, and one of the slaves who knew how to cook and mix them for medicinal uses would give the doses. For example, they used Jerusalem oak for worms, asafetida for asthma and whooping cough, cotton root tea as an abortifacient, snakeroot and boneset for malaria, and many other substances that remain in use as vegetable drugs around the world. As Goodson shows, white doctors interested in botany, such as Francis Porcher of South Carolina, born in 1824, based their own medical careers on the publication of herbal knowledge first taught them by African slaves.[49]

In addition to preparing herbal medicines and administering them, Goodson notes, "slave women routinely cared for the obstetrics cases that were a part of slave life."[50] Slave midwives usually learned through direct experience assisting an older midwife. Using minimal intervention during labor and delivery, midwives let nature take its course, sometimes with the aid of herbs, exercise, and perineal massage, sometimes incorporating birth practices based on African traditions.[51] An experienced midwife skilled at "catching" babies would be much in demand on a plantation. And, as the example of Biddy Mason demonstrates, she could easily translate these skills to practice for pay in a town, where she might charge less than half a doctor's fee and provide services not offered by physicians. In addition to attending the mother and newborn, a midwife helped the entire household by cleaning, preparing meals, and looking after other children in the family for a number of days after the delivery.[52] It is difficult to say how much Biddy Mason earned. One source reports that Dr. Griffin paid Mason $2.50 per day for her work as a midwife,[53] a good sum in that era, when many midwives might have asked that amount for an entire case and black women in general commanded considerably lower wages. It is perhaps more likely that Biddy Mason was sometimes paid in cash, sometimes in kind (bread, vegetables, chickens were common), and sometimes was without any financial compensation.[54]

As late as 1910, at least half of all the births in the United States were assisted by midwives (figures 6.6, 6.7). When childbirth came increasingly under the domain of the medical profession, white, educated writers often criticized midwives as ignorant and superstitious. Yet recent medical historians have come to respect the "outstanding maternal and infant mortality/morbidity records" of experienced granny mid-

**6.6 Midwives with bags at Penn School, Frogmore, South Carolina, in the early 1930s. (Waring Historical Library of the Medical University of South Carolina.)**

**6.7 *First Midwife Trained by Dr. White*, by Sam Doyle, housepaint on tin, 38 by 26 inches. (Red Piano Art Gallery, Hilton Head Island, South Carolina.)**

wives, records better than those of many medically trained obstetricians.[55] Today's obstetrics once again emphasizes the nineteenth-century midwives' reliance on natural childbirth, with diet, exercise, and nonintervention. In the nineteenth century, certainly some midwives continued African or Caribbean rituals to celebrate a birth, such as painting a shutter blue on the outside of a house; scattering mustard seed or hanging a sieve over the door; driving three new nails into the threshold; nailing a new board up over the door; laying a new sill; or taking down a door and turning it around, to symbolize a new order.[56] Such rituals would not have hindered their medical success, but might have attracted scorn from whites who didn't share their special meanings.

Since Biddy Mason had a busy practice as a midwife in Los Angeles, among families of all classes, it seems certain that she had a good record of medical success with her patients. As a woman of medical knowledge, she would have earned the title "Grandma" or "Aunt" for her skills. She would have gone to tend her cases, walking through the dusty, unpaved streets of Los Angeles in the 1850s, carrying a midwife's characteristic large black bag. As one woman remembered her grandmother in Texas, an ex-slave midwife in the 1860s: "Every white man or black man born in that county that's my age, my grandma *caught him*. They called it *catch em*.... Grandma kept ... a black bag, just like a doctor did, she kept it. And we wasn't allowed to touch it. We couldn't even look at it too hard, cause everything she needed was there. She had her scissors and her thread that she cut the baby's cord, and she had it right there.... Grandma had big number eight white spools of thread, and she kept it in this bag.... She caught everybody in that county, white or black. You better know she did. She had a name for herself. She was good and she was recognized."[57] While this is a contemporary of Biddy Mason's in another state, the description of the level of skill fits well.

In her practice as a successful midwife and nurse, Biddy Mason found a way to enter Los Angeles's labor market with skills developed on a plantation in the rural South, skills with African antecedents. Mason may have sharpened her medical knowledge when she lived among the Mormons, or shared her own skills, because Mormon women in Utah were often encouraged to learn midwifery in order to minister to Native Americans as well as their own women.[58] In Los Angeles, Mason may have learned from Mexican American *curanderas* and Native American herbalists.[59] Many women of different cultures found midwifery, herbal medicine, and nursing salable skills in both rural and urban settings through the first three decades of the nineteenth century. Biddy Mason was typical of such women healers, who were skilled but without formal training. Not until 1918 did Los Angeles County Hospital admit black women to nurses' training, and de Graaf notes this was "in the face of a threatened strike by white nurses."[60]

As a single mother, Mason was not unusual in Los Angeles, since at the time she arrived in the 1850s, many Mexican American families had been disrupted by the war, and female-headed households were common.[61] However, as an African American woman with three daughters, Mason was a rarity in California. In 1850, 962 African Americans were noted in the state, but only ninety were females. In 1860, in Los Angeles, there were forty-five African American males and twenty-one females reported. As late as 1900, de Graaf notes that in Los Angeles single black women were still "so scarce that Black men 'inspected' incoming trains for possible mates."[62]

Mason's skills raised her a bit above the economic level of most wage-earning Los Angeles black women, who were more likely to be domestic servants or boardinghouse keepers, and made her more equal to black men, who were likely to be small farmers, livery stable keepers, blacksmiths, or barbers, such as the men of the Owens family who befriended her, or Peter Biggs, a Los Angeles barber. Biddy Mason's occupation was one with more predictable demand than the black men's trades, and they might have to turn to less skilled work if their small businesses failed, a problem she never faced. Biddy Mason's success as a wage earner, and her prudent way of life, meant that ultimately her family was able to gain a stake in Los Angeles as urban landowners.

After ten years of work as a midwife, Biddy Mason had saved $250 to purchase land and establish a homestead for herself and her family. One of the first African American women to own property in her own right in Los Angeles, she selected a site a bit out of town on Spring Street. Her homestead was a place to unite her family and nurture her extended family, a place to earn some income from additional activities as the town grew into a city. The history of her property can reveal how one landowner dealt with urban development.

Immediately after the court proceedings in 1856, Robert Owens, with his wife, Winnie, and his children Charles, Sarah Jane, and Martha, invited Biddy Mason and her daughters to live with them temporarily.[63] The strong connections between these two families, visualized in the photograph of the Mason and Owens women on the front porch, culminated in the marriage of Charles and Ellen soon after the trial, and the birth of Biddy's grandsons, Robert Curry Owens and Henry L. Owens.[64] For much of their lives, these four lived close to Biddy, even though the two boys and their mother moved to Oakland to receive some years of schooling unavailable to them in Los Angeles.[65] Hannah's daughter, Ann, also married her sweetheart, Manuel Pepper, and lived nearby for many years. A photograph from the 1870s shows the modest wooden cottage Biddy Mason lived in as a renter, very close to the Owens' house (figures 6.8).[66]

When Biddy Mason arrived in Los Angeles in 1856, it was a small town. Before the land speculators started arriving by the trainload, a few local people were already acquiring land, among them Owens and Dr. Griffin. Both of them would have been very familiar with the Ord survey of 1849, a map showing the vineyards and groves of Los Angeles giving way to a new commercial grid. Perhaps they advised Biddy to look over the lots for sale and put her savings in land. Owens, who began his land purchases in 1854, at one point owned an entire block in the Ord survey (between Olive, Charity, Sixth, and Seventh streets), as well as his livery stable on Main

**6.8 Biddy Mason's first Los Angeles residence, near the Owens family, San Pedro Street between First and Second, 1870s. (Golden State Mutual Life Insurance Collection, UCLA Special Collections.)**

Street extending to Los Angeles Street (called the "Government Corral" during the Civil War because of his Federal contracts) and several other tracts. Griffin took enough time off from doctoring (or delegated patients to Biddy) to open a tract in East Los Angeles and to join Solomon Lazard and Prudent Beaudry in the water business. They formed the Los Angeles City Water Company, negotiated a thirty-year lease to sell water to the city in 1868, built the water system, and ultimately resold it (and the services of the engineer, William Mulholland) back to the city for $2 million.[67]

Biddy Mason, unlike Owens and Griffin, was not a speculator. She was a forty-eight-year-old working woman who wanted a home for her family, and had to save for ten years to get it. She purchased lots 3 and 8 in Block 7 of the Ord Survey on November 28, 1866, from William M. Buffum and James F. Burns for $250.[68] Her property ran between Spring Street and

Fort Street (later Broadway) in the block between Third and Fourth streets. According to Delilah Beasley, Biddy Mason "told her children that this was always to remain as their homestead, and it mattered not what their circumstances, they were always to retain this homestead."[69] Biddy Mason's use of this property shows that the way an employed woman defined "homestead" as an urban, economic base for her family's activities has little relationship to the rural, Anglo stereotypes of house with land.

The land she bought in 1866 was considered a little bit out of town, in an area of unpaved streets, interspersed with vineyards, groves, and vegetable gardens. Charles Pierce's panoramic photo of 1869 shows Spring Street and Broadway as wide, dusty streets with a collection of small one-story and two-story buildings, large yards and open spaces. Biddy's piece was described as having "a ditch of water" (irrigation from the *zanjas*) and a "willow fence." A midwife might be expected to have planted a garden of medicine herbs as well. The Britton and Rey view of Los Angeles in 1871 (republished by the Germain Seed and Plant Company in 1872) shows the city as a greener and more blossoming place, with Biddy's block bearing several small wooden houses with peaked roofs (figure 6.9). She may have erected a small wooden house or two here for rental income. It seems likely she held at least part of her land vacant while she saved more money to build a substantial commercial structure. City directories show that Biddy Mason lived in modest rental accommodations until eighteen years after her purchase, when she finally moved onto her own land.[70] By that time she was sixty-six, and the building could support her in her old age as well as her descendants.

Before 1870 the streets of the town were mostly unpaved, "dirty and dusty during the dry summer months and muddy when the rains made rivers of the rutted streets." One reporter noted that "little bare-legged urchins hire out as pilots through the mud on Alameda and Aliso Streets."[71] A sixteen-year-old boy on horseback rode around at dusk to light the city's gas lamps, which had replaced lanterns over the doors

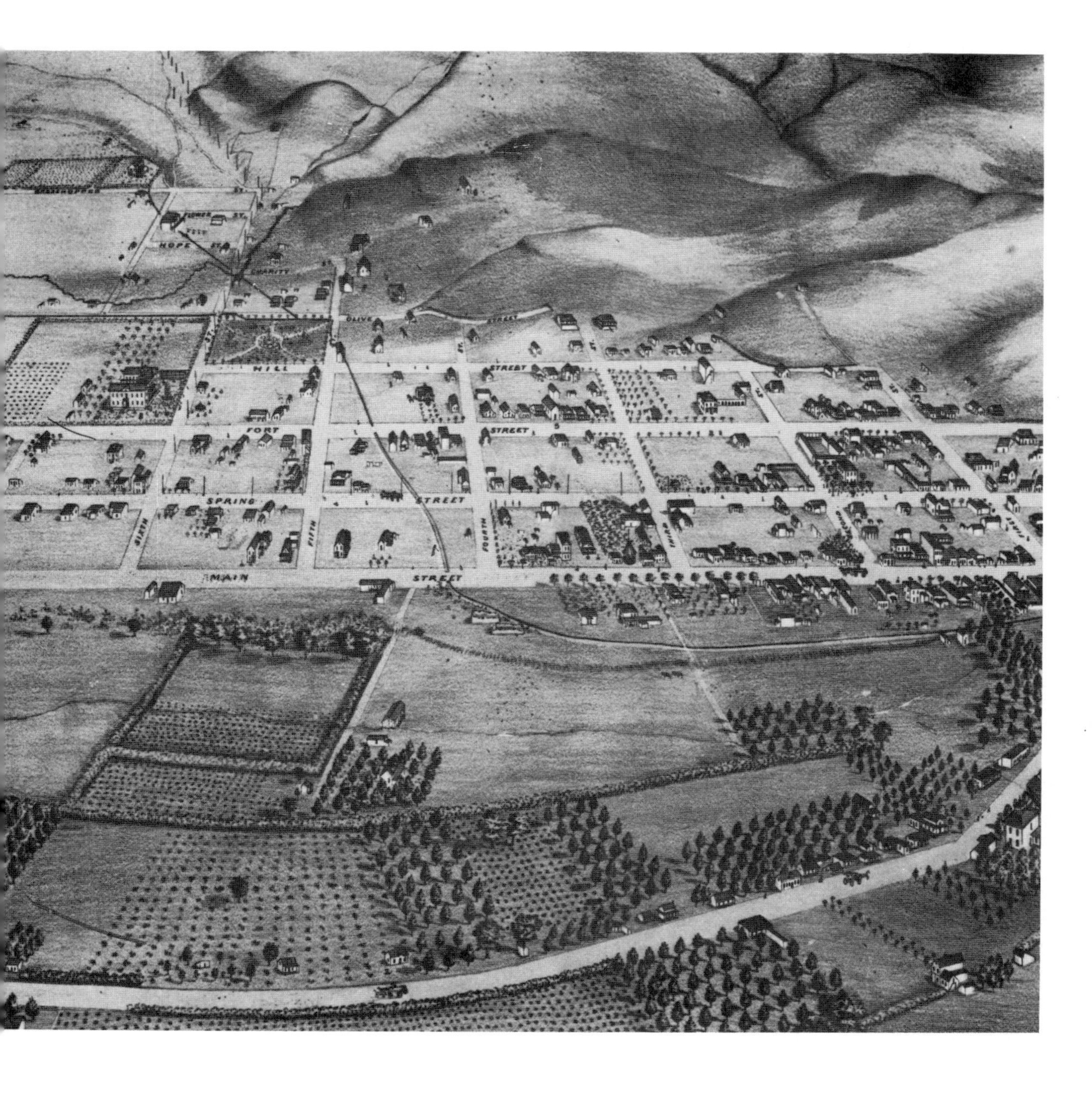


**6.9 Detail of Britton and Rey's view of Los Angeles, 1871. (UCLA Special Collections.)**

of private houses in 1870. The city could only afford one gas lamp per intersection, and staggered them on the northeast and southwest corners of alternate blocks.[72] Houses without numbers and some streets without names remained, but the first Los Angeles City and County directory of 1872 attempted to give exact addresses in a growing place.[73]

By the 1880s, the built environment of Biddy's block was dense and growing denser, changing from residential to commercial uses, and from frame to brick buildings. By 1884 she had sold one part of her land for $1,500 and had built an urban commercial building, with storerooms on the ground floor for rental and living space for her family above.[74] The building came to the sidewalk, brick-faced on the first floor, wood on the second (figures 6.10, 6.11).[75] She lived above the ground floor there, in a neighborhood of small businesses, including a nursery, bakeries, restaurants, furniture and carpet stores, offices, boardinghouses, and grocery stores.[76] It was an ethnically diverse area, similar to the ones she had been living in as a renter. By the late 1880s and early 1890s, the main financial district of Los Angeles was located on Spring, just south of her block, between Fourth and Seventh. Other landmarks such as the Bradbury Building were located on Broadway between Third and Fourth, close to the back of her lot in the 1890s.

In 1885, Mason offered her grandsons the chance to establish a business on her property, and in 1890, the venture having proved a success, she deeded them a part of her property, "in consideration of the sum of love and affection and ten dollars."[77] For Robert, the livery stable was the backup to an already successful career in politics, with a sideline in real estate. For career guidance, he recalled, "My Grandmother (Aunt Biddy) as she was known by every citizen, proved my salvation. She told my father that he could not make a farmer or a blacksmith out of a boy who wanted to be a politician, and she was right."[78] Clearly she understood the direction Los Angeles was taking, and wanted her descendants to prosper in the bustling urban center.

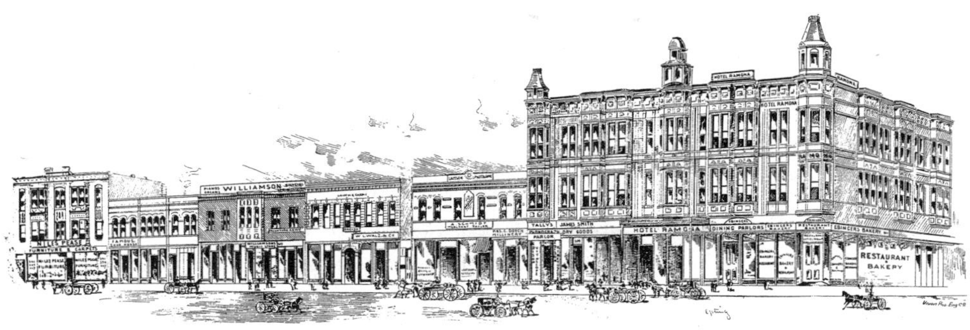


**6.10 Sketch of Spring Street, 1896, Mason homestead second from left. (Drummond Buckley.)**

**6.11 Los Angeles, Spring Street looking south from Third Street, 1900. Biddy Mason's building is at lower right center, two stories high, below "Niles Pease Furniture and Carpets" sign. This is the same block pictured in Britton and Rey's 1871 lithograph, less than three decades later. (UCLA Special Collections.)**

Employed by various families around the growing city, Biddy Mason surely gained her insights about urban jobs from observing the struggles of many rural migrants to Los Angeles in the second half of the nineteenth century, not just members of the black community. Some brought agricultural and horticultural skills, but these skills were not usually well-paid ones. Those who prospered expanded their original skills into commercial, urban ventures like the produce market or the flower market. Others who were not able to earn enough to purchase land or to educate the next generation for more urban occupations remained low-paid agricultural workers, or left the city for more rural areas. This was not the legacy Biddy Mason wished for her children and grandchildren.

## Community Builder

Biddy Mason used her homestead as a place to nurture her family and to encourage their activities. She also created many other networks that centered on her home. Together with Charles Owens, she gathered a group of people to form the Los Angeles branch of the First African Methodist Episcopal Church, and at a meeting in her home in 1872 the church was officially organized. Mason was described by many as a woman whose common sense was as strong as her religious faith, and one historian has noted that she paid the taxes for the church property from her own pocket, and called for the minister, the Reverend Jesse Hamilton. She continued to attend the Fort Street Methodist Episcopal Church, across the street from her homestead.[79]

Biddy Mason did purchase four lots besides her own homestead in 1868 for $375, all located in the block bounded by Olive and Charity Streets, which may have been the same land owned earlier by Robert Owens, since she acquired this land from Charles Owens and Martha Hall.[80] On April 7, 1884, she sold one of these lots (lot 8) for $2,800, a sum that probably enabled her to increase her work as a philanthropist, since about that time she gave orders to a small grocery in her own neighborhood to open accounts for any needy families made homeless by seasonal floods.[81]

Because she became known as a benefactor of the poor, "a frequent visitor to the jail," and a resource for settlers of all races, Biddy Mason was approached by many who wanted help: "Her home at No. 331 South Spring Street in later years became a refuge for stranded and needy settlers. As she grew more feeble it became necessary for her grandson to stand at the gate each morning and turn away the line which had formed awaiting her assistance." When she died on January 15, 1891, many in Los Angeles mourned her. After a service at the Fort Street M.E. Church,[82] she was buried without much fuss or expense in Evergreen Cemetery, in Boyle Heights. In 1988 the First African Methodist Episcopal Church erected a headstone for her there as a founding member of the first African American church in LA, a church that is still one of the city's largest and most influential, especially in the area of social activism in the community.

## The Open Hand

The legacies of Biddy Mason were legal, material, social, and spiritual. She has been celebrated in the past in a superficial way as a "good woman," a pious woman, and a slave who won her freedom. But she should be seen as a female head of a group of fourteen slaves, a woman whose intelligence and skill enabled her to provide for her family during arduous cross-country travels. She continued providing for them during her transition from rural life as a slave to independent survival in the city, at a time when women of color did not find it easy to enter the labor market and earn an adequate living.

Because of her special medical skills as a midwife and nurse, Biddy Mason succeeded. Some have characterized her medical career as an extension of her stereotyped role as a "good woman." Other historians, such as de Graaf, have classified her employment as a nurse as unskilled domestic service, but in fact the training and experience she received on plantations in the South, where female slave doctors and midwives were responsible for the health of many slave communities, were what made her exceptional in Los Angeles.[83] When white male residents and visitors passing through Los Angeles observed that Mason was "in demand" as a midwife, they were pointing to a person of high reputation for medical skill who was a founder of the professions of nursing and midwifery in the city, a medical worker who was also prepared to risk her own life nursing those with a contagious disease during an urban epidemic.

Mason's acquisition of a homestead and some other property have in the past been acclaimed because she was one of the first black women to own property in Los Angeles, and the growth of the city made the property valuable to her heirs. But Mason's homestead was for her, first of all, a place for gathering her family, helping the poor, and building social networks like the FAME Church. And second, it was a place for helping family members earn a living, with ventures like the livery stable. In this attitude toward real estate, she differed from her descendants. Mason was a woman who lived very modestly. Her children, and especially her grandchildren, put much more distance between themselves and ordinary workers of every race in Los Angeles.

As Lonnie Bunch has demonstrated, in the years between 1890 and 1930, despite its growing white majority, Los Angeles had a small, prosperous black elite, and the descendants of the Mason and Owens families were prominent in this group.[84] To the average African American family scraping by on wages from domestic service, a livery service, or laying streetcar track, the grandchildren of Biddy Mason must have seemed to be living an impossible dream of ease and wealth, people wearing elaborate Victorian dresses with lace collars, or suits with stiff collars and ties, and looking much like the white members of the business elite. Her descendants did face increasing racial segregation in the city's public places and residential areas, yet they maintained a genteel life style. Their property was considerable—they consolidated the elder Robert Owens's land, purchased beginning in the 1850s, with Biddy's holdings—and her grandson, Robert C. Owens, who became a real estate developer and political figure, tried to maximize its potential.

Mason might have been uneasy, rather than excited, had she lived to read the *Los Angeles Times* coverage in 1905 of the plans of Robert C. Owens to build a six-story building on the Broadway frontage of her homestead for $250,000. The *Times* described him as the "Richest Negro in Los Angeles," and reported that he and his mother had been feuding with his Aunt Harriet in and out of court for years.[85] In 1905, Owens planned a memorial to his grandmother Biddy in his new building, an institute run on the lines of Tuskegee, but the memorial was never built. Perhaps this was just as well—the *Times* said the new institute would assist "Los Angeles negro young men," and never mentioned young women. Owens eventually suffered financial reverses in the Depression and came to a tragic end.[86]

Biddy Mason herself had a much more lasting idea about legacies, about giving and getting in the context of a growing town. Her great-granddaughter, Gladys Owens Smith, remembers a saying the family attributed to Biddy: "If you hold your hand closed, Gladys, nothing good can come in. The open hand is blessed, for it gives in abundance, even as it receives."[87] In her words is an echo of praise for an eighteenth-century midwife, "Her Ear was open to the complaints of the Afflicted, and her Hand was open for the Supply of the Needy."[88] The traditions within midwifery were passed on from mother to daughter, generation to generation, with generosity both personal and public. Ulrich calls this practice not domestic medicine, not folk medicine, but "social medicine," a fitting profession for a woman who said, "Greet the world with an open hand."

# 7 Rediscovering an African American Homestead

**. . . all of the said persons of color are entitled to their freedom and are free forever.**

**1856 text of the Freedom Papers on the Biddy Mason wall**

By 1986, the former homestead of Biddy Mason at 331 Spring Street had become a parking lot, an unlikely site for any kind of history project. Asphalt covered the area, bounded by two busy streets in downtown Los Angeles. Spring Street itself included City Hall, the Banco Popular building (headquarters of the Community Redevelopment Agency), and blocks of ten-story commercial structures. Between the 1890s and the 1920s, Spring Street had thrived as the commercial center generated by the land boom of the 1880s, the "Wall Street of the West" in booster language. It included the Pacific Stock Exchange, the Crocker Bank, the Security National Bank Building, the headquarters of wheat farmer and rancher I. N. Van Nuys, and the offices of banker Hermann W. Hellman.[1] Their buildings flaunted the iconography of the disappearing agricultural landscape, clusters of grapes, stalks of wheat, ears of corn, heads of cattle.

By 1986 Spring Street lacked economic activity. The Alexandria Hotel hosted a few package tours. The upper floors of many office buildings were empty. The new real estate magnates of the 1980s had moved to the glass towers of Bunker Hill, if they were still in downtown at all. Spring Street had history, and National Register Historic District status, but it needed economic renewal. Broadway presented a livelier pedestrian scene, sidewalks overflowing with merchandise from small shops selling discounted electronic gadgets, calculators, boom boxes, radios, lipsticks, eye shadows, patent leather shoes, and first communion dresses. Behind glass showcases were elaborate wedding tuxedos in brilliant colors, and lacy white bridal gowns with impossibly long trains. Young and old crowded the sidewalks of Broadway, which was reputed to have higher gross sales per square foot than Rodeo Drive in Beverly Hills. Latino shoppers enjoyed the Grand Central Market's spicy sausages, chili peppers, tortillas, and fresh-peeled mangos on sticks. The grandiose Million Dollar Theatre, an old Mexican vaudeville and movie house, showed Spanish-language movies, and had once, in the 1930s, been part of the largest concentration of movie palaces in the world.[2] Broadway also included the Bradbury Building, an architectural treasure with a romantic interior courtyard, constructed by an obsessed draftsman of the 1890s who wanted to test ideas about architecture for a socialist city that were expressed in Edward Bellamy's novel *Looking Backward.*

In between Spring Street and Broadway, between Third Street and Fourth Street, Biddy Mason had built her urban homestead, the two-story brick building she had erected in the 1880s, with space for her grandson's businesses, her own living quarters upstairs, and her garden. After her death, her grandson Robert had attempted in 1905 to turn her building into a community center for African American youths, but had not succeeded. In the 1970s, an attempt led by Enola Ewing and Miriam Matthews to commemorate Biddy Mason's founding of the Los Angeles African Methodist Episcopal Church, at the first site of the church, had ended without success. Now, in this asphalt parking lot, with no visible signs of the homestead remaining, could a third attempt to mark Biddy Mason's life in Los Angeles succeed?

The parking lot was owned by the Los Angeles Community Redevelopment Agency, a public agency engaged in vast land clearance and rebuilding enterprises in nineteen different parts of the city. The CRA's operations affected nearly two hundred buildings in downtown alone.[3] Their economic development strategy for Spring Street included investment in about a dozen buildings. One of their projects was to work with several private developers to build the Broadway Spring Center, a ten-story garage with commercial space on the ground floor at 333 Spring Street.

Two planners at the CRA, Robert Chattel and Richard Rowe, had a strong interest in urban history. They had asked for a list of sites from The Power of Place's 1985 downtown walking tour to enter in the CRA's central computer. Both Chattel and Rowe were active in preservation as leaders of the local chapter of the Society of Architectural Historians. They had coauthored the Spring Street walking tour published by the Los Angeles Conservancy.[4] When they realized that the site for the Broadway Spring Center included the historic site of the Mason homestead, they asked if it might be possible for The Power of Place to sponsor some kind of commemoration as part of the new development.

Perhaps they had a bronze plaque in mind, but they were open to other possibilities. Their question came in the summer of 1986, at a time when The Power of Place's project to preserve another landmark of African American history had ground to a halt. Fire Station 30, located at Fourteenth Street and Central Avenue, was an intact craftsman building that had housed the firefighters' push for the integration of the civil service in Los Angeles in the 1950s. In 1985 The Power of Place had held a public history workshop there that had attracted about fifty retired firefighters and their families from many parts of California. After nomination by The Power of Place, the station had been designated a Los Angeles Historic Cultural landmark. The city had agreed to lease the building for $1 per year to a suitable nonprofit organization. A good deal of publicity about the station in February 1985 had resulted in several grants for its renovation and reuse as the office of The Los Angeles Community Design Center, a nonprofit organization that provided architectural and planning assistance to various community groups. In addition, The Power of Place proposed to fund and install a public history exhibit on site honoring the firefighters.

Then, following the publicity in Black History month, the station suffered a mysterious fire that destroyed part of the roof and left the second floor open to the rain. Was it arson, or just an accident? The building had been unoccupied. No blame could be fixed. But the incident made the women who worked for the Los Angeles Community Design Center wonder if the location was safe. By 1986 the area had become a mixture of warehouses and industrial spaces, as African American businesses moved further south on Central Avenue over several decades.[5] Between the additional costs imposed by the fire and the problems of safety, the plans for preservation and adaptive reuse languished. Many vernacular buildings in inner city locations have problems of location similar to this one. In 1986, the old fire station at Fourteenth and

Central simply could not justify a real estate investment, even a renovation for a nonprofit use, standing by itself. The location was not in the center city, not in a thriving ethnic minority neighborhood, not in any kind of historic district. It could not attract tenants, and probably could not attract many visitors for the same reasons. At the same time, intact historic buildings in excellent downtown locations were too interesting to real estate developers, and therefore too expensive for nonprofit organizations to get hold of for interpretive purposes. The stalled project on the firefighters provided the incentive to look at new strategies. Exploring public art as a route to public memory looked more promising than acquiring downtown real estate of any type.

The Biddy Mason site, for all its asphalt, had a superb location. Heavy pedestrian activity would be funneled through an arcade in the new building and a small park behind it, into a new pedestrian shortcut to join the two major streets, Spring Street and Broadway. The Biddy Mason site also promised a good mix of citizens of all ethnic backgrounds, economic classes, and ages, men and women, because of its location near both government offices and shopping. The construction of the Ronald Reagan State Office Building in the immediate area promised to add even more activity. The Broadway Spring Center would also have security sufficient to oversee any installation on site, because of a parking booth open at all hours.

As president of The Power of Place and project director, I recruited a team of Los Angeles artists to join in celebrating the public history of Biddy Mason's homestead through a collaborative project. We applied for a grant from the National Endowment for the Arts for project funding. The group included artist and graphic designer Sheila Levrant de Bretteville, artist Susan E. King (a specialist in letterpress books), and sculptor Betye Saar.[6] All had worked together over the years at the Los Angeles Women's Building, a center for the arts cofounded by de Bretteville. The Power of Place undertook its own fund raising; after we received the first of several NEA grants in the spring of 1987, the project began with a series of group meetings and a public history workshop. (The eventual cost of the project was about $212,000, including both cash and in-kind contributions.) In September 1987, Donna Graves, experienced in museum work, joined the project as assistant director. On November 16, 1989, the Broadway Spring Center and the new public art were dedicated.[7]

Preliminary historical research had preceded the start of the project, because Biddy Mason's site had been included in the downtown walking tour completed in 1985.[8] It was possible to consult with Lonnie G. Bunch III and Kathy Perkins, who were working on the *Black Angelenos* exhibit and video for the California Afro-American History Museum.[9] Mason's descendants, Linda Cox and Gladys Owens Smith, came forward with information. In addition, Bobi Jackson, a local writer interested in doing a screenplay on Mason, shared some of her insights and suggested using the Mormon records to track her journey west. Then the medical history on slave midwives and slave doctors opened up a range of issues. The land deeds and records connected to the built environment provided the last set of primary sources that made it possible to tell the story of a working woman of color who could neither read nor write.

On November 21, 1987, a public workshop at UCLA, cosponsored by The Power of Place, The Graduate School of Architecture and Urban Planning, and the African American Studies program, focused attention on four accounts of Mason's life and her importance for the entire city and gave interested members of the public a chance to comment on the history (figure 7.1). Presentations by artists de Bretteville, Saar, and King of the site plan (figure 7.2) and models of their proposed commemorations also generated comment by the public and the historians. About fifty people attended.

"For too long the history of the African American in Los Angeles has been restricted to small groups," noted Lonnie G. Bunch, from the California Afro-American Museum, "but there is no one who knows as much as Miriam Matthews."[10] Matthews, a retired librarian who had collected materials on

**7.1 "The Life and Times of Biddy Mason," public history workshop, run by The Power of Place at UCLA, November 21, 1987. Miriam Matthews seated with scrapbook. (Drummond Buckley.)**

**7.2 Site plan for Broadway Spring Center and the rest of the block.**

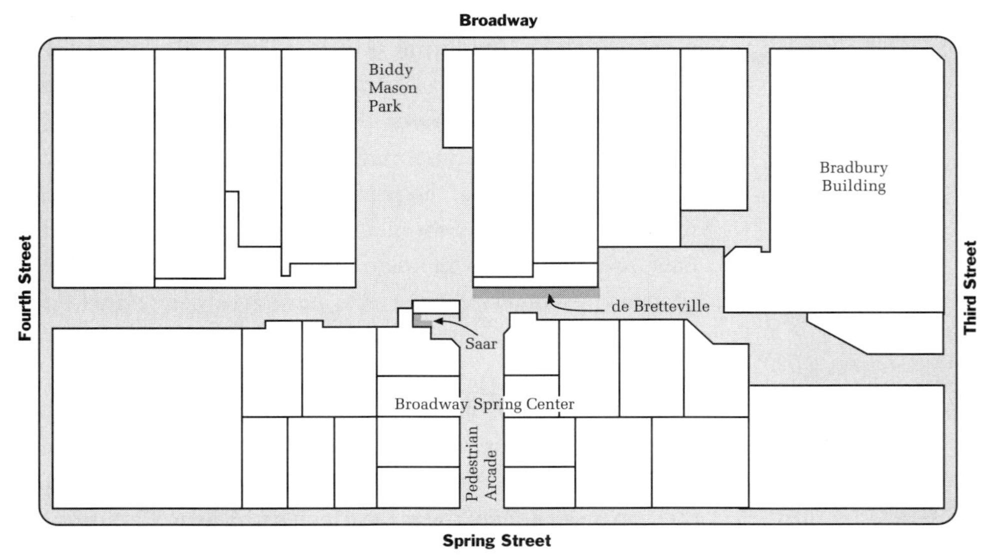

African American Los Angeles for many years, brought voluminous scrapbooks to the meeting and passed them around. "I'm happy that you are doing this. Biddy Mason *should* be remembered," she said. "I tried to get them [the CRA] to buy the lot at Eighth and Towne where the AME church had burned down and have a park with a Biddy Mason sculpture—they said it cost too much."

Passing around a photo, Matthews noted, "This photo shows that Biddy Mason was not the enormous person you think she was." Kathy Perkins brought the church history to the foreground: "I'm a recent transplant to LA from the East Coast and I came here looking for a church home at First AME. I remember going there and seeing her picture in the hall.... We have this wonderful huge mural ... a segment shows Biddy Mason with a staff in her hand standing tall and strong ... the good shepherd ... her flock became the poor in LA." Bobi Jackson added, "I found her here in UCLA Special Collections in 1981.... It's exhilarating and comforting to me that all of us can be here today linked by this one woman."

The Los Angeles AME Church, which Mason had helped found in 1872, grew to become a large, affluent, socially-minded congregation. The church's members rightly stressed Mason's role in the church as an important part of her story that the Power of Place's team had not emphasized when we focused on her role as a midwife. A missionary unit bearing Mason's name was still operating, and after the history workshop, the church decided to mark Mason's grave at the Evergreen Cemetery in Boyle Heights with a new stone and a ceremony in March 1988. (The ceremony was launched with a motorcade led by Reverend Cecil Murray, spirited renditions of "Jesus Keep Me Near the Cross" and "We Are Climbing Jacob's Ladder," plus moving tributes to Mason in a grassy, well-watered cemetery filled with Japanese American, Latino, and African American headstones, the oldest cemetery in the city, and the place most nonwhites were buried in the nineteenth century.) Meanwhile, other ideas were stirring. The California Afro-American Museum started to plan a photographic exhibit on black midwives. A storyteller from northern California's Headlands Museum of the Arts began to prepare a performance based on Mason's life. At a later date, two landscape architects employed by the Broadway Spring Center developers created a pocket park behind the Biddy Mason wall, which the city then named in Mason's honor.

The Power of Place sponsored four works of art, in addition to the public history workshop and my article on Biddy Mason (which appears here as the previous chapter).[11] The first art project, completed in August 1988, a poster designed by Sheila de Bretteville, introduced the history of the site. The text I wrote stressed the themes of midwifery and community building. It carried direct quotations from midwives about their lives and work, as well as a list of traditional midwives' remedies and architectural symbols used to mark a birth:

*Make a blue flame in the hearthfire by throwing a*
*handful of salt.*
*Paint one shutter blue in front of a house.*
*Lay a new sill for the front door to symbolize new life.*
*Take the front door down and turn it around.*[12]

As a counterpart to the poster, which was given away to school groups, Susan E. King's large-format (13-by-22-inch) letterpress artist's book, *HOME/stead*, produced in an edition of thirty-five, was donated to the Los Angeles Public Library and the City Archives and sold to a number of museums and libraries interested in Western Americana (figures 7.3, 7.4). The book combined the personal and the public. King interwove Biddy Mason's story with her own account of growing up in the South, including meditations on home and garden, southern womanhood, racism, and learning about the civil rights movement. Rubbings from gravestones in the Evergreen Cemetery included vines, ferns, and an image of the gate of heaven. The vine, reversed, showed the names of many towns Biddy Mason encountered on her journey walking west behind her master's wagon train: Fulton, Mississippi; Paris, Tennessee; Paducah, Kentucky; Metropolis, Illinois; St. Louis, Missouri; Council Bluffs, Iowa; Grand Island, Nebraska; Fort Laramie, Wyoming; Deseret, Utah; and San Bernardino, California.[13] With sensuous Rives BFK, Asuka, and Pombie

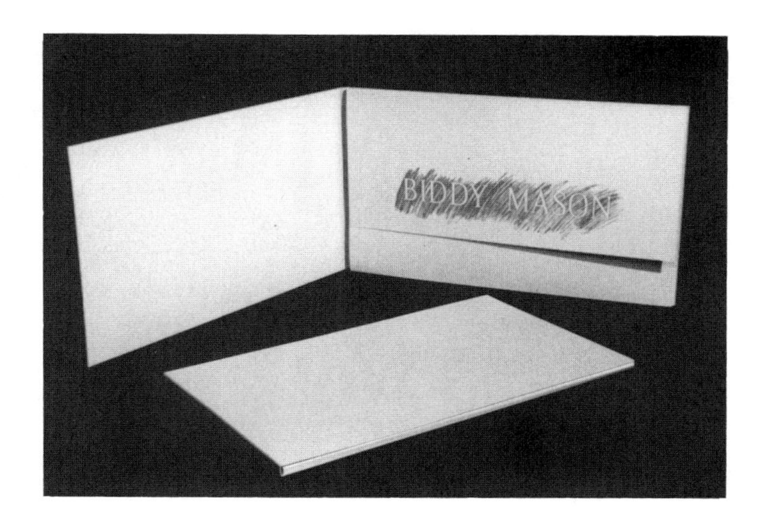


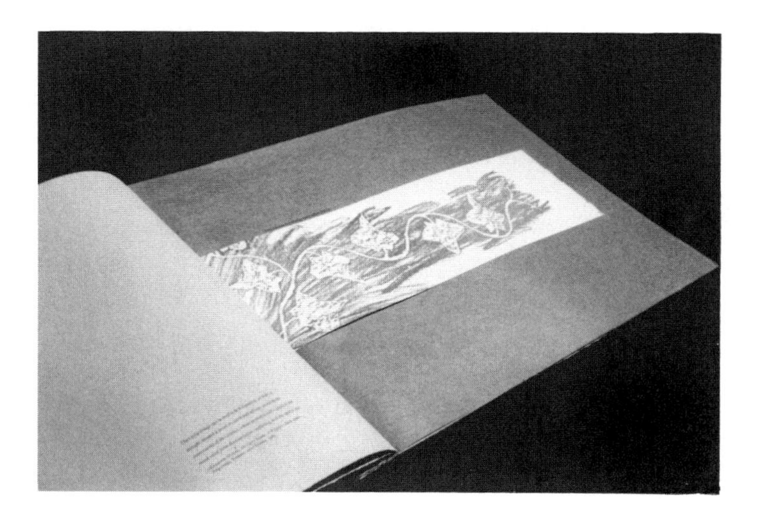

**7.3 Inside cover and a page of *HOME/Stead*, artist's book by Susan E. King, with The Power of Place, 1989.**

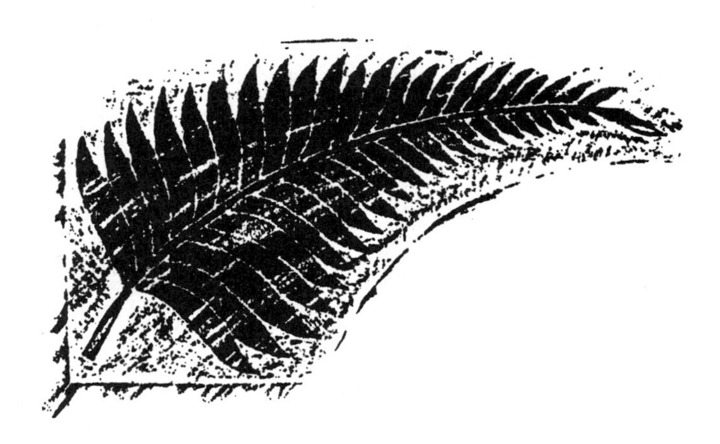

**7.4 Details of *HOME/Stead*: a rubbing from Evergreen Cemetery; the mark of Biddy Mason.**

Biddy her mark Mason

**7.5 *Biddy Mason: House of the Open Hand*, installation by Betye Saar with The Power of Place, including assemblage on left and photomural on right. (Julie Easton.)**

**7.6 Detail of *Biddy Mason: House of the Open Hand*, assemblage by Betye Saar with The Power of Place, 1989. (Julie Easton.)**

papers in greens, tans, grays, and dark red, *HOME/stead* carried the story of Biddy Mason, including the X she used to sign her deeds.

Betye Saar's assemblage, *Biddy Mason: House of the Open Hand*, was installed in the elevator lobby of the new building (figures 7.5, 7.6). One wall included a sepia-toned photomural of a surviving photograph of Biddy Mason and the women of the Owens family on the front porch of their home. The adjacent wall housed an assemblage constructed inside a window frame, including a portrait of Mason, a fan, old wallpaper, curtains, and a medicine bottle excavated during work on the site. (It was not possible to conduct any extensive archaeological research.) Motifs from vernacular building included shutters and a picket fence. (At the time, no one thought of painting one of the shutters blue, to signify a midwife's celebration of a new birth.)

By far the largest and most complicated of the installations on the site was Sheila Levrant de Bretteville's 81-foot-long wall, framing the pedestrian area at the rear of the commercial arcade, entitled *Biddy Mason: Time and Place* (figures 7.7, 7.8, 7.9). De Bretteville's wall transformed a marginal alley behind several large buildings into a significant public place.[14] Divided into decades, the wall told the story of Los Angeles's development from a tiny Mexican town to a thriving city, as well as the story of Mason's walk across the country, her arrival in Los Angeles, her suit for freedom, and her thriving practice as a midwife. Among the historic documents photographed and bonded to limestone as part of the wall were several maps and views of Los Angeles, Biddy Mason's freedom papers, and the deed to her homestead on Spring Street.

Looking at the wall, visitors could see how the homestead, located a bit out of town in 1866, in an area of gardens and groves, became part of a dense commercial district in the 1890s, and was then overshadowed by Los Angeles's Bunker Hill skyscrapers of the 1980s. The actual scale of downtown was easily perceived from the Biddy Mason wall, so that the

**7.7 Overview of *Biddy Mason: Time and Place*, by Sheila Levrant de Bretteville with The Power of Place, 1989, showing portrait of Mason, her mark (X), and an 1890s view of city. (Jim Simmons/ Annette Del Zoppo.)**

**7.8 Details of de Brettevile's wall:** ***top,*** **deed to the homestead and fence;** ***bottom,*** **freedom papers. (Simmons/Del Zoppo.)**

**7.9 Details of the wall: midwife's bag, scissors, and spool; fence; guests at the opening ceremony. (*Top left,* Simmons/Del Zoppo; *bottom left,* Drummond Buckley; *top right,* Mark Porter Zasada; *bottom right*, Dolores Hayden.)**

**7.10 Team members for the project: Betye Saar, Donna Graves, Sheila Levrant de Bretteville, Susan E. King (author behind the camera).**

small size of The Power of Place's project worked as part of the overall historical narrative. Set against a massive skyline, this small place devoted to history encouraged a viewer to contemplate change on Spring Street in both space and time.

All of us on the team (figure 7.10) hoped for an audience wider than a museum or university could provide. The opening day ceremonies were attended by a large, enthusiastic gathering including the mayor and several city council members, top officials of the redevelopment agency, students, members of the church, and several of Biddy Mason's descendants. Sheila de Bretteville's wall proved especially successful in drawing citizens to claim the history as their own. Youngsters ran their hands along the wagon wheels pressed into the wall, or traced the shapes of the midwife's bag, the scissors, and the spools of thread. Teenagers deciphered the historic maps and puzzled over the old-fashioned handwriting on the freedom papers. People of all ages asked their friends to pose for snapshots in front of their favorite parts of the wall. Today, long after the meetings and the legal negotiations are over, the wall remains as a new public place, one that connects the life of a remarkable woman with family history, community history, and the city's urban landscape changing over time.

# 8 Reinterpreting Latina History at the Embassy Auditorium

The day we signed that union contract, I knew how the signers of the Declaration of Independence must have felt.

ILGWU dressmaker, Local 96, 1933

We're getting together for the first time in our history. The problems of the Mexicans may have begun in the Southwest, but now we're present throughout the country, including all Latinos.

Participant at El Congreso national meeting, 1939

Biddy Mason's urban homestead was close to the district that boosters called the "Wall Street of the West" in the 1890s, but the center of Los Angeles's commercial development shifted southeast over the next few decades. Closer to this new center, the Embassy Auditorium (formerly named Trinity Auditorium) opened at Ninth and Grand in 1914. It housed church services, musical events, and hundreds of rallies and meetings organized by community groups, including the followers of Marcus Garvey, the promoters of Upton Sinclair's EPIC (End Poverty in California), and the Townsendites (whose campaigns led to Social Security). Here *la fuerza de unión*, the force of union, challenged Los Angeles's anti-union, open shop commercial establishment again and again. Here, in the 1930s and 1940s, three remarkable organizers, Rose Pesotta of the ILGWU (International Ladies' Garment Workers' Union), Luisa Moreno of UCAPAWA (United Cannery, Agricultural, Packing and Allied Workers Association), and Josefina Fierro de Bright of El Congreso, the first national Latino civil rights organization, reached the height of their charismatic careers. They built solidarity among women workers and coalitions between labor and community groups.

Donna Graves directed the Embassy Project for The Power of Place. She saw the Embassy, which had been designated a Los Angeles Historic-Cultural Monument, as an architectural landmark needing fuller interpretation of its women's history, labor history, and ethnic history. The team Graves recruited included two artists, Rupert Garcia (known for his silkscreen prints and posters of political and artistic figures) and Celia Alvarez Muñoz (known for her artist's books and witty gallery installations in both Spanish and English). Brenda Levin, a Los Angeles architect experienced in the renovation of many downtown buildings, joined the group with her assistant Jennifer Lee to consider how a permanent public art installation might be added to the structure, as part of a reinterpretation of its history. Historical research was contributed by Vicki L. Ruiz and George J. Sánchez as team members, as well as UCLA interns Nancy Stillger, Ronald Brooks, and Jennifer Schroeder.[1]

**8.1 Embassy Auditorium; note the showcases on sidewalk. (The Huntington Library.)**

**8.2 Embassy Auditorium, interior of the main hall. (The Power of Place.)**

**8.3 Garment workers assembled by shop names for a meeting, ILGWU Local 266, 1946, at Embassy Auditorium.**

Designed by Thornton Fitzhugh, Frank Krucker, and Henry Deckbar, the Embassy is a heavy, classical revival structure (figure 8.1).[2] It was originally a church, made more bulky by the addition of a residence with several hundred rooms, similar to a YMCA.[3] The facade includes terra-cotta trim and two massive engaged Corinthian columns. A four-story dome tops the nine-story block, a visual landmark for the neighborhood. The interior of the 1,500-seat auditorium is highlighted by a vaulted ceiling of stained glass and canvas panels stretching for over seventy-five feet (figures 8.2, 8.3). Built without artificial amplification, the main hall was, in its heyday, notable for excellent acoustics, and there are seven smaller meeting rooms as well.[4] New owners in the 1980s renovated the structure as a commercial hotel, with the support of the Community Redevelopment Agency (CRA). This venture was not a financial success. By the 1990s, the University of Southern California (USC) operated the Embassy as a residential college in downtown, apart from its more heavily landscaped campus further south.

Stodgy as the Embassy seems on the facade, social action animated its spaces. The owners' liberal rental policies were particularly important from the 1930s through the 1950s, when severe racial discrimination, increasingly strong anti-union sentiment, and McCarthyism limited the availability of meeting places for minority and progressive organizations. In those decades, nearly every major union in Los Angeles met at the Embassy—and union members often marched in rallies outside on the sidewalk.[5]

What distinguished the three organizers chosen as the subject of this project was the national importance of their careers. All three reached Los Angeles after epic journeys of the same proportions as Biddy Mason's—Pesotta came from Russia, Moreno from Guatemala, and Fierro de Bright from Mexico. And all three moved into controversial public roles that women had rarely occupied. Pesotta became the first female vice-president of the ILGWU. Moreno became a national vice-president of UCAPAWA. She was also the founder, and Fierro de Bright the executive secretary, of El Congreso, a national organization. All three experienced the peak of their careers in Los Angeles, recruiting thousands of Mexican American women and men into their organizations.[6] It must be added, however, that their work was so controversial and disturbing in its mobilization across lines of gender, race, and class that they faced intense opposition. Pesotta resigned as ILGWU vice-president in the early 1940s, and Moreno and Fierro, alleged to be communist sympathizers, left for Mexico during the red-baiting years at the end of the decade.

### The Gentle General, Rose Pesotta

Born in 1896, Rose Pesotta came from Russia to New York in 1913. She was drawn into labor organizing as a seamstress, and her interest in social justice and anarchist ideas was supplemented by training as an organizer in a summer school at Bryn Mawr. As an experienced organizer, she was sent to Los Angeles by the ILGWU in 1933 to organize dressmakers in Local 96. She formed the local with Mexican American,

Italian American, and Russian Jewish immigrants who earned an average of $10 per week.[7] In contrast to the previous male leadership, Pesotta succeeded in enrolling hundreds of new female members by making announcements on KELW, a Spanish-language radio station, and by organizing with women's issues in mind, visiting prospective members in their homes and setting up get-togethers where women could bring their children. "We got them," she wrote, "because we are the only AMERICANOS who take them into our organization as equals. They might become the backbone of the union on the West Coast."[8] (She was sensitive to ethnic issues, and spent some of her time off in San Francisco, trying to organize Chinese American seamstresses working in even more difficult conditions.)

In the year of her arrival in LA, Pesotta led a dressmakers' strike at the head of about 1,600 female garment workers in Local 96. On October 13, 1933, just one day after the strike had been declared, the Embassy Auditorium was the scene of a mass meeting between female dressmakers and male cloakmakers. The cloakmakers (coat and suit makers, mainly Anglo and Russian Jewish men in Local 65) undercut the women's efforts by announcing that they were reaching an agreement with owners that included union recognition and a closed shop. They signed on October 17. The dressmakers were disappointed in the lack of male support, but continued to strike for their own demands until November 6.

The 1933 strike refuted national skepticism about Latinas' ability to organize (figures 8.4, 8.5). Pesotta won a thirty-five-hour week with higher wages, but contract gains were difficult to enforce.[9] In May 1934, partly because of her work in LA, Pesotta became a vice-president of the ILGWU. Nicknamed the "gentle general," she went on to Puerto Rico in 1934, to Seattle, Milwaukee, and Buffalo in 1935, to the Goodyear Rubber strike in Akron, Ohio, in 1936, and to the General Motors Women's Emergency Brigade in Flint, Michigan, in 1937.[10] In 1940, Pesotta returned to Los Angeles to work with predominantly Latina dressmakers again. During the next two years she conducted some successful campaigns, although

**8.4 ILGWU picket line. (Labor Management Documentation Center, Cornell University, 5780P-N1831.)**

**8.5 Rose Pesotta, ILGWU organizer. (University of Southern California Special Collections.)**

she was increasingly at odds with the male ILGWU leadership. In 1942 she returned to New York and a job at a sewing machine. In June 1944 she resigned from her post as vice-president of the ILGWU.

## The California Whirlwind, Luisa Moreno

**8.6 Luisa Moreno, UCAPAWA organizer. (The Power of Place.)**

Luisa Moreno (figure 8.6), born in Guatemala, was a poet and journalist who came to New York with an artist husband in 1928. Poverty led her to a job at a sewing machine in Depression-era Spanish Harlem. She soon became a labor leader of exceptional effectiveness.[11] She organized cigar workers in Florida and pecan shellers in San Antonio before coming to Los Angeles to work with cannery women under the guidance of Dorothy Ray Healy. Moreno eventually became a national vice-president of UCAPAWA as well as vice-president of the Los Angeles Industrial Council (later the Los Angeles CIO Council) and vice-president of the California CIO Executive Board. With a fluent speaking style and a strong grasp of tactics, she earned the nickname the "California whirlwind." Like Pesotta's, her organizing was geared to women in effective ways, with an understanding of the importance of child care and freedom from sexual harassment as well as better hours and wages.

Long experience in union work, during the years when Mexican Americans in Los Angeles were coming to see that their identity was as much tied to the United States as it was to Mexico, turned Moreno's interests to civil rights. Taking a leave from union responsibilities in 1938, she spent $500 of her own savings traveling across the country to recruit members for what became the first national Latino civil rights organization, El Congreso Nacional del Pueblo de Habla Española, or the Spanish Speaking People's Congress.[12] Establishing chapters in many cities across the country, she was active in its first national convention in Los Angeles in 1939. This event drew members of diverse Puerto Rican, Cuban, Mexican, and other Latin American backgrounds into the first national organization to discuss common community and labor issues for Spanish-speaking people.

### Josefina Fierro de Bright

Working with Moreno on El Congreso was Josefina Fierro de Bright, born in Mexico in 1920. She grew up in farm labor camps as the daughter of a *bordera* who served meals to migrant workers in Madera, California (figure 8.7). Fierro de Bright gave up her studies at UCLA to become an organizer, and her style was described by veteran longshoremen's leader Bert Corona as gutsy, flamboyant, and tough.[13] As executive secretary of El Congreso, Josefina Fierro de Bright's activities brought her time and again to the Embassy Auditorium from 1939 to the mid-1940s. She organized protests against racism in the LA schools, against the exclusion of Mexican American youths from public swimming pools, and against police brutality. In 1942 Fierro de Bright was a key figure in organizing the Sleepy Lagoon Defense Committee, to support the seventeen Mexican American youths held without bail on little

**8.7 Josefina Fierro de Bright, community organizer. (The Power of Place.)**

evidence for the alleged killing of one youth. With Moreno, she helped to coordinate El Congreso's support for Spanish-speaking workers in the furniture, shoe manufacturing, electrical, garment, and longshoremen's unions.

In the late 1940s, as red baiting stirred up many investigations of labor and community leaders associated with militant unions and with Popular Front organizations, both Moreno and Fierro were targeted. As Latinas, they found that few resources were allocated to their defense by their male, American-born labor allies. Fierro de Bright left for Mexico in the late 1940s; Moreno fought deportation but eventually left as well.[14]

In February 1991, The Power of Place hosted "La Fuerza de Unión," a public workshop at the Embassy Auditorium, to explore the published and unpublished history behind Pesotta's, Moreno's, and Fierro de Bright's campaigns and careers. About two hundred people attended, including residents of the building, members of various labor unions, members of union retirees' groups, students from USC and UCLA, and members of Latino community organizations. Interns at The Power of Place had done extensive public outreach work and visited with many small retirees' groups in advance. They also arranged for discussions on Spanish-language radio before the event. For publicity, the project's first work of public art was created, a four-color poster by Rupert Garcia including portraits of Josefina Fierro de Bright, Luisa Moreno, and Rose Pesotta (figure 8.8).

The workshop began with a welcome by historian Kevin Starr, head of the residential college and professor at USC, who noted that "we who live in the Embassy day by day feel this power of place . . . the echoes, the ghosts, the moral presence." He added, "The best way to preserve a building is to keep it in proper use." Bill Robertson of the Los Angeles AFL-CIO, a cosponsor of the event, noted, "this project . . . educates people with a realism you don't find elsewhere. . . . I went through the school system and I didn't learn these lessons." Maria Cuevas of the UCLA Chicano Studies Research Center, also a cosponsor, introduced Kathleen Ochoa, who said, "The history of Latina women in Los Angeles is largely unwritten. I'm excited that today my daughters can come to know these histories when they are young, an opportunity that many Latinas of my generation did not have."[15]

Historian George Sánchez from UCLA, a specialist in Mexican American Los Angeles, followed with a vivid account of the dressmakers' meeting at the Embassy in October 1933, explaining Rose Pesotta's career and her success in organizing women workers said to be unorganizable by the men. He showed how the Depression hit the Mexican community of

**8.8 Detail of the poster designed by Rupert Garcia for The Power of Place history workshop "La Fuerza de Unión," November 4, 1991, showing Josefina de Bright, Luisa Moreno, and Rose Pesotta.**

Los Angeles particularly hard, and how the dressmakers were struggling to hold their jobs in an era when the Los Angeles County Welfare Bureau was campaigning to repatriate Mexicans to Mexico, offering one-way train tickets.

Nancy Stillger then provided a look at the history of the surrounding urban neighborhood. She evoked the 1930s garment factories, often located in ten-story buildings, and the weary seamstresses who would take the elevator to the top floor and then walk down the stairs, asking for work on every floor. She mentioned the daughters who first went into the paid labor force as seamstresses, and the mothers who often followed them into the shops when the men of the family were unemployed in the Depression. During the 1933 dressmakers' strike, at least one USC student played a supporting role: Stillger told of a fashionable young woman who visited local department stores, tried on various dresses, and then indignantly rejected them if they did not carry the union label.

Historian Albert Camarillo from Stanford, who was working on a biography of Moreno, focused on her and her protégé, Fierro de Bright. "When I realized I'd be standing on the very stage she spoke from, there was no question that I would come today." As a doctoral student at UCLA in 1976, Camarillo had learned that Luisa Moreno was still alive and living in Mexico under an assumed name. In an atmosphere of great secrecy, he arrived in Mexico with a letter of introduction from Bert Corona. He began the first of many conversations with her, coming to see her as "the most important Latina union organizer in the U.S. in the twentieth century," crucial to the "Mexican working-class movement in the Southwest in which she played a fundamental part."

Camarillo evoked the living and working conditions of the 1930s for Latinos in the Los Angeles area, women who did laundry, made tortillas, picked and shelled walnuts, men who laid streetcar tracks, dug irrigation ditches, worked in construction. "Talk to the old-timers, they'll tell you these stories." Following Camarillo's talk, members of the audience came forward to say how they remembered the struggles to get union recognition, and how they feared the "zoot suit riots," when military personnel beat up anyone they thought might be Mexican in downtown. Because this audience was a very large group, the feeling of the discussion was less intimate and focused than the workshop on Biddy Mason had been, but it had more citywide scope. One immediate result was to convey a heightened sense of the importance of women's work and women's issues to ongoing, unpublished research, as well as to current organizing.[16]

At the workshop, artist Celia Muñoz presented her proposal for *If Walls Could Speak/ Si Las Paredes Hablaran*, a 32-page artist's book in English and Spanish, interweaving the story of one garment worker with an account of the campaigns to unionize in the 1930s. As she completed it a year later, the text of her book begins: "If walls could speak, these walls would tell/ in sounds of human voices, music and machines/ of the early tremors of the City of Angels." And on the same three pages, the personal narrative starts, "As a young child, I learned my mother had two families./ One with my grandmother, my aunt and I./ The other at la fábrica, the factory." (The weaving together of public and private texts, begun on Sheila de Bretteville's wall and in Susan King's book, is also an explicit strategy here.)

The book's endpapers capture the union logos of the period, with the CIO sun rising on UCAPAWA's agricultural landscape, the heroic sewing machines of the ILGWU, the scissors of the cutters, the steering wheels of the trainmen, the tools of the boot and shoe workers. Photographs of the Embassy building and its main meeting space are interspersed with portraits. A typical spread includes a photograph of Rose Pesotta with her arm around a dressmaker, and a drawing of another worker stitching a banner with the slogan "Win the War." It concludes with an ILGWU poster, "Knowledge is Power" (figures 8.9, 8.10, 8.11). Oral histories provide an informal counterpart to the logos:

*I come in the morning, punch my card, work for an hour, punch the card again. I wait for two hours, get another bundle, punch card, finish bundle, punch card again. Then I wait some more—the whole day that way.*

*When I caught the foreman cheating me he said, "I love you like a daughter, Carmen, but who's the foreman, me or you?"*

Photographs of garment workers celebrating Labor Day and sitting in the auditorium organized by dress shops (Ideal, Clarabelle, Carol Modes) join photos of students supporting strikers, and portraits of Pesotta, Moreno, and Fierro de Bright

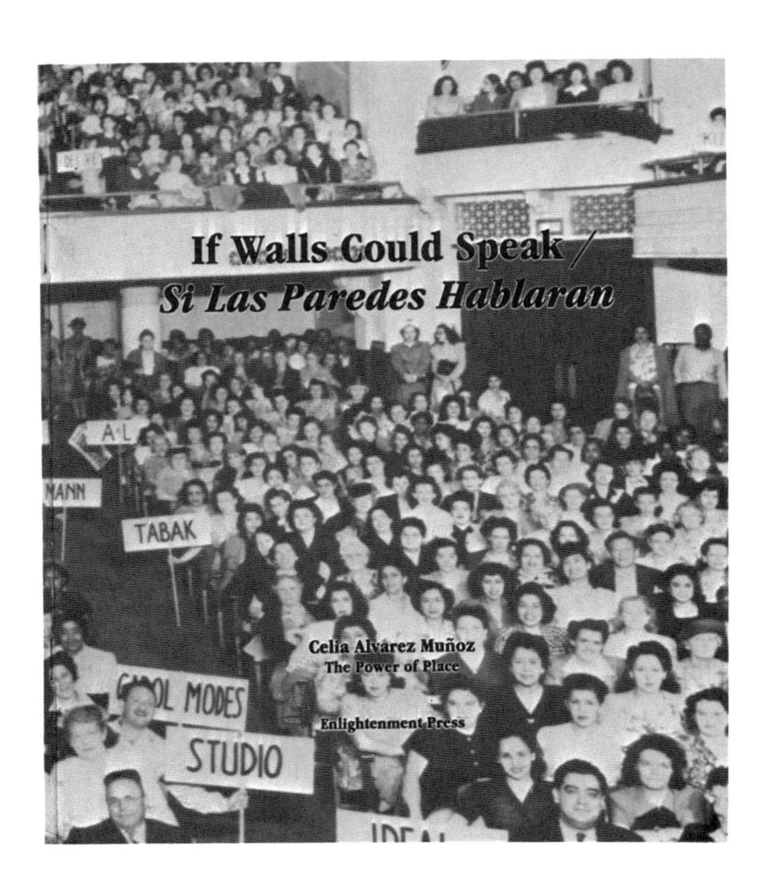


**8.9 Celia Alvarez Muñoz, *If Walls Could Speak/Si Las Paredes Hablaran*, artist's book with The Power of Place, 1991. (Arlington, Texas: Enlightenment Press.)**

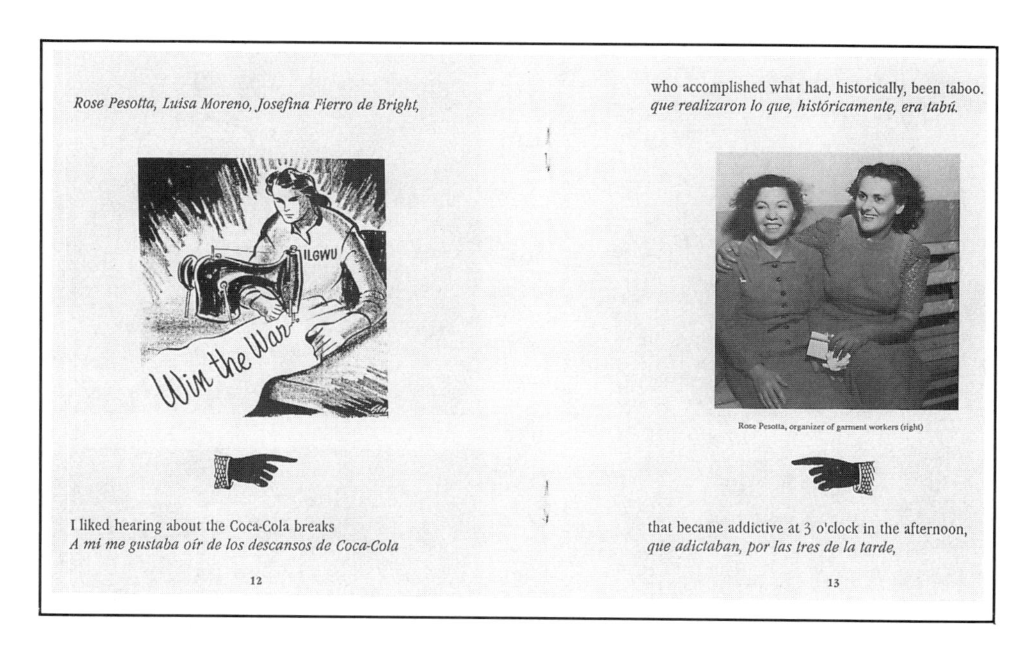

Rose Pesotta, Luisa Moreno, Josefina Fierro de Bright,

*Rose Pesotta, Luisa Moreno, Josefina Fierro de Bright,*



I liked hearing about the Coca-Cola breaks
*A mi me gustaba oír de los descansos de Coca-Cola*

12

who accomplished what had, historically, been taboo.
*que realizaron lo que, históricamente, era tabú.*

Rose Pesotta, organizer of garment workers (right)

that became addictive at 3 o'clock in the afternoon,
*que adictaban, por las tres de la tarde,*

13

**8.10 A two-page spread from Muñoz's book.**

**8.11 Endpapers of Muñoz's book with union and community logos. A similar pattern was proposed for the sidewalk in front of the auditorium.**

in action, to complement Garcia's poster. Several thousand copies of both Garcia's poster and Muñoz's book were distributed free to union groups and educational groups, and these two artists' works, along with the public workshop, became the most successful parts of the project that the team created (figure 8.12).

**8.12 Participants in the Embassy workshop, 1991.** ***Opposite page, clockwise from top left:*** **Rupert Garcia; George Sánchez; Albert Camarillo; Celia Alvarez Muñoz.** ***Above, top to bottom:*** **Garcia, Muñoz, Jennifer Lee (architect), Brenda Levin, Sánchez, Nancy Stillger, Dolores Hayden, Donna Graves; UCLA student interns Stacy Patterson, Sebastian Hardy, Scott Figenshow, Reginald Chapple, Nancy Stillger, Amalie Courvesior; discussion. (Photos by Garo Enjain for The Power of Place.)**

At the workshop, there was also enthusiasm for the proposal of architect Brenda Levin to recreate two metal showcases that had been used to publicize events in front of the theater in the 1920s and 1930s (figure 8.13). These showcases could carry text about the history of the building on the back and publicity for new events on the front. With molded terra-cotta bases including sewing machines and bobbins for the garment workers, hammers for the furniture workers, and canning tools for the cannery workers, they would have alerted pedestrians to the building's political past. Union logos stamped in the concrete of the sidewalk would mark the spot where many workers had marched, and would resonate with the endpapers of Muñoz's book.

The energy of the public history workshop also generated another physical proposal for the building. Abel Amaya of

**8.13 Showcase design for the Embassy Auditorium sidewalk by Brenda Levin, architect, with The Power of Place, 1991.**

USC offered to donate his personal collection of rare books, pamphlets, and other printed materials on the history of community and labor organizing in Los Angeles to USC, if the university would create a "Luisa Moreno Reading Room of Latino and Chicano Labor History," open to students and the public, in a storefront that was part of the building. His idea had immediate resonance. The Power of Place saw this as a way to create a new publicly accessible space within the historic building, to provide ongoing activities, and to support new showcases installed on the sidewalk (figure 8.14).

Although Donna Graves raised funding for the showcases and their installation appeared to be on track in the spring of 1991, there were several setbacks, all typical of the difficulties of negotiating the installation of public art in public space.[17] Brenda Levin began to have trouble getting a permit for the position of the showcases on the public sidewalk. Earlier the Public Works authorities had offered no opposition, but there had been a change of personnel. Then USC had some problems with new sidewalk locations for the showcases, closer to the building, because they had recently waterproofed their basement and did not want to interfere with the work that had been done (One reason Brenda Levin had chosen the showcases was to leave the facade of the historic building alone. As she pondered alternatives that did not disrupt the sidewalk, the architectural preservation officials of the city complained about anything that directly affected the rather mediocre facade.) After some months of haggling about the legal issues necessary for an agreement about where to put the showcases, a more serious problem emerged.

USC officials told The Power of Place in September 1991 that the university's real estate division had decided to put the building up for sale. Commercial real estate was in a slump in the city, and they may have thought a new work of public art might make the building harder, rather than easier, to sell. A permanent installation would also be vulnerable because there was no way of knowing if the showcases would be properly maintained. It was a great disappointment to us all when The Power of Place decided it was necessary to return

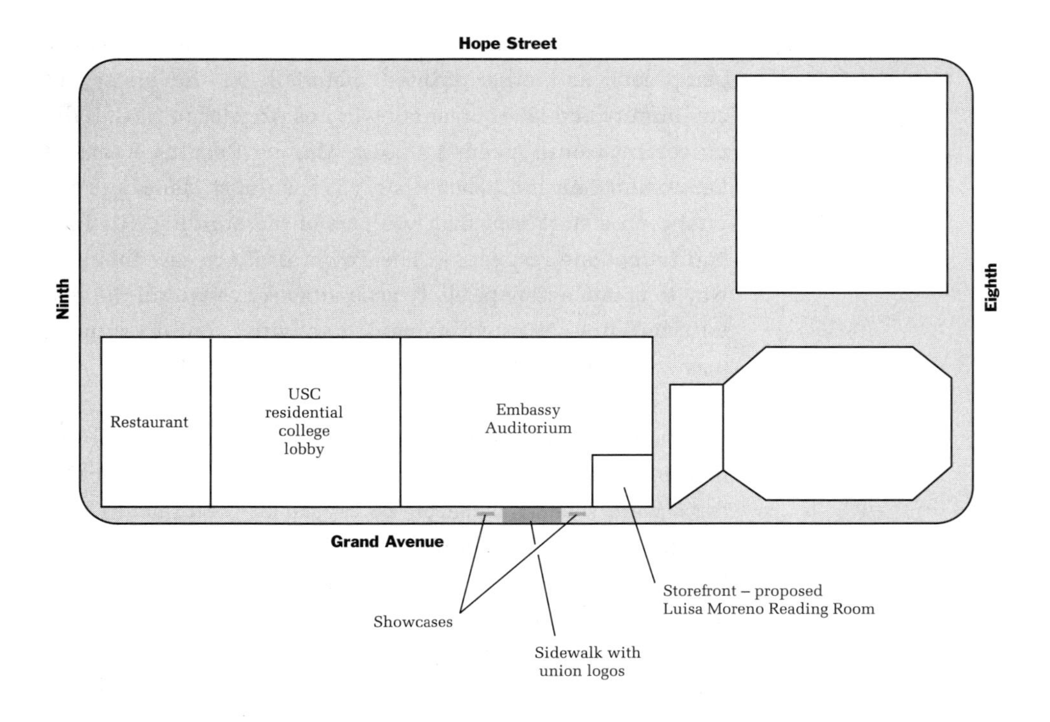


**8.14 Block plan showing Embassy Auditorium, showcases, sidewalk, and storefront to be used as reading room.**

the showcase grants to the funders. Even the internal proposal for the reading room in the storefront did not survive. Sadly, the University of Southern California seemed to be having the same problems as the creator of the structure, Trinity Methodist Church, had experienced in 1914. An organization with an idea about the city as a place filled with possibilities for education and social improvement, USC found the building was difficult to manage because of its diverse spaces. In 1993 USC still owned the property, not having found a buyer.

Further developments made the failure to install expensive public art on site less upsetting. The earthquake of January 1994 caused substantial damage and the building had to be evacuated. At the moment its future is uncertain, and its past as a center for labor and community organizing has not yet been marked in a physical way. Donna Graves and her team uncovered and represented three significant figures at the Embassy, making it very clear that a commemoration of their work, on that site or elsewhere in public space in Los Angeles, would have strong support.

# 9 Remembering Little Tokyo on First Street

**It's a small town set in the middle of a metropolis.**

**Katsumi Kunitsugu**

Close to City Hall, in the heart of downtown Los Angeles, stands Little Tokyo, a district that has been home to Japanese Americans since the late nineteenth century. By 1915 there were over seven thousand Japanese in Los Angeles, the largest Japanese settlement in the mainland United States, a distinction it retains today. By 1930, thirty-five thousand persons of Japanese descent lived in Los Angeles County, most of them close to Little Tokyo (figures 9.1–9.4).[1] They ran grocery and produce shops, sold bamboo, cultivated vineyards, citrus groves, and commercial flower fields, and owned labor contracting firms, clothing stores, boardinghouses, billiard parlors, cafes, nurseries, florists, and a local newspaper.

**9.1 Little Tokyo, First Street between San Pedro and Central. (Toyo Mitayake.)**

**9.2 Little Tokyo home of Sokichi Kataoka, posed with his family and employees of his watch store, 1919. (Visual communications.)**

**9.3 Japanese American family and their employees in a flower field. (Japanese-American Cultural and Community Center.)**

**9.4 Sun Nursery, 3425 South San Pedro Street, Japanese American proprietor K. Kamada and his employees, ca. 1910. (Visual Communications.)**

Smaller Japanese American communities developed in Boyle Heights, West Los Angeles (Sawtelle), Hollywood, and Gardena, but Little Tokyo was the center that pulled these residents together, a place for community and connection. Little Tokyo also drew Japanese Americans working in the fishing industry on Santa Monica Beach or Terminal Island near San Pedro, as well as families working in agriculture in the San Fernando Valley. "The San Fernando Valley farmer didn't relate to the San Pedro fisherman," noted one urban planner, "but they did both relate to Little Tokyo."[2] There Japanese Americans of all classes and occupations could attend religious services, learn traditional sports, or take classes in kimono etiquette and flower arranging (figure 9.5) There, too, Nisei week parades transformed the city streets with Japanese pattern and color, starting in 1934.

**9.5 Kimono class, Japanese Union Church, Los Angeles, 1934. (Tanaka Photo Studio, courtesy Visual Communications.)**

During World War II, Japanese Americans lost Little Tokyo completely. Forcibly relocated, most inhabitants were first transported to the Santa Anita Racetrack, where stables provided inadequate temporary quarters for as many as eighteen thousand people.[3] Then the detainees were moved to ten crudely built prison camps throughout the West, including Manzanar, California, where they were held between 1942 and 1945. Dorothea Lange's remarkable photographs convey the desolation of these internment camps (figure 9.6).[4] The empty buildings of Little Tokyo became "Bronzeville," home to African Americans from the South who had migrated to Los Angeles in search of wartime jobs in defense industries. The Japanese Union Church became a black community center. Jazz clubs thrived where small Japanese American businesses had once flourished.

**9.6 Dust storm at War Relocation Authority Center, Manzanar, California, July 3, 1942. (Photograph by Dorothea Lange, National Archives 210-G10-C839.)**

After the war, Japanese Americans returned to Little Tokyo, but the former businesses run by the first-generation immigrants had been devastated and many younger members of the community needed to obtain employment elsewhere. While younger Japanese Americans dispersed in the search for jobs, Little Tokyo remained the best location for the elderly, for cultural organizations, and for stores emphasizing traditional Japanese products. Public history was not a priority or even a possibility for many years. As one resident put it, "It wasn't to our advantage to be a visible minority in the past." Many Japanese Americans turned away from remembering the loss of Little Tokyo and the experience of the internment camps. Then in the 1980s, when the Presidential Commission on the Wartime Relocation and Internment of Civilians held hearings and authorized reparations to former internees, the entire community had to deal with the bitter past in a public way.[5]

As a result of public discussion of the internment among several generations of Japanese Americans, preserving the remaining historic buildings of Little Tokyo began to seem more important. Several younger authors concluded: "These hearings took place during a time when many of the Issei generation were passing away and many Nisei were nearing retirement age. Increased sentiment has grown to preserve their history and leave some monument which Sansei and later generations can retain as the legacy of their people. The physical structures of Little Tokyo were the place from which the reality of the experience sprang, a way for the 'stories' to be validated and grounded in reality."[6] But how much of thriving, prewar Little Tokyo remained to reflect their history?

The city demolished part of First Street for a new police station in 1950 and relocated a thousand people. Then the CRA began a redevelopment project in Little Tokyo in 1970 and introduced many high-rise projects that created dramatic conflicts of scale, as commercial investment from both Japan and the United States overlaid the traditional blocks of modest housing and small businesses. With the new buildings came higher rents that forced many small shops to close and poorer tenants to move. Redevelopment was the push of the

1970s and 1980s and made any type of preservation difficult to negotiate. The showdown between the community and the CRA finally occurred in the mid-1980s with the remaining buildings on the north side of First Street. The CRA proposed a major office development right behind them, and cosponsored an architectural competition with the Museum of Contemporary Art for the design, although many members of the Japanese American community felt cut off from this process.

Meanwhile, on February 23, 1985, The Power of Place ran a public history workshop, "Japanese Americans in the Flower Fields and the Flower Market." Held in Little Tokyo, at the Japanese American Cultural and Community Center, which cosponsored the event, it included myself and William Mason, curator of the Los Angeles Museum of Natural History, talking about the first commercial flower fields in Los Angeles, and Frank Kuwahara, former president of the Southern California Flower Market, recalling the early days of the market.[7] He had begun working there in 1925, when he was only twelve, driving in with his father from Montebello where the family flowers were grown.[8]

The special character the flower fields contributed to Los Angeles's urban landscape is equal to the vineyards and the citrus groves. Flower fields began to be an essential part of the city in the 1890s, when the spicy scent of carnations filled the first commercial field on the corner of Jefferson and Main. Today one has to cross the line to San Diego or Ventura counties to see the broad stripes of violet, pink, white, and dark red on the landscape, snapdragons grown for the market. Today no one seeks out the wild species in the woods or the marshes that Japanese American women once brought to the Flower Market. No one sees a flower grower with the traditional basket, the *kori* on his shoulders. And most of all, the language of flowers, the coded meanings of a bouquet of different species, scents, and hues that together might say "I miss you," or something much more complicated, has been forgotten, even by many florists.

Could public history reconnect the spicy scent of carnations and the landscapes of the flower industry with downtown? Everyone who had attended the workshop agreed that the *kori*, the traditional basket carried by the flower growers, would be a strong symbol of the industry's history. Early growers had carried the *kori*, full of flowers, on the streetcars to sell their wares in downtown. At one point this was declared illegal, and the growers retaliated by forming the cooperative Southern California Flower Market in 1913. Following the workshop, The Power of Place tried for several years to plan a public art installation focused on the families in the flower fields and the theme of the *kori* that could be sited in the busy market. The building is now much enlarged and still active in the same location on Wall Street. But in 1985 the status of the building was in doubt. Possibly the market would move to a more convenient location. No one there thought that the building was an appropriate place for a permanent installation.

Donna Graves then attempted to develop a plan for an Asian American project celebrating the City Market, a joint endeavor of Chinese American, Japanese American, Russian American, and Italian American entrepreneurs of the same era. The City Market was still an intact financial entity, and installed in an interesting building, but it too had outgrown its space and was considering a move further out of downtown. While the owners were delighted that their market was considered important to the city's economic and cultural history, the last thing they wanted was a designation of their structure as a Los Angeles Cultural Historic Landmark, since this might hinder their ability to sell the property.[9] (This designation would impose a 180-day stay of demolition for themselves or any possible buyer.)

The Power of Place had been wary of tackling a project directly in the Little Tokyo commercial area since many groups were contesting the CRA's plans for the area, and various developers were also involved.[10] However, in October 1986, through the combined efforts of the Little Tokyo Citizens Development Advisory Committee and the Los Angeles

Conservancy, the buildings on the north side of First Street, between San Pedro Street and Central Avenue, were nominated as a National Register Historic District (figure 9.7). The question of how to deal with the interpretation of an entire historic district was a fascinating one raised by the new district status.[11]

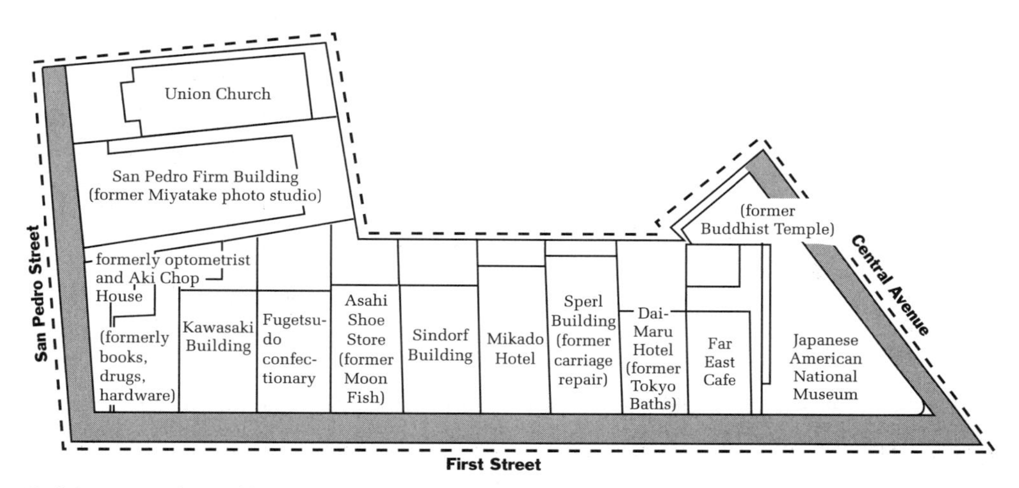


**9.7 Little Tokyo, plan of First Street National Register Historic District, 1986. (Based on research by Susan Sztaray and National Register of Historic Places Inventory.)**

Thirteen buildings (nine contributing) comprised the district, the last intact block in Little Tokyo, reflecting the scale of the neighborhood in the 1920s and 1930s, before redevelopment had generated the New Otani Hotel, Weller Court, or Japanese Village Plaza. At the San Pedro end stands the Union Church, a Japanese American Church built in a neoclassical style in 1923, resulting from the merger of three Japanese Christian congregations.[12] For many years it served as a social and community center. It was also used as an internment processing center during the war. At the opposite end, on Central Avenue, stands the former Nishi Hongwanji Buddhist Temple, a brick building from 1925 planned with some commercial space on First Street to generate revenue for the congregation.

Between the two was the San Pedro Firm Building, constructed in 1924 by shareholders from the Southern California Flower Market. Among its tenants was the courageous photographer Toyo Miyatake, who smuggled a camera lens into the Manzanar detention camp to document conditions. Also in the block was the Kawasaki Building, the only continuously Japanese American–owned building in the district, built on land purchased by Yajusiro Kawasaki in the name of his three American-born daughters in 1933. (The Alien Land Act of 1913 prohibited the ownership of land by anyone who was not a citizen.) In the same building was the Futaba Nisei Beauty Shop. Fugetsu-do, a Japanese confectionery store, sold traditional bean cake and rice paste candy next door. Then came the Asahi Shoe store, specializing in small sizes and Japanese footgear. In the same building was Moon Fish. The Dai Maru Hotel was once Tokyo Baths. A noodle shop, a Japanese restaurant, and a Japanese restaurant rented the commercial space attached to the temple. A German American blacksmith's building and a Chinese restaurant completed the block.

In 1988–1989, Susan Sztaray, a UCLA graduate student in urban planning, wrote both a historic walking tour and a public art proposal for Little Tokyo. She had lived in Japan and spoke Japanese, although she was not a Japanese American. Sztaray's "A Proposal for Public Art: Little Tokyo's Historic District," drew on the rich historical research provided for the National Register nomination as well as on the Biddy Mason project to suggest the possibilities of public art contributing to effective public history here.[13] Sztaray recognized that retaining the existing small-scale businesses in this historic block posed a difficult economic problem, since the scale of real estate development usually promoted by the CRA was not supportive of old-fashioned family businesses. Certainly it would be preferable to support the survival of these traditional shops, as a living dimension of the cultural landscape, rather than to rely on public art to recall recently lost businesses. However, effective public art might call attention to businesses that were surviving, despite the years of clearance and large-scale redevelopment in surrounding blocks.

Sztaray proposed that a new public art sidewalk be used to unify the block and represent the commercial and political history it embodied. Using Japanese publications similar to Chamber of Commerce directories, she traced the histories of the small businesses in the block and illustrated their specialized Japanese products such as sweets or kimonos. Upon her graduation from UCLA, Sztaray continued to work on the proposal with Gloria Uchida at the CRA. By 1990 the CRA had formed a Little Tokyo First Street public art initiative, based on Sztaray's detailed program. Working as an individual artist, Sheila de Bretteville, the designer of the Biddy Mason wall, submitted her qualifications in the CRA's competition. Her winning proposal was a design for a new terrazzo and concrete sidewalk wrapping the block, combining residents' personal statements about remembering Little Tokyo (in both Japanese and English) with the names of the small businesses that had flourished there, and the imagery of wrapped bundles such as a traditional Japanese trunk, a bamboo basket, and sushi.

Working in collaboration with some Japanese-speaking assistants and two Japanese American artists, Sonya Ishii and Nobuho Nagasawa, de Bretteville began a four-year process of meeting with many residents and creating a final design for the pavement, *Omoide no Shotokyo* (Memories of Little Tokyo), that would carry the history of the street into the twenty-first century (figures 9.8, 9.9). She was forced to revise some aspects of the project by the Public Works Department of the city which oversees sidewalks (they had a ban on terrazzo, and required that she substitute concrete), an experience similar to Brenda Levin's difficulties on the Embassy project. Nevertheless, de Bretteville's concept remains intact and construction is expected to begin in 1995, with her sidewalk carrying many quotations from residents, time lines for the historic buildings, drawings by Sonya Ishii, and an oversize replica of the camera Toyo Miyatake used at Manzanar, constructed by Nobuho Nagasawa.

In the meantime, on May 15, 1992, the Japanese American National Museum opened with a major exhibit on the Issei,

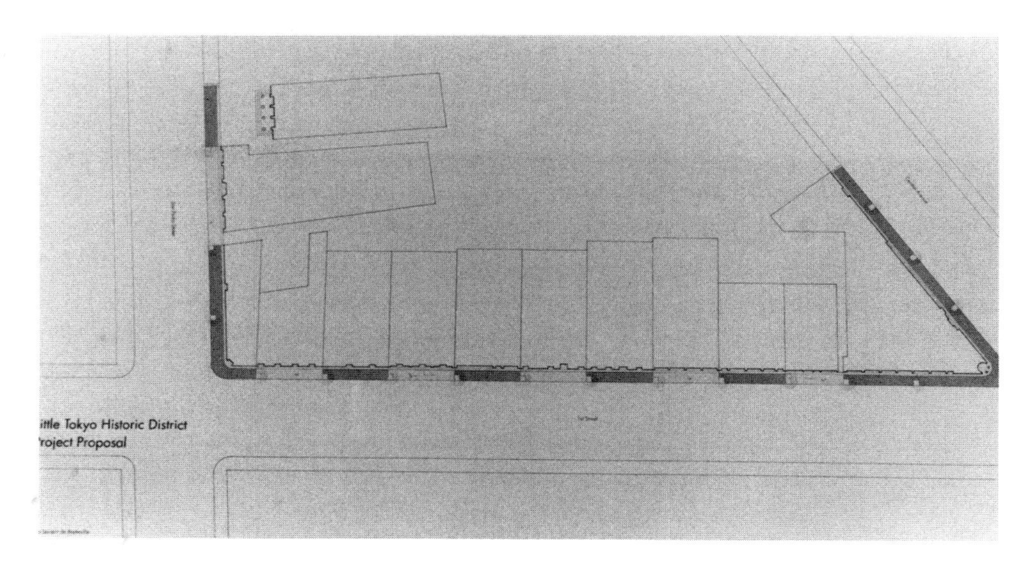

**9.8 Sheila de Bretteville, artist, *Omoide no Shotokyo*, proposal, 1991. This work, with contributions by Sonya Ishii and Nobuho Nagasawa, should be under construction in 1995. (Community Redevelopment Agency, Los Angeles.)**

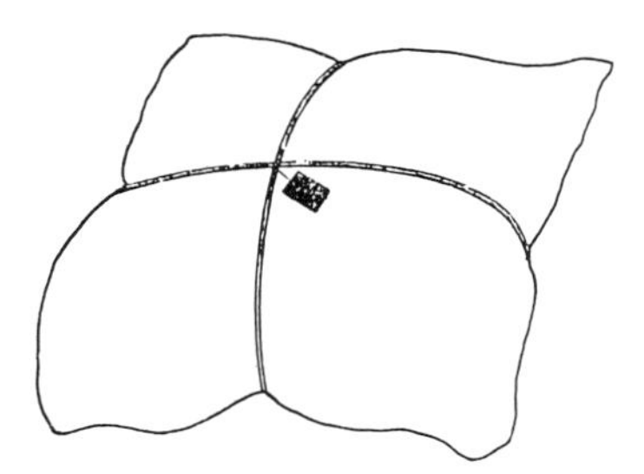
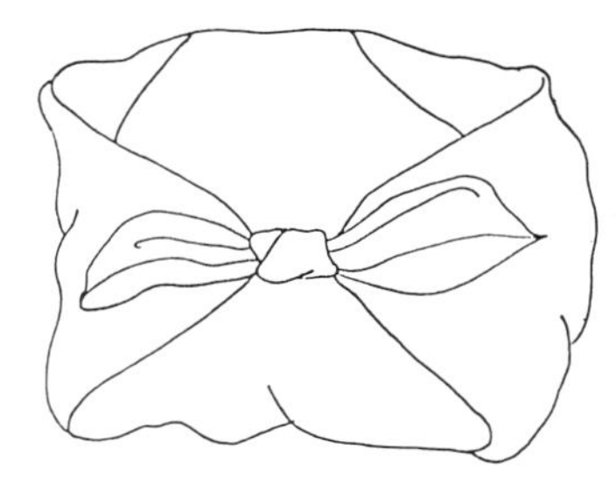

**9.9 Sonya Ishii, detail of detention bundle and wrapped bundle for sidewalk. These will be outlined in brass and filled with colored concrete. (Community Redevelopment Agency, Los Angeles.)**

and a Legacy Center where visitors can engage in interactive programs about ethnic history (figures 9.10, 9.11). The museum occupies the former Nishi Hongwangi Buddhist Temple and anchors one end of the historic district. The Union Church is on the other. De Bretteville's sidewalk is an encompassing work that will serve as a public path connecting the doorways of the row of modest preserved buildings, the church, and the museum. Her design will help to make the whole more than the sum of the parts.

Involving hundreds of residents, and dozens of organizations, including a group of Japanese American World War II veterans, the Little Tokyo Citizens Development Advisory Committee, the Japanese American Cultural and Community Center, the Los Angeles Conservancy, and the CRA, as well as three artists and a small role for The Power of Place, the Little Tokyo Historic District epitomizes an important urban place whose historic significance is finally recognized. In 1976 and 1977, a county survey had deemed the area ineligible for National Register status, and in 1986 the California state historic preservation officer deemed it of state rather than national importance. Times change: in 1993, the National Park Service nominated it for National Landmark status.[14]

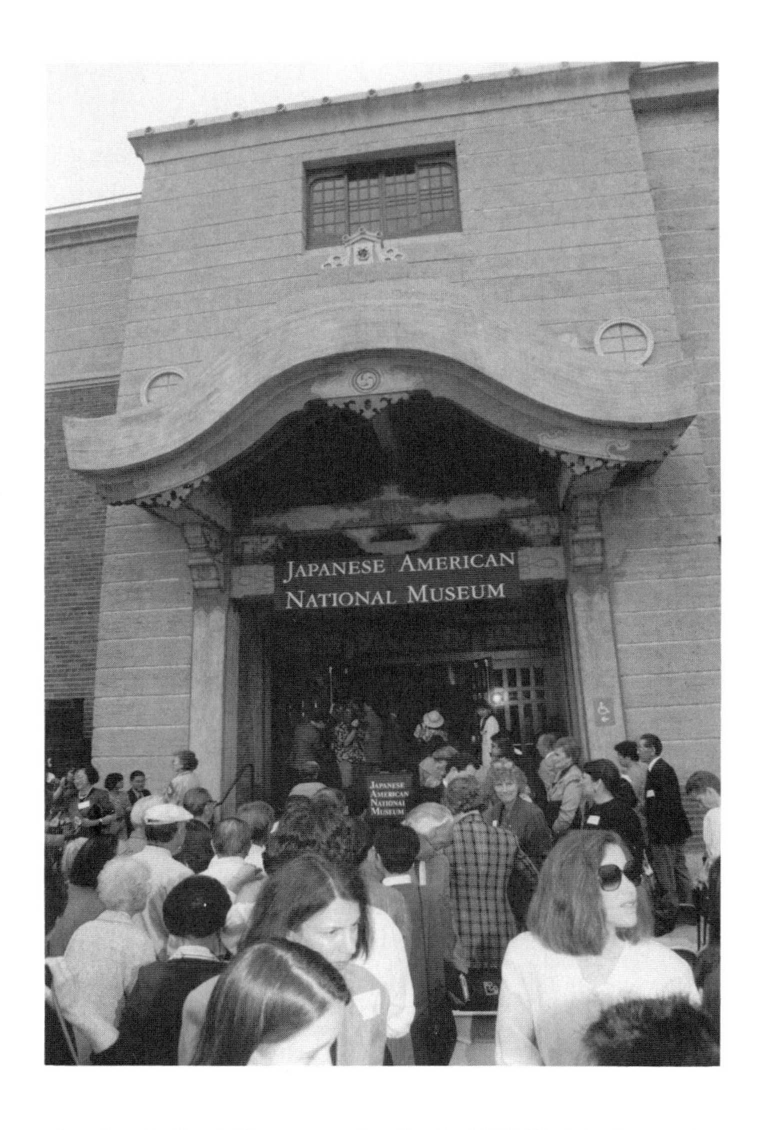


**9.10 Little Tokyo, Japanese American National Museum, restoration by KSNU Architects, opening May 15, 1992. (Community Redevelopment Agency, Los Angeles.)**

**9.11 Grant Murata Sunoo honoring Katsuma Mukaeda, 101-year-old Issei pioneer, at museum opening of exhibit on Issei, 1992. (Toyo.)**

Even in a difficult situation where much demolition has occurred and bitterness and denial about the past exists, preservation, public art, and ethnic history museums can complement each other in retrieving urban memories. As John J. Miyauchi wrote, the museum and the historic district provide a place where "old people can go to remember; where young people can go to learn, lest they grow up in ignorance of their own past; it will be a place to teach other people about the Japanese American people. . . ." Another resident put it even more simply, calling the place "the family album of the Japanese American community."[15]

# 10 Storytelling with the Shapes of Time

**We must reckon with the artifice no less than the truth in our heritage. Nothing ever made has been left untouched, nothing ever known remains immutable; yet these facts should not distress but emancipate us.**

**David Lowenthal, *The Past Is a Foreign Country***

**Choosing a past helps us to construct a future.**

**Kevin Lynch, *What Time Is This Place?***

Storytelling with the shapes of time uses the forms of the city, from the curve of an abandoned canal to the sweep of a field of carnations, to connect residents with urban landscape history and foster a stronger sense of belonging. The places of everyday urban life are, by their nature, mundane, ordinary, and constantly reused, and their social and political meanings are often not obvious. It takes a great deal of research, community involvement, and inventive signing and mapping to bring these meanings out, but this process can lead from urban landscape history into community-based urban preservation, as understanding the past encourages residents to frame their ideas about the present and future. Scale and cost are not the defining elements of a public, urban language. Rather it is shared process leading to shared public meanings that contributes most to an American sense of place.

Many types of organizations can work collaboratively with the shapes of time in the city, drawing together people with different specialties—historians, preservationists, environmentalists, community planners, and artists among others—around a common purpose and a shared project. Projects can be sponsored by small nonprofit corporations dedicated to planning for public history or public art. But there might be more logistical support available if a project team were located within an existing university or school system, a labor union, an environmental group, a nonprofit development corporation, a preservation organization, a municipal department of city planning or cultural affairs, an art museum, or an urban history museum. The process of reclaiming urban cultural landscapes as people's history touches all of these fields, and redefines parts of them.

Historians are just beginning to explore the intricate relationships among history, place-specific memory, and the preservation of the urban landscape. The power of place—the power of historic urban landscapes to help nurture ordinary citizens' collective memory—remains untapped until these relationships are better understood. The urban landscape is not a text to be read, but a repository of environmental memory far richer than any verbal codes. An evocative public program, using multiple sites in the urban landscape itself, can build upon place memory, in all of its complexity, to bring local history, buildings, and natural features to urban audiences with a new immediacy as part of daily life. Projects as diverse as those on Biddy Mason, Fire Station 30, the organizers at the Embassy Auditorium, the flower growers, or the residents of Little Tokyo suggest that working within an inclusive urban landscape history can connect diverse people, places, and communities, without losing a focus on the process of shaping the city. Within this framework, certain special opportunities may arise—to connect with a church congregation and with midwives across the city, or to work with both students and union retirees—that are unique to certain projects. Yet their common ground is the history of the city.

Beyond the experimental projects undertaken by The Power of Place, many organizations of different kinds are moving to similar goals. As the examples in chapter 3 suggest, a new kind of urban preservation is emerging in the 1990s in community-based public history, architectural preservation focusing on vernacular buildings, landscape preservation, and commemorative public art. These areas offer new models of collaborations between professionals and communities, as well as new alliances among practitioners concerned with urban landscape history. Artists and designers are also active in the public work of connecting memory into the built fabric of the city. Their interventions in the urban landscape (if handled with skill) can strengthen urban storytelling and enhance citizens' interest in history. But community process is crucial to the future of all these efforts.

## Creating Community Processes

Diverse urban audiences—such as the brass workers of Waterbury, the laundry workers of Chinatown in New York, or the people of Little Tokyo in Los Angeles—have accepted conflict and bitterness as part of the story necessary to understand their communities. Coming to this point through a community process requires the steady investment of time and energy by historians or artists involved in any project team. It is often a face-to-face process, although this should be supported by written communication. It is about giving respect to members of a community, listening to them and talking to them as equals, and earning their trust.[1] As in research, there are no shortcuts and no substitutes for quality. A good process builds the audience for the projects as well as gathering essential information. The team may be working with a sponsoring organization that has a built-in constituency—such as a neighborhood group—but it is always good to reach out to other organizations, such as women's groups, labor unions, or school systems, to increase the range of people who participate.

Through mapping as well as interviewing, it is possible to find out what residents of a city think about the meaning of urban history in their lives and in the places they go. People in a neighborhood have unique understanding of its landmarks, its sights, sounds, smells, its pedestrian patterns and social organization. As the Common Ground projects demonstrate, along with many others in the United States, community mapping projects can gather this material in abundance when citizens of all ages draw cognitive maps, exhibit them in public places, and discuss their multiple meanings.[2] Residents can also lead professionals on walking tours or bus tours to teach them how insiders perceive a place. Both residents and outsiders can take photographs of a place and then analyze them together, to share perceptions of places.

All kinds of public meetings offer opportunities for discussion of places (figure 10.1). Everyone on a project team—historians, artists, administrators—needs contact in open public meetings. It is also important to know how neighborhoods have reacted to history projects, landmark projects, or public art projects in the past: which ones succeeded, which ones failed, and why. And while any public history or public art project will sponsor its own public meetings, there are also opportunities for historians or artists working on a project, and their community collaborators, to carry the discussion of

*Japanese-Americans in a flower field*
*from* History & the Flower Industry
in Southern California, *JACCC Library*

Yes, I will come on February 23rd and my sense of place includes material I can bring with me:

____ memories of Los Angeles
____ memories of early Flower Fields
____ memories of City Market
____ old photographs
____ family history

Name Phone

Address

*Funding provided by the California Council for the Humanities,*
*a state-based affiliate of the National Endowment for the Humanities.*

HUMANITIES

*Fire Station No. 30, 1401 South Central Avenue,*
*Los Angeles, California, 1925. (Photograph from the collection of Miriam Matthews.)*

Yes, I will come on February 9th and my sense of place includes material I can bring with me:

____ memories of Los Angeles
____ memories of Central Avenue
____ memories of Fire Station No. 30
____ old photographs
____ fire fighters' lore
____ family history
____ ideas about how to enhance the sense of place in downtown Los Angeles

Name Phone

Address

*Funding provided by the California Council for the Humanities,*
*a state-based affiliate of the National Endowment for the Humanities.*

HUMANITIES

**10.1 Letterpress postcards enclosed with invitations to workshops, designed by Susan E. King, The Power of Place, 1985.**

history into public meetings reviewing environmental quality, zoning, or future development plans.

A specialist in urban landscape history can bring to a neighborhood an analysis of the city as a succession of historic cultural landscapes. This shared knowledge of the urban landscape may allow a neighborhood group to plan small projects that still contain broad urban themes. A historian can also bring to a neighborhood a good knowledge of the published work on its economic and physical history. But, "Never forget that *you* are an expert on your place," said Common Ground. Residents are often more expert than historians by virtue of daily life in the area. Learning about the lives of working people—women, men, and children of all ethnic groups within the city—is a slow process. A new oral history project can draw out fresh material, but for the purposes of engaging buildings and public art in the city, it is often easier to choose projects where a substantial amount of social history research is in hand at the start. (Some social history research or oral history will always be necessary on any new project, but ambitious documentary projects—*The Baltimore Book* and *Brass Valley* are excellent examples—take years in themselves.)[3]

Often, listening to residents will reveal intersecting themes of ethnic history, workers' history, and women's history. These intersectional stories may connect into local places in the most resonant way. Residents may feel that certain places whose significance is invisible to outsiders need to be marked. For African Americans in one midwestern city, a corner where blacks could secure a nonsegregated taxi was such a spot. Women may see spaces such as kitchens or nurseries needing interpretation. Sometimes, destroyed places are the most important to people. When the remains of the past are few in architectural terms, so that preservation is not possible, and when landscapes are battered in ecological terms, so that environmental protection is not possible, public art may hold the key to making new forms in the city that interpret the past in resonant ways. Artists can work with missing pieces, or erasures of important aspects of history, so as to reestablish

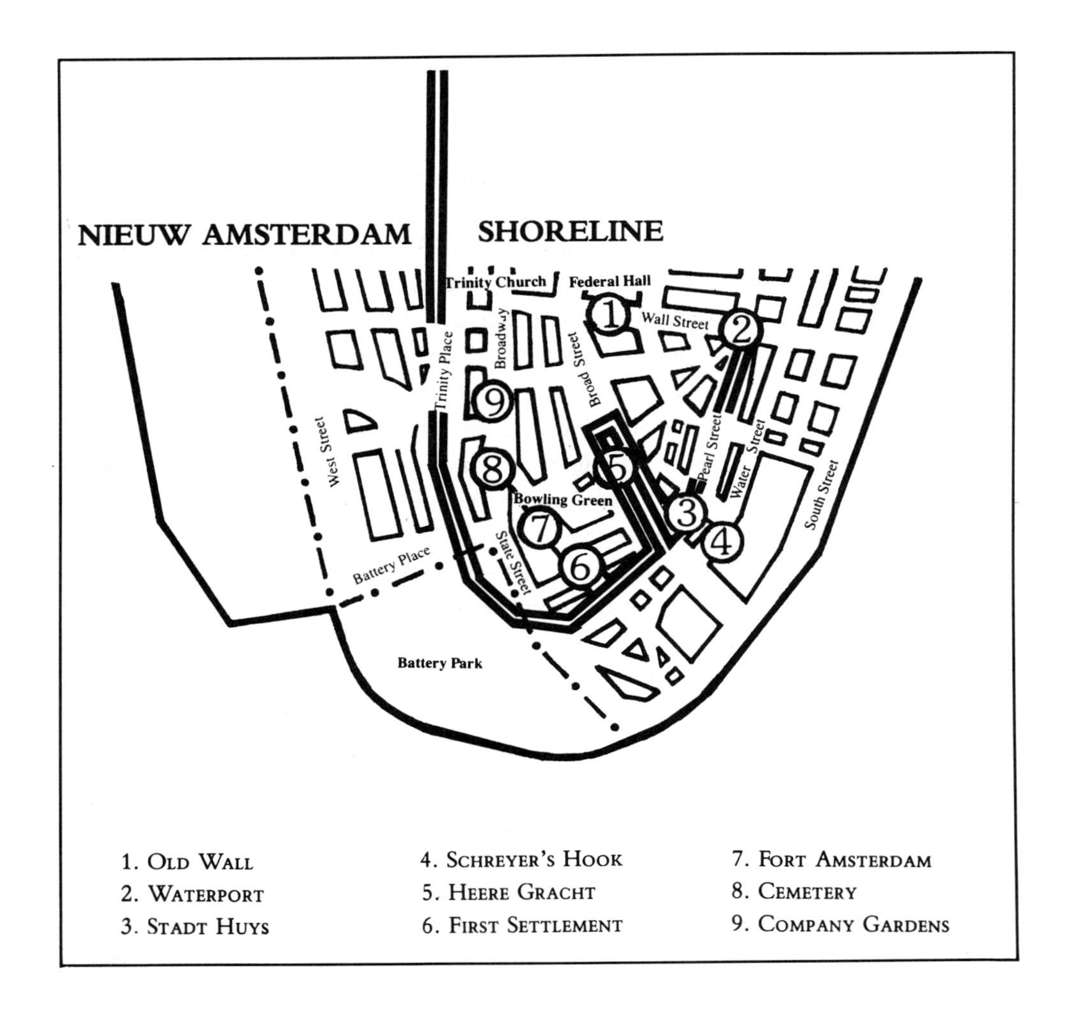


**10.2 Making the invisible visible: A. Eric Arctander, *Nieuw Amsterdam Shoreline*, 1980. In his celebration of Dutch heritage, line-striping machines followed the actual shoreline of lower Manhattan in 1627, blue for water, green for land. (A. Eric Arctander, sponsored by the Public Art Fund and Lower Manhattan Cultural Council.)**

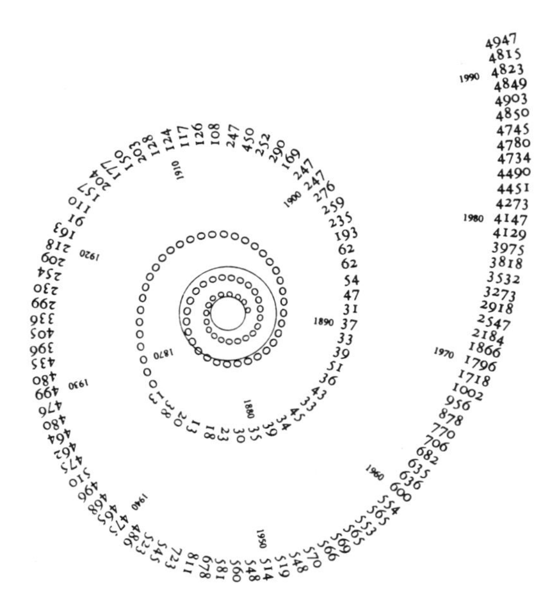


**10.3 Making visible: Maya Lin, *The Women's Table*, 1993 graphic for the top of a fountain, Yale University. The spiral shows the number of women in the university, by year, beginning with a series of zeroes. (Copyright Maya Lin.)**

**10.4 Making visible: Judy Baca, *Division of the Barrios*, section from the mural *The Great Wall of Los Angeles*, located in the Tujunga Wash, 1983. It shows the destruction of Chavez Ravine and the construction of freeways separating Latino neighborhoods in the 1950s. (Social and Public Art Resource Center.)**

missing parts in a story, from the scale of a coastline (figure 10.2), to the presence of women (figure 10.3), to the destruction of a barrio (figure 10.4). New works of public architecture and landscape architecture may also involve the reconstruction of public meanings in the urban landscape, and may transcend traditional disciplinary lines.

## Connecting Community Processes into Urban Planning

In addition to creating a good rapport with community members (who are potential collaborators on urban public history projects, as well as sources and audiences for these projects) a project team needs to establish working relationships with elected officials and urban planners. These relationships may range from collegial to adversarial, depending on the city and the agency involved. Team members need to know the scope of the city's future plans and the possibilities of their implementation, in order to think about where resonant parts of the past exist that should be protected, or where reminders of lost pasts may be reinserted into the changing urban landscape. If it is possible for a project team to convey its findings to a planning agency, and enter new research on historic resources into their central computer mapping system, this can be of benefit to both sides, as these resources will receive more official consideration in routine planning processes. At the same time the team may receive more detailed briefings about impending projects that could affect their own plans either positively or negatively.

Urban planning agencies, or redevelopment agencies, often serve as centers for the coordination of factual data (past and present) about every piece of land in the city. Computer systems that scan images and plot physical data and print new maps, such as Geographic Information Systems, are often housed there as an aid to the agencies' regulatory functions, such as zoning. City planning departments are also the centers for future plans that involve all aspects of the city's physical space and public infrastructure. Planners have often informed themselves about elected officials, private real estate developers, preservation groups, and community organizations, on their way to setting the city's timetable of future projects. They can be extremely helpful in pointing out spatial conflicts that might lie ahead for new history projects.

## Confronting Urban Design

Public interpretation of historic places requires a broad understanding of urban history, yet the practice is usually incremental and experimental. Its best measure is shared meanings, Native American, African American, Latino, Asian American, and Anglo American meanings, female as well as male values, children's experiences as well as grown-up patterns of life. It is city dwellers' shared lifetimes that create an American sense of place. In scale and approach, this is the opposite of the top-down thinking that underlies urban design as grand-scale redevelopment planning practiced by American cities. There the understanding of history is often minimal, the practice often involves vast areas of demolition and new construction, and the accepted measures of success are developer profits and increased tax base.

The Power of Place's approach to the public landscape has more in common with a formal approach to urban design that prizes context, the restoration of street grids, the preservation of buildings, and the respectful study of building types. Yet this second, more aesthetic approach to urban design often holds meaning only for limited cultural elites and affluent neighborhoods, and it is still a top-down process, though one with more highly skilled consultants, more rules, and less freedom for commercial builders. In contrast, we struggled to focus on social and political issues, rather than physical ones, as the center of urban landscape history. Our teams worked hard to develop what public historian Michael Frisch has called "a shared authority," a willingness to listen and learn from members of the public of all ages, ethnic backgrounds, and economic circumstances. This approach gives primary importance to the political and social narratives of the neighborhood, and to the everyday lives of working people. It assumes that every inhabitant is an active participant in the making of the city, not just one hero-designer. It is rooted in an aesthetic of nurturing and connection.

## New Roles, Relationships, Rewards

Historians, preservationists, environmental activists, artists, and citizens who undertake public urban projects will experience the transformation of roles and expectations discussed at length in chapter 3, as everyone searches for a satisfactory public process and a possible project. There are many ways to work together with citizens who will be living with the physical expression of people's history in public space, and a good process depends on recognizing the opportunities, as well as the limitations, in any given social and physical situation. Many of the projects discussed in this book were undertaken by teams from the humanities, arts, design, and planning professions. Teamwork is difficult, especially across disciplines. Differences of gender, class, race, and educational background affect perceptions of the urban landscape, as well as differences based on urban life experience, aesthetic preferences, and individual personalities. (The Power of Place teams were multiethnic as well as multidisciplinary, and we tried to balance insider-outsider views in this way.)

Happily, there are rewards for undertaking such complex collaborations and inventing new public processes. First, for scholars interested in history, public space has a resonance for urban, environmental history that no other medium can match. Second, locking history into the design of the city exploits a relatively inexpensive medium. Over time the exposure can be as great as a film or an exhibit. Third, when you have a significant urban public place, important to many constituencies, there is no need to divide history into academic categories like women, ethnic, or labor, categories that often trivialize and marginalize urban stories.

For the city itself there are also rewards. Putting working people's history into downtown expands the potential audience for all urban preservation and public art. The awareness that every citizen's history is important—firefighters', garment workers', streetcar drivers'—can renew family pride in connection to the larger urban community. The recognition of important cultural heritage in diverse working people's neighborhoods can also support other kinds of community organizing—including neighborhood economic development, environmental protection, and affordable housing. Seeing each and every urban neighborhood as part of the landscape of the city, past and present, widens support for public memory in the multicultural city. A city with a network of public places tied to resonant social history can start educational projects for children, from kindergarten on, that use the humanities and the arts to inform young citizens about urban life, its tough choices, its rewards.

Last, but not least, public space dedicated to women's history and to ethnic history, especially to projects focused on working women of color, claims political territory in tangible ways. Citizens can meet in these historic places and work together on new issues with the collective knowledge of earlier struggles. And this fosters a public realm where, at last, women are free to be ourselves and to see ourselves as strong and wise people, because we have represented ourselves this way.

Today, I and many of my colleagues work in other cities besides Los Angeles. Across the country, many Americans are starting to reevaluate collective life in inner cities' poorer neighborhoods. Ghettos, barrios, Chinatowns, Little Tokyos, Little Manilas, and Little Italys are places imbued with bitter memories, such as slavery, internment, deportation, and segregation, as well as more positive stories of hard work and community organizing. A new American sense of identity is emerging as we begin to recognize a diverse society where cultural differences are respected. With acceptance of diversity can come a new sense of place. Americans are just starting to realize the need for public places to celebrate the history of ordinary citizens and the collective significance of our working lives. When we know our own engaging and difficult history as a nation of women and men, drawn from many ethnic backgrounds, we can begin to create public places, in all parts of our cities, to mourn and to celebrate who we really are.

# Epilogue: Los Angeles after April 29, 1992

**The fact of the matter is,**

**whether we like it or not,**

**riot**

**is the voice of the unheard.**

**Maxine Waters, Congresswoman, in *Twilight: Los Angeles, 1992***

**Watts bleeds**

**as I bled**

**getting laid-off from work,**

**standing by my baby's crib,**

**touching his soft cheek**

**and fingering his small hand**

**as dreams shatter again,**

**dreams of fathers**

**for little men.**

**Luis J. Rodriguez, "Watts Bleeds,"**

***The Concrete River*, 1991**

Los Angeles burned on April 29, 1992. Following the "not guilty" verdict in the trial of several Anglo American policemen accused of brutality against African American Rodney King, fires were set in many different parts of the city. Especially devastated areas included South Central Los Angeles (the African American neighborhood torn by the Watts uprisings in 1965, which by 1992 was also home to many Latino families and small Korean American businesses); Koreatown, an area of mixed Korean and Latino residence; and Pico-Union, a Latino community.

As flames consumed grocery stores, liquor stores, bookstores, and homes, schools closed and roadblocks were erected to stop looters. Mayor Tom Bradley issued a dusk-to-dawn curfew. When the local police and the state government could not preserve order, President Bush sent in federal troops. After five days of civil unrest, calm was restored. Dozens were dead, hundreds wounded, acres in ashes (figure E.1).[1] Many commentators compared the events to the 1965 Watts uprising, saying nothing had changed. But for some, the frustration was not that nothing had changed but that conditions had worsened, and that decades of conservative policy making had weakened the job base in the inner city and pitted poor and unemployed against each other and against new immigrants.[2] The city had failed to redevelop and revitalize South Central LA after Watts, preferring to encourage international investment in downtown and the westside. The hopes of residents that Los Angeles could become the nation's most thriving, diverse city turned to fear of even more intense ethnic conflict.

What defined Los Angeles residents' responses during the civil unrest? It could be the team spirit at the emergency fire headquarters where African American, Anglo American, Latino, and Asian American men and women worked side by side to control the flames. But it might be better expressed by the bulletproof vests the firefighters had to wear to protect themselves against snipers of all ethnic backgrounds. It could be the determination of the Latino who spray-painted on the ruins of his office, "You burned my place, but not my spirit!!!/

**E.1 Burned-out block, Vermont and Manchester, after the civil unrest of 1992. (Jim Mendenhall, *Los Angeles Times* photo.)**

Han quemado mi negocio pero no mi espiritu!!!" But it might also be the anxiety of Korean American businessmen who stood on the roofs of their small stores armed with AK47 assault rifles to stop looters. Or the desperation of mothers who stole shoes for their children.

Throughout the events of April and May 1992, commentators repeated phrases like "devastated urban landscapes," or "vast landscapes of human despair," as if somehow the terrain of South Central Los Angeles could, in itself, explain just why angry mobs gathered there. The area was lacking in jobs and amenities, but not in history. It was a dangerous place to live, yet the poverty and the drug dealing and the gangs were familiar newspaper fare. What shocked Americans, and the rest of the world, was the spectacle of urban people setting fire to their own landscape, destroying the only neighborhood they had.

In the aftermath of the events, committees were appointed and commissions convened. As if he could recapture the buoyant spirit of the 1984 Olympic Games, hosted by Los Angeles, Mayor Bradley asked Peter V. Ueberroth, businessman and former Olympics head, to chair an "extra-governmental task force" on rebuilding the city, Rebuild L.A. (RLA). Many activist groups called this "business as usual." Other groups, like the editors of *L.A. Architect,* asked for fifty-word nuggets of advice for Ueberroth. The architects and planners consulted were surprisingly frank: "We need to reinvent L.A., not rebuild it. We don't need another wake up call," said Julia Thomas. "The devastated Hispanic neighborhood of Pico-Union has been largely ignored. The civic leadership must be accountable for the entire community regardless of ethnicity," argued Carlos Araujo Garcia de Paredes.[3]

A year later, very little economic reconstruction had been done. In April 1993, tension continued during the second trial of the police officers who had beaten Rodney King, but this time the jury delivered some convictions and calm prevailed. In October 1993, the process wound down with the trial of two African American youths accused of beating a white truck driver, Reginald Denny. By March 1994, disillusion with RLA filled reports and the local papers. "A consultant hired by RLA reported that 75,000 to 90,000 jobs are needed in South L.A. alone. Yet today . . . the growing perception is that the best jobs RLA has created are in its own P.R. department."[4] Even by its own estimates, RLA seemed better at getting buildings cleaned up and training programs and volunteers in place than at creating new jobs with decent wages.[5]

The larger urban questions remain unanswered. Is it inevitable for Los Angeles to be torn by conflicts of race, ethnicity, gender, and class? Or is it still possible to argue that the citizens of Los Angeles are learning to develop an American city based on diversity? These are issues of more than local importance. The largest cities of the United States are all changing demographically. In the past twenty-five years the proportion of white citizens has declined from about three-quarters to about two-fifths.[6] Groups previously called "minorities"—African American, Latino, or Asian American—together outnumber the former majority in some cities; and in some, like Los Angeles, Latinos, a former minority, are becoming the largest group in a diverse population.[7] If the American city is going to survive, let alone thrive, it is critical to absorb the lessons of Los Angeles, and the economic, spatial, and cultural conflicts scrawled across its urban landscape.

Any American city split between affluent suburbs, a glossy downtown business area, and a maze of ghettos and barrios is not going to work. This book has addressed just one aspect of that problem, how to understand diverse social history as part of the public landscape of the American city. To look at ethnic and women's history as the missing mainstream experience means respecting the urban places that house ordinary working people. It means caring for the urban landscapes of South Central and East Los Angeles, Chinatown, or Little Tokyo as part of understanding of what it means to live in a city.

Most of the authors of the outdated "melting pot" literature on American ethnicity presented collective life in the inner city's poorer neighborhoods (ghetto, barrio, Chinatown, Little Tokyo, Little Manila, Little Italy) as a prelude to the individual acquisition of an American dream house, an experience most nonwhite families have never achieved. By stressing assimilation, these authors implied that Americans did not need to care much about the condition of the urban landscape as the working poor experienced it. Today, inner-city neighborhoods are places that still house large groups of urban Americans. They are places with complex and often bitter political histories, places that could foster important public memories.

Listening to the resonant stories of working people in inner-city neighborhoods is the first step. Connecting the stories to reclaim the landscape as people's history is the next. "Stalking with stories," a practice of the Western Apache, has been recounted by anthropologist Keith Basso. "Learn the names. Learn the names of all these places," insists his Apache guide. "All these places have stories. We shoot each other with them, like arrows." In historical tales, "mountains and arroyos step in symbolically for grandmothers and uncles ... even if we go far away from here to some big city, places around here keep stalking us." N. Scott Momaday, Kiowa poet and novelist, stresses the importance of this kind of memory, rooted in landscape, to the Native American who "invests himself [or herself] in the landscape, and at the same time incorporates the landscape into his [or her] own most fundamental experience.... This appropriation is primarily a matter of imagination which is moral in kind."[8]

In the United States, some historians may have expected "moral imagination" to happen at a historic military landscape like Gettysburg, or a historic urban political site like Independence Hall. What would be new is making moral imagination work in ordinary urban landscapes like those of the South Bronx or South Central Los Angeles. In places like these, especially for women and members of diverse ethnic groups, memory is inevitably going to involve issues of isolation and exploitation, as well as connectedness. But these difficulties can remind citizens that, as historian T. H. Breen suggests, "We are what we were even when we most passionately reject our own history."[9] Choosing to engage the difficult memories, and the anger they generate, we can use the past to connect to a more livable urban future.

Creating public history within the urban landscape can use the forms of the cultural landscape itself, as well as words and images, to harness the power of places to connect the present and the past. The work is time-consuming, interdisciplinary, and politically controversial, but it is not particularly expensive. Historians Susan Porter Benson, Stephen Brier, and Roy Rosenzweig suggest that "people's history projects can be a potent force for sustaining a vision of social change ... [and] can be used to teach people that the social, political, economic, and cultural institutions that delimit contemporary life are not timeless but rather the products of human agency and historical choices. Grasping the contingent nature of the past can break the tyranny of the present; seeing how historical actors made and remade social life, we can gain a new vision of our own present and future." Public historian Michael Frisch puts it even more directly: "Whether one is talking about the history of a war or the memories of old residents in a crumbling ethnic neighborhood, what we need are works that will search out the sources and consequences of our own active ignore-ance. We need projects that will involve people in exploring what it means to remember, and what to do with memories to make them alive and active, as opposed to mere objects of collection."[10]

While this is a book about cultural possibilities, urban Americans need to find a new kind of political will to pursue them. Can Americans learn how to respect and nurture a diverse urban public? In every city and town across the United States, there are resources waiting to be tapped. Based on the available resources, Americans can have urban historic public places with personal resonance for large numbers of people who are not now represented—ordinary workers, women, men, and children of every ethnic group. Or we can shrug and buy the twenty-dollar ticket to "heritage" in Disneyland, agreeing with Charles Moore that "you have to pay for the public life." But public space should not be a luxury that American cities fail to provide their residents. Whether public space is created as part of community-based social history, architectural preservation, environmental protection, or public art, diverse citizens need places to spend time that connect them to the possible meanings of city life as a social bond.

Beyond ethnicity, race, gender, and class lies a new kind of urban landscape. If it is designed to contain conscious historical mapping of the commonalities and differences in American urban experience, it might be able to convey the Los Angeles firefighters' team spirit—and the difficult history that went into forging that team spirit—as well as their need for bulletproof vests. If, back in 1985, The Power of Place had been able to save Fire Station 30, in what is now a difficult neighborhood halfway between downtown and South LA, it might have been a place where Angelenos could remember the vibrant, commercially successful African American neighborhood that had flourished at 12th and Central in the 1920s. It might have been a place to remember the African American firefighters who struggled for change in the city's employment practices, and won, in the 1950s. It could also have become a place where the struggle of 1992, between the citizenry and the angry mobs, between the firefighters and their attackers from every ethnic group, could be recorded, pondered, and perhaps debated. Any historic place, once protected and interpreted, potentially has the power to serve as a lookout for future generations who are trying to plan the future, having come to terms with the past.

Angelenos didn't get to occupy this particular lookout. But other projects were possible, and they suggest varied models for public projects that connect to Native American, African American, Latina, and Asian American history. There are a hundred other possibilities. The city is constantly changing, and yet it retains potent memories in its streets and sidewalks, fences and alleys, buildings and vacant lots. Some of those memories—painful ones—are now located on the corner of Florence and Normandie, April 29, 1992.

# Notes

## Preface

1. Hazel V. Carby, "The Multicultural Wars," *Radical History Review* 54 (Fall 1992), 16–17.

2. Patricia Nelson Limerick, "Disorientation and Reorientation: The American Landscape Discovered from the West," *Journal of American History* 79 (December 1992), 1049.

3. Previous articles by the author about the projects and the ideas behind them include: "The Power of Place," *Journal of Urban History* 20 (August 1994), 466–485; "Using Ethnic History to Understand Urban Landscapes," *Places* 7 (Fall 1990), 11–17 (reprinted in Paul Groth, ed., *Vision, Culture, Landscape* [Berkeley: University of California, Berkeley, 1990], 69–76); "Biddy Mason's Los Angeles, 1856–1891," *California History* 68 (Fall 1989), 86–99; "The Power of Place: A Proposal for Los Angeles," *Public Historian*, 10 (Summer 1988), 5–18 (reprinted in *Journal of Architectural Education*, 41 [Spring 1988], 45–51); "The Power of Place: The Impact of Los Angeles' Multi-Ethnic History on Public Art," *Passage* (Spring/Summer 1987), 1–3; "The American Sense of Place and the Politics of Space," in Robert A. M. Stern, David de Long, and Helen Searing, eds., *American Architecture: Innovation and Tradition* (New York: Rizzoli, 1986), 184–197; "The Meaning of Place in Art and Architecture," SITE II, *Design Quarterly* 122 (Summer 1983), 18–20 (reprinted as "An American Sense of Place," in Sally Webster and Harriet Senie, eds., *Critical Issues in Public Art* [New York: HarperCollins, 1992], 261–269).

## 1 Contested Terrain

1. Herbert J. Gans, "Preserving Everyone's Noo Yawk," *New York Times*, January 28, 1975, op-ed page.

2. Ada Louise Huxtable, "Preserving Noo Yawk Landmarks," *New York Times*, February 4, 1975, op-ed page.

3. Herbert J. Gans, "Elite Architecture and the Landmarks Preservation Commission: A Response to Ada Louise Huxtable" *New York Times*, February 25, 1975, editorial page, letters column. Gans supplied me with the complete text of his article, which appeared in very abbreviated form.

4. Huxtable, *New York Times*, February 4, 1975.

5. Gans wrote *Popular Culture and High Culture* (New York: Basic Books, 1975) but didn't anticipate ethnic diversity as a focus. The Organization of American Historians is holding its 1995 meeting on "Public Pasts and Public Processes." An overview of some current museum efforts is Ivan Karp, Christine Mullen Kreamer, and Steven D. Lavine, eds., *Museums and Communities: The Politics*

*of Public Culture* (Washington, D.C.: Smithsonian Institution Press, 1992). Also see Karp and Lavine's *Exhibiting Cultures: The Poetics and Politics of Museum Display* (Washington, D.C.: Smithsonian Institution Press, 1991); Warren Leon and Roy Rosenzweig, eds., *History Museums in the United States* (Urbana: University of Illinois Press, 1989).

6. Henry G. Cisneros ed., *Interwoven Destinies: Cities and the Nation* (New York: W. W. Norton, 1993) provides a good summary of changing demographics. Also see Mike Davis, "Who Killed L.A.? The War Against the Cities," *Crossroads* 32 (June 1993), 9–10.

7. Davis, "Who Killed L.A.?," 9.

8. Steven Lee Myers, "Politics of Present Snags Remembrance of Past," *New York Times*, July 20, 1993, B1, 2. Geneviève Fabre and Robert O'Meally, eds., *History and Memory in African-American Culture* (New York: Oxford University Press, 1994).

9. See Karp, Kreamer, and Lavine, *Museums and Communities*, for examples.

10. "Focus-on Cultural Diversity II," *Historic Preservation Forum* 7 (January/February 1993), 4–5; also see *Cultural and Ethnic Diversity in Historic Preservation*, Information Series Number 65 (Washington, D.C.: National Trust for Historic Preservation, 1992), for an extensive list of ongoing projects.

11. "Historic Store Slated to Become Civil-Rights Museum," *Historic Preservation News* 34 (February/March 1994), 2–3.

12. Jurate Kazickas and Lynn Scherr, *Susan B. Anthony Slept Here* (New York: Times Books, 1994).

13. Betsy Wade, "New Guides to Landmarks of Black History," *The New York Times*, February 13, 1994, section 5, 4.

14. Inter-University Project for Latino Research, Hunter College, Working Group, Concept Paper, 1988, quoted in John Kuo Wei Tchen, "The Chinatown-Harlem Initiative: Building a Multicultural Understanding in New York City," in Jeremy Brecher and Tim Costello, eds., *Building Bridges: The Emerging Grassroots Coalition of Labor and Community* (New York: Monthly Review Press, 1990), 189.

15. Colin Rowe and Fred Koetter, *Collage City* (Cambridge, Mass.: MIT Press, 1978), 49. They are quoting Frances Yates's term from *The Art of Memory.*

16. Frederick Turner, *Spirit of Place: The Making of an American Literary Landscape* (San Francisco: Sierra Club Books, 1989), is an admirable account of several American writers coming to terms with American places. Rick Simonson and Scott Walker, eds., *Multi-Cultural Literacy: Opening the American Mind* (Saint Paul, Minn.: Greywolf Press, 1988), is a good introduction to current writing. Lucy Lippard, *Mixed Blessings: New Art in a Multicultural America* (New York: Pantheon, 1990), is an excellent analysis of how American artists are dealing with ethnic heritage.

17. Kevin Lynch, *What Time Is This Place?* (Cambridge, Mass.: MIT Press, 1972).

18. George Kubler, *The Shape of Time: Remarks on the History of Things* (New Haven: Yale University Press, 1962), 12–13.

## 2 Urban Landscape History: The Sense of Place and the Politics of Space

1. John Brinckerhoff Jackson, *Discovering the Vernacular Landscape* (New Haven: Yale University Press, 1984), xii.

2. Yi-Fu Tuan sees both biology and culture forming the human connection to place, in *Space and Place: The Perspective of Experience* (Minneapolis, Minn.: University of Minnesota Press, 1977), 6. He also notes that these terms may be elusive: "Architects talk about the spatial qualities of place; they can equally well talk about the locational (place) qualities of space." Tuan describes place as a pause in the flow of time: "If we see the world as a process, constantly changing, we should not be able to develop any sense of place." He argues that the experience of place engages all five senses in seeing, smelling, feeling, hearing, and tasting the essence of places.

3. Cross-cultural studies reveal heightened sensitivities to certain kinds of places. The Aivilik of northern Canada can describe many kinds of snowy landscapes; the Puluwat Islanders of the Pacific can read minute variations in ocean currents. Yet it would be wrong to say that sense of place is primarily determined this way. Among the Aivilik gender accounts for marked differences. Settlements and trading posts appear on cognitive maps drawn by women, while coastline is the key to those made by men, according to Tuan, *Space and Place*, 79–84.

4. Tuan, *Space and Place*, 30, 79–84.

5. Irwin Altman and Setha M. Low, eds., *Place Attachment* (New York: Plenum Publishing, 1992). Also see Denise L. Lawrence and Setha M. Low, "The Built Environment and Spatial Form," *Annual Review of Anthropology* 19 (1990), 453–505, a review essay covering several hundred works.

6. Herbert J. Gans, *The Urban Villagers: Group and Class in the Life of Italian-Americans*, 2d ed. (New York: Free Press, 1982); Peter H. Marris, *Family and Social Change in an African City* (Evanston: Northwestern University Press, 1962); Peter H. Marris, *Loss and Change*, 2d ed. (London and New York: Routledge and Kegan Paul, 1986).

7. Sauer said: "Culture is the agent, the natural area is the medium, the cultural landscape is the result." See "Landscape," in Robert P. Larkin and Gary L. Peters, eds., *Dictionary of Concepts in Human Geography* (Westport, Conn.: Greenwood Press, 1983), 139–144. Among the scholars who have helped shape cultural landscape studies are John Brinckerhoff Jackson and Donald Meinig. See Jackson's essays in *Landscapes* (Amherst: University of Massachusetts Press, 1980), *Discovering the Vernacular Landscape* (cited above), and *A Sense*

*of Place, a Sense of Time* (New Haven: Yale University Press, 1994); and Meinig's edited volume, *The Interpretation of Ordinary Landscapes* (New York and Oxford: Oxford University Press, 1979) as well as his *The Shaping of America*, 2 vols. (New Haven: Yale University Press, 1986 and 1993). More recent edited volumes include Dell Upton and John Michael Vlach, eds., *Common Places: Readings in American Vernacular Architecture* (Athens, Georgia: The University of Georgia Press, 1986) and Michael Conzen, ed., *The Making of the American Landscape* (New York: HarperCollins, 1990), both with extensive bibliographies. Conzen's is the more urban of the two, and the broader in focus. Also see Wayne Franklin and Michael Steiner, eds., *Mapping American Culture* (Iowa City: University of Iowa Press, 1992).

Landscape architect Anne Whiston Spirn, in a forthcoming book, *The Language of Landscape*, will provide a more thorough grounding in aesthetics and environmental science for landscape studies and design. See her articles "From Uluru to Cooper's Place: Patterns in the Cultural Landscape," *Orion* 9 (Spring 1990), 32–39, and "The Poetics of City and Nature: Towards a New Aesthetic for Urban Design," *Landscape Journal* 7 (Fall 1988), 108–127.

8. Two collections of essays on ethnic spatial patterns and vernacular architecture in the American rural landscape exist, but there is nothing comparable focusing on vernacular building in urban ethnic places: Allen G. Noble, ed., *To Build in a New Land: Ethnic Landscapes in North America* (Baltimore: Johns Hopkins University Press, 1992); Dell Upton, ed., *America's Architectural Roots: Ethnic Groups That Built America* (Washington, D.C.: The Preservation Press, 1986).

9. See Michael Dear and Jennifer Wolch, eds., *The Power of Geography* (Boston: Hyman Unwin, 1990); Kay Anderson and Fay Gale, eds., *Inventing Places* (New York: John Wiley, 1992); John A. Agnew and James S. Duncan, eds., *The Power of Place: Bringing Together Geographical and Sociological Imaginations* (Boston: Unwin Hyman, 1989); James Duncan and David Ley, eds., *Place / Culture / Representation* (London and New York: Routledge, 1993); Derek Gregory, *Geographical Imaginations* (Cambridge, Mass., and Oxford: Blackwell, 1994); Neil Smith, *Uneven Development: Nature, Capital, and the Reproduction of Space* (Cambridge, Mass., and Oxford: Blackwell, 1990); Gillian Rose, *Feminism and Geography: The Limits of Geographical Knowledge* (Minneapolis: University of Minnesota Press, 1993); Doreen Massey, *Space, Place, and Gender* (Minneapolis: University of Minnesota Press, 1994).

10. William Cronon, "A Place for Stories: Nature, History, and Narrative," *Journal of American History* 78 (March 1992): 1347–1376.

11. John A. Agnew, "The Devaluation of Place in Social Science," examines the way that ideas about class and community have become more central to social science research than ideas about place, in Agnew and Duncan, eds., *The Power of Place*. Also see David Ley, "Modernism, Post-Modernism, and the Struggle for Place," in the same volume, 44–65.

12. Edward Relph, *Place and Placelessness* (London: Pion, 1976), promoted the term "placeless," which is misleading since he really meant bad place. Melvin Webber, an urban planner, used "non-place urban realm" earlier in a way that

was neither positive nor negative but referred to the decline of face-to-face activities and the rise of telephone, television, etc. More recent commentators stress the "information highway" as a non-place.

13. Mira Engler, "Drive-Thru History: Theme Towns in Iowa," *Landscape* 32 (1993), 8–18; Patrick Wright, *On Living in an Old Country* (London: Verso, 1985).

14. But terminology is in flux. Alexander Wilson describes his *The Culture of Nature: North American Landscape from Disney to Exxon Valdez* (Cambridge, Mass.: Blackwell, 1992) as "a cultural history of nature in North America," 12.

15. Henri Lefebvre, *The Production of Space*, tr. Donald Nicholson-Smith (Oxford, England, and Cambridge, Mass.: Basil Blackwell, 1991).

16. Fredric Jameson, *Postmodernism, or, The Cultural Logic of Late Capitalism*, (Durham: Duke University Press, 1991), 364–365.

17. For a more complex look at these issues, see Gregory, *Geographic:al Imaginations*, and David Harvey, *The Condition of Postmodernity* (Cambridge, Mass., and Oxford: Blackwell, 1989), especially Table 3.1.

18. To list just a few examples of works that deal with political contestation: on city plans, Gwendolyn Wright, *The Politics of Design in French Colonial Urbanism* (Chicago: University of Chicago Press, 1991); and on parks, Galen Cranz, *The Politics of Park Design* (Cambridge, Mass.: MIT Press, 1982), and Roy Rosenzweig and Elizabeth Blackmar, *The People and the Park* (Ithaca: Cornell University Press, 1992).

19. Patricia Nelson Limerick, "Disorientation and Reorientation: The American Landscape Discovered from the West," *Journal of American History* 79 (December 1992), 1031–1034.

20. Denis Wood's atlas of the Boylan Heights neighborhood of Raleigh, North Carolina, is a wonderful example of the evocation of an entire urban neighborhood, achieved through drawings that record the contours of its landscape and the patterns of its roads, alleys, bridges, sewers and water mains, manhole covers, street trees, street signs, and stop signs. Denis Wood, *Dancing and Singing: A Narrative Atlas of Boylan Heights*, proof copy from the author, 1990, School of Design, North Carolina State University. A basic text that explores some of these materials for teachers undertaking school projects is Gerald Danzer, *Public Places: Exploring Their History* (Nashville, Tenn.: Association for State and Local History, 1987.)

21. John Stilgoe, *Metropolitan Corridor: Railroads and the American Scene* (New Haven: Yale University Press, 1983).

22. At the scale of bodily space, in the middle third of the nineteenth century, some middle-class women fought for dress reform and access to birth control, while African American women fought slavery as a system that required them to bear

children as a source of new wealth for their owners. At the scale of housing space, by the last third of the century, some middle-class women, who were usually political activists and housewives, were looking for ways to reorganize the home economically as a domestic workplace. In the same period, some African American women, who were employed as domestics, organized a major strike of household workers in Atlanta in 1881. At the scale of urban space, in the late nineteenth and early twentieth centuries, middle-class white women's movements for "municipal housekeeping" challenged corrupt government by men; suffrage also brought broad coalitions of women, across lines of class and race, into public space to demand this right. At the same time, while African American women participated in these wider movements, they would have experienced more limited access to space in the city. Dolores Hayden, *The Grand Domestic Revolution: A History of Feminist Designs for American Homes, Neighborhoods, and Cities* (Cambridge: MIT Press, 1981); Mary P. Ryan, *Women in Public: Between Banners and Ballots, 1825–1880* (Baltimore: Johns Hopkins University Press, 1990).

23. Dear and Wolch, *The Power of Geography*, 4.

24. For example, Rina Swentzell, "Conflicting Landscape Values," *Places* 7 (Fall 1990), 19–27; Dell Upton, "Black and White Landscapes in Colonial Virginia," in Robert Blair St. George, ed., *Material Life in America 1600–1860* (Boston: Northeastern University Press, 1988), 357–369; Manuel Castells, "Cultural Identity, Sexual Liberation and Urban Structure: The Gay Community in San Francisco," *The City and the Grassroots* (Berkeley: University of California Press, 1983), 138–172; George Chauncey, *Gay New York: Gender, Urban Culture and the Makings of the Gay Male World, 1890–1940* (New York: Basic Books, 1994).

25. For example, Allen Scott and Michael Storper, eds., *Production, Work, and Territory: The Geographical Anatomy of Industrial Capitalism* (London: Allen and Unwin, 1986); Dear and Wolch, eds., *The Power of Geography.*

26. Interview with Loren Miller, Jr., in Charles Perry, "When We Were Very Young," *Los Angeles Times Magazine* (February 4, 1990), 13–14.

27. Lynell George, *No Crystal Stair: African Americans in the City of Angels* (London and New York: Verso, 1992), 222–223.

28. Such photographs are often surprisingly difficult to locate since only certain archives are willing to preserve them. Lonnie G. Bunch's *Black Angelenos* includes a good selection (Los Angeles: California Afro-American Museum, 1989).

29. For a sociological look at these spatial issues in world perspective, see Daphne Spain, *Gendered Spaces* (Chapel Hill: University of North Carolina Press, 1992).

30. Miller, in Perry, "When We Were Very Young," 13, includes a photograph of an African American women's social club his mother belonged to in Los Angeles in the 1950s.

31. Kevin Lynch, *The Image of the City* (Cambridge, Mass.: MIT Press, 1960).

32. Peter Orleans discusses this study by Tridib Bannerjee and others in "Urban Experimentation and Urban Sociology," in *Science, Engineering, and the City*, publication 1498 (Washington, D.C.: National Academy of Sciences, 1967), 103–117; also see Peter Gould and Rodney White, *Mental Maps* (Boston: Allen and Unwin, 1986).

33. Jameson, *Postmodernism*, 54. But how this could operate in terms of global capitalisn is more difficult to say. Also see Doug Aberley, ed., *Boundaries of Home: Mapping for Local Empowerment* (Gabriola Island, B.C., and Philadelphia: New Society Publishers, 1993).

34. Thomas Hubka, "In the Vernacular: Classifying American Folk and Popular Architecture," *The Forum* (Society of Architectural Historians) 7 (December 1985), 1.

35. As Michel Foucault has suggested, "Both architecture and urban planning, both designs and ordinary buildings, offer privileged instances for understanding how power operates." Cited in Gwendolyn Wright and Paul Rabinow, "Spatialization of Power: A Discussion of the Work of Michel Foucault," *Skyline* (March 1982), 14.

36. Barbara Wyatt, "The Challenge of Addressing Vernacular Architecture in a State Historic Preservation Survey Program," in Camille Wells, ed., *Perspectives in Vernacular Architecture II* (Columbia, Missouri: University of Missouri Press, 1986), 37–43.

37. Camille Wells, "Old Claims and New Demands" in Wells, *Perspectives*, 9–10. She refers to the potential conflict between vernacular scholarship and interpretation for a museum audience. The study of ordinary buildings and neighborhoods offers a bridge between academics (in the fields of history and history of architecture) and practitioners (in public history and in historic preservation planning), but those in the latter group, such as the museum curators and preservationists, may be under pressure to serve certain audiences and funders, and may be asked to avoid conflict and exploitation as themes of research. This is also frequently a problem for architectural journalists.

38. Sam Bass Warner, Jr., is one urban historian who pioneered the use of evidence based on buildings, in his *Streetcar Suburbs: The Process of Growth in Boston, 1870–1900* (Cambridge: Harvard University Press, 1962). Warner's *The Urban Wilderness, The Private City: Philadelphia in Three Stages of Its Growth*, and *To Dwell Is to Garden* are all classics of urban history that use the built environment well. Other examples include James Borchert, *Alley Life in Washington: Family, Community, Religion and Folklife in the City, 1850–1870* (Champaign, Ill.: University of Illinois Press, 1980); Elizabeth Blackmar, *Manhattan for Rent, 1785–1850* (Ithaca: Cornell University Press, 1989).

39. Dolores Hayden, *Seven American Utopias: The Architecture of Communitarian Socialism, 1790–1975* (Cambridge, Mass.: MIT Press, 1976); Margaret Crawford, *Building the Workingman's Paradise: The Architecture of American Company Towns* (New York and London: Verso, 1994); Wright, *The Politics of Design*.

40. One recent example of a study of community space is Gerald L. Pocius, *A Place to Belong: Community Order and Everyday Space in Calvert, Newfoundland* (Athens, Georgia: University of Georgia Press, 1991). *Perspectives in Vernacular Architecture I, II, III, IV* (Columbia, Mo.: University of Missouri Press, 1982–1989) gives a selection of work by members of the Vernacular Architecture Forum. On the importance of process to vernacular building studies, see Dell Upton, "Vernacular Buildings," in Diane Maddex, ed., *Built in the USA: American Buildings from Airports to Zoos* (Washington, D.C.: The Preservation Press, 1985), 167–168. He has also made a plea for architectural historians to turn away from studying single buildings by master designers (thus serving as the architectural profession's press agents) in favor of looking at landscape history, in "Architectural History or Landscape History?," *Journal of Architectural Education* 44 (August 1991), 195–199.

41. Daniel Bluestone, *Constructing Chicago* (New Haven: Yale University Press, 1991); Abigail Van Slyck, *Free to All: Carnegie Libraries and American Culture* (Chicago: University of Chicago Press, forthcoming). Paul Groth's choice of the single-room-occupancy hotel, as a vernacular building type of great importance in analyzing both urban renewal and homelessness, is an example of the new kinds of work possible using these older methods: " 'Marketplace' Vernacular Design: The Case of Downtown Rooming Houses," in Wells, ed., *Perspectives*, 179–191; Paul Groth, *Living Downtown: The History of Residential Hotels in the United States* (Berkeley: University of California Press, 1994). Also see Gwendolyn Wright, *Building the Dream: A Social History of Housing* (New York: Pantheon, 1981), for an overview of 13 housing types.

42. Jules David Prown, "Mind in Matter: An Introduction to Material Culture Theory and Method," in St. George, ed., *Material Life in America*, 17–34. Also see essays by Thomas J. Schlereth in *Cultural History and Material Culture: Everyday Life, Landscapes, Museums* (Ann Arbor, Michigan: UMI Research Press, 1990); and by Dell Upton, "The City as Material Culture," in Anne E. Yentsch and Mary C. Beaudry, eds., *The Art and Mystery of Historical Archaeology: Essays in Honor of James Deetz* (Boca Raton, Fla.: CRC Press, 1992), 51–74, and "Another City: the Urban Cultural Landscape in the Early Republic," in Catherine Hutchins, ed., *Everyday Life in the Early Republic, 1789–1829* (Winterthur, Del.: Winterthur Museum, forthcoming).

43. One social history research team associated with the New York Lower East Side Tenement Museum is working on a tenement located at 97 Orchard Street on the Lower East Side of New York City. (A fluke in the occupancy laws closed the dwelling units but kept small stores in the building operating, and thus saved it from any modifications for several decades.) Now the researchers are tracking the more than 7,000 immigrants of Irish, German, Italian, Russian, Greek, and Turkish descent who are known to have lived there between 1863 and 1935.

Other housing types might also lead to larger social analyses. For example, on the tract house, see Dolores Hayden, *Redesigning the American Dream: The Future of Housing, Work, and Family Life* (New York: W. W. Norton, 1984); and Gwendolyn Wright, *Moralism and the Model Home: Domestic Architecture and Cultural Conflict in Chicago, 1873–1913* (Chicago: University of Chicago Press, 1980).

44. Anthony Jackson, *A Place Called Home: A History of Low-Cost Housing in Manhattan* (Cambridge, Mass.: MIT Press, 1976), 1–29, outlines the issue but does not run the numbers.

45. 97 Orchard Street, the Lower East Side Tenement Museum, has been included in the National Register of Historic Places for its social importance. (The old storefronts in the building, but not the dwelling units, are open to the public as the Lower East Side Tenement Museum. Similarly, the National Trust for Scotland has a tenement apartment in Glasgow, home to a milliner and dressmaker, open to the public. It is one of their most popular attractions.)

46. Christine Stansell, *City of Women: Sex and Class in New York City, 1789–1860* (New York: Knopf, 1986), explores these issues; also Sarah Deutsch, "Reconceiving the City: Women, Space, and Power in Boston, 1870–1910," *Gender and History* (forthcoming, 1994).

47. Upton, ed., *America's Architectural Roots*, 14.

48. For an excellent study of this kind in a rural context, see Richard Westmacott, "Pattern and Practice in Traditional African-American Gardens in Rural Georgia," *Landscape Journal* 10 (Fall 1991), 87–104, and his *African American Gardens and Yards in the Rural South* (Knoxville: University of Tennessee Press, 1992). A new documentation of the gardens of the homeless in New York is Diana Balmori and Margaret Morton, *Transitory Gardens, Uprooted Lives* (New Haven: Yale University Press, 1993). Because many of the homeless they document are African American, there may be some patterns that recall Westmacott's rural gardens. Morton also has an independent project on homeless dwellings, "The Architecture of Despair," forthcoming. Also see Joseph Sciorra, "Yard Shrines and Sidewalk Altars of New York's Italian Americans," *Perspectives in Vernacular Architecture III*, 185–198.

49. James T. Rojas, "The Enacted Environment of East Los Angeles," *Places* 8 (Spring 1993), 42–53.

50. See Gail Lee Dubrow, "Property Types Associated with Asian/Pacific American Settlement in Washington State," in Gail Lee Dubrow, Gail Nomura, et al., *The Historic Context for the Protection of Asian/Pacific American Resources in Washington State* (Olympia, Washington: Department of Community Development, 1993); Gail Lee Dubrow, "Asian Pacific Imprints on the Western Landscape," in Arnold R. Alanen and Robert Z. Melnick, eds., *preserving Cultural Landscapes in America* (Baltimore: Johns Hopkins University Press, forthcoming); David Chuenyan Lai, *Chinatowns: Towns within Cities in Canada* (Vancouver: University of British Columbia Press, 1988); *Places*, special issue on Latino spaces, Spring 1993; Kay J. Anderson, *Vancouver's Chinatown: Racial Discourse in Canada, 1875–1980* (Montreal and London: McGill-Queens University Press, 1991); and Borchert, *Alley Life.*

51. Joseph Sciorra, "'I Feel Like I'm in My Country': Puerto Rican Casitas in New York City," photographs by Martha Cooper, *The Drama Review* 34 (Winter 1990), 156–168.

52. Dorothy Noyes, *Uses of Tradition: Arts of Italian Americans in Philadelphia* (Philadelphia: Samuel S. Fleisher Art Memorial, 1989).

53. Joseph Sciorra, "Religious Processions in Italian Williamsburg," *The Drama Review* 29 (Fall 1985), 65–81. Also see Geneviève Fabre and Ramón Gutiérrez, eds., forthcoming book on ethnic celebrations in the United States.

54. Susan Davis, *Parades and Power: Street Theatre in Nineteenth-Century Philadelphia* (Berkeley: University of California Press, 1986); David Glassberg, *American Historical Pageantry: The Uses of Tradition in the Early Twentieth Century* (Chapel Hill: University of North Carolina Press, 1990).

55. Temma Kaplan, "Making Spectacles of Themselves," an essay drawn from her forthcoming book on women's use of public space as a part of political protest, develops this point.

56. William Serrin, "Shifts in Work Put White Men in the Minority," *New York Times*, July 31, 1984, 1. In 1954, white men made up 62.5 percent of the paid labor force.

57. Hayden, *Redesigning the American Dream*; Sam Bass Warner, Jr., "When Suburbs Are the City" (paper delivered at symposium "The Car and the City," UCLA, 1988); Kenneth T. Jackson, *Crabgrass Frontier: The Suburbanization of the United States* (Oxford and New York: Oxford University Press, 1985).

58. For example, Ricardo Romo, *East Los Angeles: The History of a Barrio* (Austin, Tex.: University of Texas Press, 1983). Or, for a historical geographer's perspective, see Kay J. Anderson, "The Idea of Chinatown: The Power of Place and Institutional Practice in the Making of a Racial Category," *Annals of the Association of American Geographers* 77 (December 1987), 580–598. Forthcoming work on "Chocolate Cities" by Robin Kelley will look at African American cities across the country.

"Ethnic" is perhaps the hardest of all words to use consistently. Although "ethnic" in its linguistic roots suggests "the people," it is often used in the United States to suggest an outsider, specifically an outsider to the English white Protestant immigrants of seventeenth- and eighteenth-century New England and the eastern seaboard. (Rarely has anyone of that tradition been described as ethnic, and as a result some community groups think the word "ethnic" is a coded way to imply nonwhite or working class and try not to use it.) However, ethnic will be used here to indicate a shared cultural tradition, whether that of an indigenous Native American tribe or of an immigrant group—English, African, Irish, Mexican, German, Japanese, Chinese, or Polish, to name a few possibilities. "Ethnic minority" is a term always defined by time and place that often outlives its accuracy. Sometimes "ethnic minorities" has been used to describe all of the nonwhite groups in a population; in this case, the terms multicultural or multiethnic will be used instead to refer to a diverse population. See Stephan Thernstrom, Ann Orlov, and Oscar Handlin, eds., *Harvard Encyclopedia of American Ethnic Groups* (Cambridge, Mass.: Harvard University Press, 1980), and Werner Sollors, *Beyond Ethnicity: Consent and Descent in American Culture* (New York: Oxford University Press, 1986).

59. Toni Morrison, *Playing in the Dark: Whiteness and the American Literary Imagination* (New York: Vintage, 1990), 6.

60. American Social History Project, *Who Built America?*, 2 vols. (New York: Pantheon, 1992).

61. Gloria T. Null, Patricia Bell Scott, and Barbara Smith, *All the Women Are White, All the Blacks Are Men, but Some of Us Are Brave: Black Women's Studies* (Old Westbury, N.Y.: Feminist Press, 1981).

62. For example, Elizabeth Higginbotham, "Laid Bare by the System: Work and Survival for Black and Hispanic Women," in Amy Swerdlow and Hanna Lessinger, eds., *Class, Race and Sex: The Dynamics of Control* (Boston: G. K. Hall, 1983); also see Higginbotham's excellent *Selected Bibliography of Social Science Readings on Women of Color in the United States* (Memphis, Tenn.: The Center for Research on Women, Memphis State University, 1989).

63. William Cronon, *Nature's Metropolis: Chicago and the Great West* (New York: W. W. Norton, 1991).

64. Lefebvre, *The Production of Space*, 286.

65. David Brodsly, *LA Freeway: An Appreciative Essay* (Berkeley: University of California Press, 1981); Mark Rose, *Interstate: Express Highway Politics 1939–1989*, rev. ed. (Knoxville: University of Tennessee Press, 1990). Also see Martin Wachs and Margaret Crawford, eds., *The Car and the City: The Automobile, the Built Environment, and Daily Urban Life* (Ann Arbor: University of Michigan Press, 1992), and Virginia Scharff, *Taking the Wheel: Women and the Coming of the Motor Age* (New York: Free Press, 1991).

66. Castells, *The City and the Grassroots*, 314; David Harvey, "From Space to Place and Back Again: Reflections on the Condition of Postmodernity," UCLA Graduate School of Architecture and Urban Planning Colloquium, May 13, 1991, 39.

67. There is not space for a complete review. Sharon Zukin, *Landscapes of Power: From Detroit to Disney World* (Berkeley: University of California Press, 1992), is one good study from the sociology of culture; John M. Findlay, *Magic Lands: Western Cityscapes and American Culture after 1940* (Berkeley: University of California Press, 1992), treats a variety of western places, including Disneyland and Sun City, Arizona. Michael Sorkin, ed., *Variations on a Theme Park: The New American City and the End of Public Space* (New York: Noonday Press, 1992), is uneven, but contains a wonderful essay on shopping malls by historian Margaret Crawford. Joel Garreau, *Edge City: Life on the New Frontier* (New York: Doubleday, 1991), and James Howard Kunstler, *The Geography of Nowhere: The Rise and Decline of America's Man-Made Landscape* (New York: Simon and Schuster, 1993), are journalists who agree with Sorkin that Americans face the end of meaningful places and public space.

68. Harvey, "From Space to Place," 39.

1. John Kuo Wei Tchen, "Historical Amnesia and Collective Reclamation: Building Identity with Chinese Laundry Workers in the United States," in *Vers des Sociétés Pluriculturelles: Études Comparatives et Situation en France* (Paris: Éditions de l'Orstom, 1987), 242–250; Michael Wallace, "Visiting the Past: History Museums in the United States," in Benson, Brier, and Rosenzweig, eds., *Presenting the Past*, 160; M. Christine Boyer, *The City of Collective Memory: Its Historical Imagery and Architectural Entertainments* (Cambridge, Mass.: MIT Press, 1994), 367–476; David Lowenthal, *The Past Is a Foreign Country* (Oxford and New York: Oxford University Press, 1985), xvi. For other examples of recent work on this topic, see Michael Kammen, *Mystic Chords of Memory: The Transformation of Tradition in American Culture* (New York: Knopf, 1991); John Bodnar, *Remaking America* (Princeton: Princeton University Press, 1992); Michael Frisch, "The Memory of History," in Susan Porter Benson, Stephen Brier, and Roy Rosenzweig, eds., *Presenting the Past: Essays on History and the Public* (Philadelphia: Temple University Press, 1986); Lois Silverman, ed., *A Bibliography on History-Making* (Washington, D.C.: American Association of Museums, 1989); Peter Fowler, *The Past in Contemporary Society* (London: Routledge, 1992); Martha Norkunas, *The Politics of Public Memory: Tourism, History, and Ethnicity in Monterey, California* (Albany: State University of New York, 1993); David Thelen, *Memory and American History* (Bloomington, Ind.: Indiana University Press, 1990); Melissa Keane, "Asking Questions about the Past," *Mosaic: The Newsletter of the Center on History Making in America*, 1 (Spring/Summer 1992), 9.

2. Paul Connerton, *How Societies Remember* (Cambridge and New York: Cambridge University Press, 1989), 36. He cites Maurice Halbwachs, *Les cadres sociaux de mémoire* (Paris, 1925), and *La mémoire collective* (Paris: Presses Universitaires de France, 1950). See Maurice Halbwachs, *The Collective Memory*, tr. Francis J. Ditter, Jr., and Vida Yazdi Ditter (New York: Harper and Row, 1980) . On the importance of social memory, also see Lowenthal, *The Past Is a Foreign Country*, xix; Boyer, *The City of Collective Memory* (especially chapters 1 and 4); Edmund Blair Bolles, *Remembering and Forgetting* (New York: Walker and Company, 1988); George Lipsitz, *Time Passages: Collective Memory and American Popular Culture* (Minneapolis: University of Minnesota Press, 1989); Pierre Nora, "Between Memory and History: *Les Lieux de Mémoire*," *Representations* 26 (Spring 1989), 7–24.

3. Edward S. Casey, *Remembering: A Phenomenological Study* (Bloomington, Ind.: Indiana University Press, 1987), 186–187. See also his chapters on "Body Memory," "Place Memory," and "Commemoration."

4. Frances A. Yates, *The Art of Memory* (Chicago: University of Chicago Press, 1966), traces the classical art of memory building. Jonathan D. Spence, *The Memory Palace of Matteo Ricci* (New York: Viking, 1984), is a fascinating account of a Jesuit missionary transmitting these ideas to the Chinese in 1596.

5. Connerton, *How Societies Remember*, 27.

6. For an account of some of these differences, see Michael J. Ettema, "History Museums and the Culture of Materialism," in Jo Blatti, ed., *Past Meets Present:*

*Essays about Historic Interpretation and Public Audiences* (Washington, D.C.: Smithsonian Institution Press, 1987), 62–86.

7. Linda Shopes, "Oral History and Community Involvement: The Baltimore Neighborhood Heritage Project," in Benson, Brier, and Rosenzweig, eds., *Presenting the Past*, 253. Also see Elizabeth Fee, Linda Shopes, and Linda Zeidman, eds., *The Baltimore Book: New Views of Local History* (Philadelphia: Temple University Press, 1991).

8. Paul Buhle, "Popular Memory, the Landscape, and Photo History," *Radical History Newsletter* 66 (May 1992), 1.

9. Some projects seem to have cultivated these bodily social memories. Long ago, Jane Addams's Hull House Labor Museum introduced craft demonstrations of Irish and Italian spinning techniques as a part of preserving ethnic identities, and many museums do craft demonstrations today—blacksmithing and weaving, for instance. At Lowell National Historic Park in Massachusetts, The Boott Cotton Mills Museum of industrial history runs turbines and power looms to show visitors old technologies and explain how fast the operatives had to work. The curators ordered ten thousand pairs of earplugs to spare them the shattering noise.

10. Casey, *Remembering*, 214–215.

11. Michael Frisch, *A Shared Authority: Essays on the Craft and Meaning of Oral and Public History* (Albany: SUNY Press, 1990); John Kuo Wei Tchen, "Creating a Dialogic Museum: The Chinatown History Museum Experiment," in Ivan Karp et al., eds., *Museums and Communities: The Politics of Public Culture* (Washington, D.C.: Smithsonian Institution Press, 1992), 285–326.

12. This approach gained ground in England in the early 1970s with historian Raphael Samuel and the journal *History Workshop* and then spread to the United States; it has been supported by *Radical History Review* and many other journals and organizations. The People's Autobiography of Hackney, founded in England in 1972, is one early example of a very creative, entrepreneurial group that presented itself to urban audiences in unusual ways. Ken Warpole started this project at Centerprise, a community bookstore in a working-class neighborhood in the East End of London. A dressmaker, a cab driver, and two fifteen-year-olds who hated school were the first local authors to write vivid accounts of their everyday lives in Hackney. As many as 5,000 to 10,000 copies of these autobiographies were sold to neighborhood residents, advertised by word of mouth. To meet the demand for more, the group began taping accounts of the lives of other residents, using oral history as a route to generating more autobiographies, and involving both professional historians and local residents in their production.

    Combining a series of local history publications with a cafe and bookstore enabled each to enhance the others. The storefront, located on a busy pedestrian street, attracted people. Visitors interested in one aspect of the work would often meet others with similar interests in the cafe or store. Hackney was enriched by the bookstore, the cafe, the exhibits, and the opportunity they provided to organize with others, as well as the special line of books by local authors. Ken Warpole, *Local Publishing and Local Culture* (London: Centerprise Trust Ltd., 1977).

13. Jeremy Brecher, Jerry Lombardi, and Jan Stackhouse, comps. and eds., *Brass Valley: The Story of Working People's Lives and Struggles in an American Industrial Region* (Philadelphia: Temple University Press, 1982).

14. Jeremy Brecher, "A Report on Doing History from Below: The Brass Workers History Project," in Benson, Brier, and Rosenzweig, eds., *Presenting the Past*, 275–276. Also see the longer version of this text, Jeremy Brecher, "How I Learned to Quit Worrying and Love Community History: A 'Pet Outsider's' Report on the Brass Workers' History Project," *Radical History Review* 28–30 (1984), 187–201.

15. *Brass Valley* (videotape distributed by Cinema Guild, 1697 Broadway, New York, N.Y. 10019).

16. *Brass City Music* (videotape coproduced by Lisa Bothwell and Jeremy Brecher and produced by The Waterbury Traditional Music Project of Stone Soup and Connecticut Public Television).

17. Brecher, "A Report on Doing History from Below"; Jeremy Brecher, " 'If All the People Are Banded Together': The Naugatuck Valley Project," in Jeremy Brecher and Tim Costello, eds., *Building Bridges: The Emerging Grassroots Coalition of Labor and Community* (New York: Monthly Review Press, 1990), 93–105.

18. "Why History? An Introduction to the New York Chinatown History Project," in *New York Chinatown History Proiect* (New York: New York Chinatown History Project, n.d.), unpag. For accounts of the work also see J. Tevere MacFadyen, "Exploring a Past Long Locked in Myth and Mystery," *Smithsonian* (January 1983), 70–78, and Candace Floyd, "Chinatown," *History News* 39 (June 1984), 6–11. Also see John Kuo Wei Tchen, "Towards Building a Democratic Community Culture: Reflections on the New York Chinatown History Project" (paper delivered at the Fifth International Oral History Conference, March 29–31, 1985).

19. Tchen, "Towards Building a Democratic Community Culture," 2–4.

20. John Kuo Wei Tchen, "The Chinatown-Harlem Initiative: Building Multicultural Understanding in New York City," in Brecher and Costello, eds., *Building Bridges*, 186–192. A permanent center for the project was created in New York in 1984 in four rooms of a former city school at 70 Mulberry Street, and included a gallery, a book shop, archives, and an office. The project continued in 1989 with the lively exhibit "On Both Sides of the Cloth," on the history of garment workers in past and present sweatshops of Chinatown. In 1991 they opened a permanent exhibit, "Remembering New York Chinatown." The project also offers walking tours of Chinatown. A Chinatown-Harlem initiative to promote multicultural understanding includes discussions with East Harlem and the Latino community there. In 1991 the project renamed itself the Chinatown History Museum.

21. Tchen, "Creating a Dialogic Museum," 285–320.

22. At the Mattatuck Museum in Waterbury, an exhibit was mounted that included one section comparing workers' and managers' dwellings as a follow-up to *Brass Valley.*

23. See "The National Park Service and History," in John Bodnar, *Remaking America*, for a full critique.

24. Antoinette J. Lee, "Discovering Old Cultures in the New World: The Role of Ethnicity," in Antoinette J. Lee and Robert E. Stipe, eds., *The American Mosaic: Preserving a Nation's Heritage* (Washington, D.C.: US/ICOMOS, 1986), 203; Antoinette J. Lee, ed., *Past Meets Future* (Washington, D.C.: The Preservation Press, 1992).

25. Page Putnam Miller, ed., *Reclaiming the Past: Landmarks of Women's History* (Bloomington: Indiana University Press, 1992), raises these issues. See especially Gail Lee Dubrow, "Women and Community," in that volume, and Gail Lee Dubrow, "Claiming Public Space for Women's History in Boston: A Proposal for Preservation, Public Art, and Public Historical Interpretation," *Frontiers: A Journal of Women's Studies* 13 (Winter 1992), 111–148; as well as Dubrow's forthcoming *Planning for the Preservation of American Women's History* (New York: Oxford University Press).

26. *Black Heritage Trail* (brochure, Boston African American National Historic Site, n.d.). There is a newer African American heritage trail planned for Cambridge, Massachusetts.

27. Dubrow, "Claiming Public Space," discusses how to do this in the context of a review of women's history landmarks in Boston.

28. *A Vision Realized: The Design Competition for the Women's Rights National Historical Park* (Seneca Falls, N.Y.: National Park Service, 1990).

29. Michael Wallace, "Reflections on the History of Historic Preservation," in Benson, Brier, and Rosenzweig, eds., *Presenting the Past*, 189. Also see his "Industrial Museums and the History of Deindustrialization," *The Public Historian* 9 (1987), 9–19; "Mickey Mouse History: Portraying the Past at Disneyworld," in Warren Leon and Roy Rosenzweig, eds., *History Museums in the United States: A Critical Assessment* (Urbana: University of Illinois Press, 1989), 158–180.

30. But of course there are limits to what any one site can convey. As Jo Blatti has warned, "we tend to look at a 'George Washington' site, likely to have been developed in the late nineteenth century or the first third of the twentieth century, wanting to know about the rest of the cast—women, blacks, soldiers, children—who may have been present as well. The next question is whether that particular site can shoulder the weight of our contemporary concerns." Blatti, *Past Meets Present*, 4–5. She suggests referring visitors to related sites of the same era, and describes curators in Minnesota who manage a nineteenth-century Anglo American settler's rural farmstead and refer visitors to an urban market garden in St. Paul and immigrant farmsteads at Old World Wisconsin.

Taking this approach one step further in 1991, the state of Wisconsin's Ethnic Corridor Project proposed to link inner-city neighborhoods with rural farmsteads to show the state's diverse past: German, Finnish, Swedish, Belgian, Luxembourgian groups in the countryside; Italian, Latino, and African American neighborhoods in the city. Alan C. Pape, "Preserving Cultural Landscapes," *Historic Preservation Forum* 5 (January–February 1991), 26–29. This kind of agenda gives curators opportunities to save vernacular buildings in ordinary urban ethnic neighborhoods—the modest homes, workplaces, and public spaces that have formed the urban landscape framing the daily lives of working people in the past.

31. "Once Is Never Enough," *Historic Preservation News* (November 1990), 6.

32. Heather Huyck, "Beyond John Wayne: Using Historic Sites to Interpret Western Women's History," in Lillian Schlissel, Vicki L. Ruiz, and Janice Monk, eds., *Western Women, Their Land, Their Lives* (Albuquerque, N.M.: University Press of New Mexico, 1988), 303–329.

33. See, for example, Paul M. Bray, "The City as a Park," *American Land Forum* 5 (Winter 1985), 23–27; *The Urban Cultural Park (UCP) Program* (Albany: New York State Office of Parks and Recreation, 1980); Allen Freeman, "Lessons From Lowell," *Historic Preservation* 42 (November–December 1990), 38; *Five Views: An Ethnic Sites Survey for California* (Sacramento: State of California Department of Parks and Recreation, 1988).

34. For example, Gail Dubrow, Gail Nomura, Shawn Wong, et al., *The Historic Context for the Preservation of Asian/Pacific American Resources in Washington State* (Olympia: Washington Office of Archaeology and Historic Preservation, 1993).

35. See, for example, "Focus on Landscape Preservation," special issue of *Historic Preservation Forum* 7 (May–June 1993); "Conserving Historic Landscapes," special issue of *APT Bulletin, The Journal of Preservation Technology* 24 (1992); and Arnold R. Alanen and Robert Z. Melnick, eds., *Preserving Cultural Landscapes in America* (Baltimore: Johns Hopkins University Press, forthcoming).

36. The Nature Conservancy has a project of this kind in a rural area around the village of Oster on the Eastern Shore of Virginia, with 6,200 acres of mainland property as well as 35,000 acres of undeveloped barrier islands. Denis Drabelle, "Design for an Ecosystem," in *The Art of Landscape Architecture* (Washington, D.C.: Partners for Livable Places, 1990). The Hanalei Valley Federal Wildlife Refuge on the Hawaiian island of Kauai is another rural example, "sugar cane and coffee plantations, cattle ranches, missions, and the villages of fishermen and farmers of Chinese, Japanese, Filipino, Korean, and Spanish ancestry"; William J. Murtagh, *Keeping Time: The History and Theory of Preservation in America* (Pittstown, N.J.: The Main Street Press, 1988), 126–127.

37. Anne Whiston Spirn, report of the West Philadelphia project, unpublished.

38. Susan Clifford and Angela King, "Preface," in Richard Mabey, ed., with Susan Clifford and Angela King for Common Ground, *Second Nature* (London: Jona-

than Cape, 1984), vii. Also see Sue Clifford, *Places: The City and the Invisible* (London: Public Art Development Trust, 1993).

39. Angela King and Sue Clifford, "Common Ground," in *An Introduction to the Deeds and Thoughts of Common Ground* (London: Common Ground, 1990).

40. "The Parish Maps Project," in *An Introduction to the Deeds and Thoughts*, n.p.

41. Terry Friedman and Andy Goldsworthy, eds., *Hand To Earth: Andy Goldsworthy Sculpture, 1976–1990* (New York: Abrams, 1990).

42. Clifford, *Places*, 11.

43. *Local Distinctiveness* (London: Common Ground, 1990), n.p.

44. *Mayday!Mayday!* (London: Common Ground, 1988).

45. John Ashberry, "A Call for Papers," *Yale Review* 80 (April 1992), 44.

46. On statues, see Eric Hobsbawm, "Mass-Producing Traditions: Europe, 1870–1914," in Eric Hobsbawm and Terence Ranger, eds., *The Invention of Tradition* (Cambridge: Cambridge University Press, 1983), 272–280; for Baca, see Suzanne Lacy, "Mapping the Terrain: The New Public Art," *Public Art Review* 8 (Spring/Summer 1993), 16.

47. Hafthor Yngvason, "The New Public Art: As Opposed to What?" *Public Art Review* 8 (Spring/Summer 1993), 8.

48. Ibid. Also see Lucy Lippard, *Mixed Blessings: New Art in a Multicultural America* (New York: Pantheon, 1990).

49. Lacy, "Mapping the Terrain," 16–17.

50. Some recent works on public art include: Pam Korza and Jeffrey Cruickshank, *Going Public: A Field Guide to Developments in Art in Public Places* (Amherst, Mass.: University of Massachusetts Arts Extension Service, 1988); Richard Andrews, Jim Hirschfield, and Larry Rauch, *Artwork/Network: A Planing Study for Seattle, Art in the Civic Context* (Seattle, Wash.: Seattle Arts Commission, 1984); Richard Andrews, "Artists and the Visual Definition of Cities: The Experience of Seattle," in Stacy Paleologos Harris, ed., *Insights/On Sites: Perspectives on Art in Public Places* (Washington, D.C.: Partners for Livable Places, 1984), 16–23; Ronald Fleming and Renata von Tscharner, *Place Makers: Public Art That Tells You Where You Are*, 2d ed. (New York: Harcourt Brace Jovanovich, 1987); Martha Rosler, *If You Lived Here: The City in Art, Theory, and Social Activism* (Seattle: Bay Press, 1991); Myrna Margulies Breitbart and Pamela Worden, *Beyond a "Sense of Place": New Roles for the Arts and Humanities in Urban Revitalization* (Boston: Urban Arts, 1993); Harriet Senie and Sally Webster, eds., *Critical Issues in Public Art* (New York: HarperCollins, 1992); Harriet Senie, *Contemporary Public Sculpture: Tradition, Transformation, and Controversy* (New York: Oxford University Press, 1992); Arlene Raven, ed., *Art in the Public Interest* (Ann Arbor: UMI Research Press, 1989);

Donna Graves, "Sharing Space," *Public Art Review* 8 (Spring/Summer 1993), 10–13; Rosalyn Deutsche, "Uneven Development: Public Art in New York City," *October* 47 (Winter 1988), 34. Also see the journals *Passage*, *On View*, and *Public Art Review*.

51. Mary Jane Jacob, *Places with a Past: New Site-Specific Art at Charleston's Spoleto Festival* (New York: Spoleto Festival U.S.A. and Rizzoli International Publications, Inc., 1991). See also *Program Guide: Culture in Action* (Chicago: Sculpture Chicago, 1993).

52. Edgar Heap of Birds, lecture, Yale University, April 6, 1992.

53. The 14 are: Sullivan's Island Pest Houses (the initial quarantine holding places for enslaved Africans); Sullivan's Island, site of Cato's Insurrection (one of the first sites of resistance among enslaved Africans); Boone Hall Plantation (site of enslaved Africans' quarters); Middleton Place Plantation (burial site for enslaved Africans); Johns Island Progressive Club (established by activist Esau Jenkins as a literary and citizenship training center); Moving Star Hall (oldest Praise House on Johns Island and home of the Moving Star Singers); Morris Island (burial site of Colonel Robert Gould Shaw and the 54th Massachusetts Regiment, the first African American military unit to fight in the Civil War); Fort Sumter (where the first shot of the Civil War was fired); Charleston Harbor (where Robert Smalls commandeered a transport steamer, carrying his family north to freedom); Jenkins Orphanage (established by the Reverend Daniel Jenkins in 1893 to aid troubled African American youth and famous for its jazz band); Slave Market (where thousands of enslaved Africans endured the auction block); Emanuel A.M.E. Church (built by the congregation of Denmark Vesey, who, inspired by the Haitian Revolution, masterminded an unsuccessful insurrection); The Hanging Tree (site of numerous executions of enslaved Africans and African Americans); and last af all, Avery Normal Institute, now Avery Research Center for African-American History and Culture, established for the education of African American children. Jacob, *Places with a Past*, 147.

54. Ibid., 148–150.

55. Sigfried Giedion, *Mechanization Takes Command: A Contribution to Anonymous History* (New York: W. W. Norton, 1969), 77–99. See especially plates 49 and 50.

56. The testimony was taped by Harriet Baskas, "The Place of Place in Public Art" (Seattle, Wash.: Reel Women Productions, for National Public Radio, 1989). Also see the brief reference to the city council testimony in Ruth Eckdish Knack, "Painting the Town Red and Green and Blue and Yellow and . . . ," *Planning* (May 1988), 13.

57. Baskas, "The Place of Place."

58. David Harvey, "From Space to Place and Back Again: Reflections on the Condition of Postmodernity," text for UCLA GSAUP Colloquium, May 13, 1991, p. 39.

1. *1990 Census of Population: General Characteristics of Population (California)* (Washington, D.C.: Bureau of the Census, 1992). Census categories are white, black, Hispanic (any race) American Indian, and Asian/Pacific Islander. They make consistent use of material difficult. I'm using Anglo American, African American, Latino, Native American, and Asian American. All the terminology about ethnicity and race is evolving.

2. *1990 Census of Population and Housing, Summary Tape File 3A* (cd rom) (Washington, D.C.: Bureau of the Census, 1992).

3. Zena Pearlstone, *Ethnic L.A.* (Beverly Hills, Calif.: Hillcrest Press, 1990), 27.

4. Ibid., 33.

5. Ibid., 44.

6. Guillermo Gómez-Peña, "Documented/Undocumented," in Rick Simonson and Scott Walker, eds., *The Graywolf Annual Five: Multi-Cultural Literacy, Opening the American Mind* (Saint Paul, Minn.: Graywolf Press, 1988), 130–131.

7. Pearlstone, *Ethnic L.A.*, 83.

8. Ibid., 71, quoting an Alhambra city planner.

9. Gail Lee Dubrow, "Preserving Her Heritage: American Landmarks of Women's History" (unpublished paper, UCLA Urban Planning Program, 1986), 23–25. One of the African American monuments she counted was Fire Station Number 30, a Power of Place nomination approved in 1985.

10. Charles W. Moore, "You Have to Pay for the Public Life," *Perspecta* (1964), 63–65.

11. Reyner Banham, *Los Angeles: The Architecture of Four Ecologies* (New York: Harper & Row, 1971), 23.

12. Adam Gopnik, "Paradise Lost," *New Yorker* (February 22, 1993), 160.

13. James Thomas Rojas, "The Enacted Environment: The Creation of 'Place' by Mexicans and Mexican Americans in East Los Angeles" (M.C.P. and M.S.A.S. thesis, MIT, Cambridge, 1991); and "The Enacted Environment of East Los Angeles," *Places* 8 (Spring 1993), 42–53.

14. Carey McWilliams, *Southern California: An Island on the Land* (Salt Lake City, Utah: Peregrine Smith Books, 1983); Robert Fogelson, *The Fragmented Metropolis: Los Angeles, 1850–1930* (Cambridge: Harvard University Press, 1967; new edition, with an introduction by Robert Fishman, Berkeley: University of California Press, 1993), 83. Fishman's otherwise capable introduction lacks attention to the new ethnic histories of the city. Other recent works include Scott Bottles, *Los Angeles and the Automobile: The Making of the Modern City*

(Berkeley: University of California Press, 1987); Kevin Starr, *Material Dreams: Southern California through the 1920s* (New York: Oxford University Press, 1990); and Mike Davis, *City of Quartz: Excavating the Future in Los Angeles* (New York: Verso, 1990). For maps and photographs, William Wilcox Robinson, *Maps of Los Angeles* (Los Angeles: Plantin Press, 1966); David L. Clark, *Los Angeles: A City Apart* (Woodland Hills: Windsor Publications, 1981); Bruce Henstell, *Los Angeles: An Illustrated History* (New York: Knopf, 1980); Ichiro Mike Murase, *Little Tokyo: One Hundred Years in Pictures* (Los Angeles: Visual Communications/Asian American Studies Central, Inc., 1983); Antonio Riós-Bustamante and Pedro Castillo, *An Illustrated History of Mexican Los Angeles, 1781–1985* (Los Angeles: Chicano Studies Research Center, UCLA, 1986). On literature, see Gerald W. Haslam, *Many Californias: Literature from the Golden State* (Reno: University of Nevada Press, 1992).

15. Two historical geographers, Howard J. Nelson and William V. Clark, *Los Angeles: The Metropolitan Experience* (Cambridge, Mass.: Ballinger, 1976), provided an overview of the ethnic history. For a few examples of more detailed ethnic histories: Lucie Cheng, Suellen Chang, et al., *Linking Our Lives: Chinese American Women of Los Angeles* (Los Angeles: Chinese Historical Society of Southern California, 1984); Albert Camarillo, *Chicanos in a Changing Society: From Mexican Pueblos to American Barrios in Santa Barbara and Southern California, 1848–1930* (Cambridge: Harvard University Press, 1979); Rudolfo Acuña, *A Community under Siege: A Chronicle of Chicanos East of the Los Angeles River, 1945–1975* (Los Angeles: UCLA Chicano Studies Center, 1980); Richard Griswold del Castillo, *The Los Angeles Barrio, 1850–1890: A Social History* (Berkeley: University of California Press, 1979); Ricardo Romo, *East Los Angeles: History of a Barrio* (Austin: University of Texas Press, 1983); Lonnie G. Bunch III, *Black Angelenos* (Los Angeles: California Afro-American Museum, 1989); Noritaka Yagasaki, "Ethnic Cooperativism and Immigrant Agriculture: A Study of Japanese Floriculture and Truck Farming in California" (Ph.D. diss., Department of Geography, University of California, Berkeley, 1982); George J. Sánchez, *Becoming Mexican American: Ethnicity, Culture, and Identity in Chicano Los Angeles, 1900–1945* (New York: Oxford University Press, 1993); Timothy P. Fong, *The First Suburban Chinatown: The Remaking of Monterey Park, California* (Philadelphia: Temple University Press, 1993); Hector L. Delgado, *New Immigrants, Old Unions: Organizing Undocumented Workers in Los Angeles* (Philadelphia: Temple University Press, 1993); Sucheng Chan, ed., *Entry Denied: Exclusion and the Chinese Community in America, 1882–1943* (Philadelphia: Temple University Press, 1991); Norman M. Klein and Martin J. Schiesl, eds., *20th Century Los Angeles: Power, Promotion and Social Conflict* (Claremont, Calif.: Regina Books, 1990); and "Japanese Americans in California," special issue of *California History* (Spring 1994).

16. The voices of Gabrieleño Indians are not often heard in public debates today, but they spoke against a real estate development on ancestral lands at Ballona Creek in Marina del Rey in 1988 (Pearlstone, *Ethnic L.A.*, 19). For an overview, see the "Indians of California" issue of *California History* 71 (Fall 1992).

17. Antonio Riós-Bustamante, "The Once and Future Majority," *California History* 60 (Spring 1981), 24.

18. Nelson and Clark, *Los Angeles*, 34.

19. Lawrence B. DeGraaf, "The City of Angels: Emergence of the Los Angeles Ghetto, 1890–1930," *Pacific Historical Review* 39 (August 1970), 327–330.

20. Nelson and Clark, *Los Angeles*, 36.

21. Richard G. Lillard, "Problems and Promise in Tomorrowland," *California History* 60 (Spring 1981), 93.

22. Don and Nadine Hata, "The Far East Meets the Far West," *California History* 60 (Spring 1981), 90.

23. William Mason, "The Chinese in Los Angeles," Los Angeles Museum of Natural History *Quarterly* 6 (Fall 1967), 16. Also see "Special Issue: The Chinese in California," *California History* 57 (Spring 1978), and Raymond Lou, "The Chinese American Community of Los Angeles, 1870–1900" (Ph.D. diss., University of California, Irvine, 1982).

24. Hata and Hata, "The Far East," 91.

25. Murase, *Little Tokyo*, 8.

26. Kanichi Kawasaki, quoted in Fogelson, *Fragmented Metropolis*, 200.

27. But this does not mean the bland rhetoric of *LA 2000*: "Think of Los Angeles as a mosaic with every color distinct, vibrant, and essential to the whole" (Los Angeles: Los Angeles 2000 Committee, 1988), 51.

## 5 Workers' Landscapes and Livelihoods

1. Raymond Williams, "Between Country and City," in Richard Mabey, ed., with Susan Clifford and Angela King for Common Ground, *Second Nature* (London: Jonathan Cape, 1984), 219.

2. Edward Soja, *Postmodern Geographies: The Reassertion of Space in Critical Social Theory* (London: Verso Press, 1989); Fredric Jameson, "Postmodernism, or the Cultural Logic of Late Capitalism," *New Left Review* 146 (July–August 1984), 53–92.

3. Soja, *Postmodern Geographies*, 248.

4. Both Soja and Davis devote their considerable energies to the white, male power structure of Los Angeles and its uses of territory and symbols. While they repeatedly mention ethnic diversity as a demographic issue, both books might have been improved by more sustained attention to ethnic and gender issues. Mike Davis, *City of Quartz: Excavating the Future in Los Angeles* (London and New York: Verso, 1990). He does map the machismo of Crips and Bloods, 283–308. Also see Davis's excellent "Cannibal City: Los Angeles and the Destruction

of Nature," in Elisabeth Smith, ed., *Urban Revisions* (Cambridge, Mass.: MIT Press, 1994).

5. Soja, *Postmodern Geographies*, 216–217. On the conflation of residents and immigrants also see Edward Soja, Rebecca Morales, and Goetz Wolff, "Urban Restructuring: An Analysis of Social and Spatial Change in Los Angeles," *Economic Geography* 59 (April 1983), 219. "If one includes the increasing Black population (now approaching one million) the county of Los Angeles has become a Third World metropolis." On women, critics complain that Soja's Marxist postmodernism, and that of David Harvey, is out of date (modern, not postmodern) because of an unwillingness to engage feminist theory and take account of women in the city. Doreen Massey, "Flexible Sexism," *Environment and Planning D: Society and Space* 9 (1991), 31–57; Rosalyn Deutsche, "Boys Town," in the same issue, 5–30.

6. Iris Marion Young, *Justice and the Politics of Difference* (Princeton: Princeton University Press, 1990), 240; Jameson, "Postmodernism," 90–92.

7. Carolyn Flynn and Gail Dubrow provided research assistance on a 1985 walking/driving tour that laid the foundation for parts of this chapter: Dolores Hayden, Gail Dubrow, and Carolyn Flynn, *The Power of Place: Los Angeles* (Los Angeles: The Power of Place, 1985). UCLA students whose research contributed included Daniel Hernandez, Susan Ruddick, Mary Beth Welch, John Condas, Ronald Brooks, Guadelupe Compean, Rudolph Brown, Jo Ann Victor, Judy Liss, Vivian Rescalvo, Mary Merritt, Sherry Katz, Gordon Howard, Margaret Crawford, and since 1985, Donna Graves, Nancy Stillger, Drummond Buckley, Sebastian Hardy, Stephanie Eyestone, Christine McPherson, Marc Norman, Timothy Sales, Rick Rosen, and Bill Doebler.

8. Howard J. Nelson and William V. Clark, *Los Angeles: The Metropolitan Experience* (Cambridge, Mass.: Ballinger, 1976), 124–125.

9. Robert F. Heizer and Albert B. Elsasser, *The Natural World of the California Indians* (Berkeley: University of California Press, 1980); Marc Norman, "History of the Los Angeles River" (unpublished paper, Graduate School of Architecture and Urban Planning, UCLA, 1990); Mary La Lone, *Gabrieleño Indians of Southern California: An Annotated Ethnohistoric Bibliography* (Los Angeles: UCLA Institute of Archaeology, 1980); Robert F. Heizer, *Indians of Los Angeles County* (letters of Hugo Reid of 1852) (Los Angeles: Southwest Museum, 1968); Stanley Young, *The Missions of California* (San Francisco: Chronicle Books, 1988); W. W. Robinson, *Los Angeles from the Days of the Pueblo*, rev. ed. (Los Angeles: California Historical Society, 1981).

10. Edward O. C. Ord, *The City of the Angels and the City of the Saints, or A Trip to Los Angeles and San Bernardino in 1856*, ed. Neal Harlow (San Marino: The Huntington Library, 1978), 8–9.

11. Ibid., 9.

12. Leonce Jore, "Jean Louis Vignes of Bordeaux, Pioneer of California Viticulture," tr. L. Jay Oliva, *Southern California Quarterly* 45 (1963), 297; Julius L. Jacobs,

"California's Pioneer Wine Families," *California Historical Quarterly* 54 (Summer 1975), 140; parts of this section are based on the walking tour, Hayden, Dubrow, and Flynn, *Los Angeles: The Power of Place.*

13. Jore, "Jean Louis Vignes." Also see Mary J. Merritt, "Vignes Vineyard, Los Angeles, California" (unpublished paper, UCLA, 1984).

14. Iris Wilson, *William Wolfskill* (Glendale, Calif.: Clark Company, 1965), 99.

15. J. Eliot Coit, *Citrus Fruits: An Account of the Citrus Fruit Industry* (New York: MacMillan Company, 1915), 3.

16. Carey McWilliams, *Factories in the Field* (Boston: Little, Brown & Co., 1939), 57.

17. Ibid., 71.

18. Stephanie Eyestone, "A History of the Built Form of California's Wineries" (unpublished paper, UCLA, 1991); Thomas Pinney, *A History of Wine in America* (Berkeley and London: University of California Press, 1989).

19. Carey McWilliams, *Southern California: An Island on the Land* (Salt Lake City, Utah: Peregrine Smith Books, 1983), 218.

20. Ibid., 207.

21. George and Elsie Yee, "The Chinese and the Los Angeles Produce Market," *Los Angeles Chinatown Souvenir Book* (Los Angeles: Chinese Historical Society, 1983), 33; parts of this section rely on Hayden, Dubrow, and Flynn, *Los Angeles: The Power of Place.*

22. Yee, "The Chinese," 35; "City Market," Historic Resources Inventory, State of California, 1980.

23. Thomas A. McDannold, "Development of Los Angeles Chinatown: 1850–1970," M.A. thesis, California State University, Northridge, Department of Geography, 1973, 53. Also see Ichiro M. Murase, *Little Tokyo: One Hundred Years in Pictures* (Los Angeles: Visual Communications, 1983), 9, and Masakazu Iwata, "The Japanese Immigrants in California Agriculture," *Agricultural History* 36 (January 1962), 27–28.

24. Donna Graves, "Los Angeles' City Market: An Historic Cultural Resource," unpublished report, 1989, 4.

25. Ibid., 5.

26. Ibid., 5–6. Also see "City Market," Historic Resources Inventory, Department of Parks and Recreation, State of California.

27. Mark Singer, "The Chinos' Artful Harvest," *The New Yorker* (November 30, 1992), 142–156.

28. Dick Mount, ed., "Los Angeles Terminal Markets" (Los Angeles: Associated Produce Dealers and Brokers of Los Angeles, 1969); "City Market."

29. Yee, "The Chinese," 41.

30. Donna Graves notes that this firm was founded in 1889 and is "the oldest continually operating architectural firm in Los Angeles." Octavius Morgan emigrated from England and came to Los Angeles in 1873. He was in partnership with E. P. Kysor, and then with J. A. Walls during the City Market's design and construction. Later the firm was Morgan Walls and Clemens. Graves, "Los Angeles' City Market," 9–10.

31. Drummond Buckley, "Context Statement: History and Historic Preservation in Chinese American Los Angeles," unpublished paper, UCLA, 1989, figure 13.

32. Landmark designation might affect their ability to dispose of their property as commercial real estate; they wish to remain viable as a social and economic institution. Donna Graves and Christine MacPherson, interviews with Peter Fleming, 1989 and 1991.

33. Noritaka Yagasaki, "Ethnic Cooperativism and Immigrant Agriculture: A Study of Japanese Floriculture and Truck Farming in California" (Ph.D. diss., Department of Geography, University of California, Berkeley, 1982), 412; Judy Liss, JoAnn Victor, and Vivian Rescalvo, "The Japanese Influence in Floriculture" (unpublished paper, 1983); parts of this section are drawn from Hayden, Dubrow, and Flynn, *Los Angeles: The Power of Place.*

34. Yagasaki argues that previous transcriptions of his name as Kamataro Endo are in error.

35. Yagasaki, "Ethnic Cooperativism and Immigrant Agriculture," 111.

36. Ibid., 152, 439.

37. Ibid., 411; Kuwahara, interview with the author, February 23, 1985.

38. Yagasaki, "Ethnic Cooperativism and Immigrant Agriculture," 412. For additional references see William M. Mason and John A. McKinstry, "The Japanese of Los Angeles," Los Angeles Museum of Natural History, Contribution no. 1 (1969); Iwata, "The Japanese Immigrants in California Agriculture," 27–28; and "Southern California Flower Market," Historic Resources Inventory, State of California, 1980.

39. Remi Nadeau, "When Doheny Struck Oil," *Westways* 52 (October 1960), 11.

40. Drummond Buckley, "City Oil Field" (unpublished paper, UCLA, 1988); John Condas, "The Early Oil Boom in L.A." (unpublished paper, UCLA, 1984); Charles Lockwood, "In the Los Angeles Oil Boom, Derricks Sprouted Like Trees," *Smithsonian* 11 (October 1980), 190; William Rintoul Spudding, "Oil in the Streets of Los Angeles," *Recollections of Pioneer Days in Los Angeles* (San Francisco: California Historical Society, 1976), 83–91. For comparison, Brian

Black, "Petrolia," *Landscape* 32 (1994), 42–48, covers the Pennsylvania oil boom after 1859.

41. R. E. Crowder, "L.A. City Oil Field," *California Oil Fields* 47 (1960–1961), 69; California State Mining Bureau, *Thirteenth Report of the State Mineralogist* (Sacramento, 1896), 579–581.

42. Charles Lockwood, "The Oil of L.A.," *New West* 4 (September 1979), 96.

43. *Los Angeles Times*, May 8, 1895, quoted in Buckley, "City Oil Field," 2–3.

44. Spudding, "Oil in the Streets," 89–90. Also see Kenny Franks and Paul F. Lambert, *Early California Oil: A Photographic History, 1865–1940* (College Station, Texas: Texas A & M University Press, 1985).

45. Spudding, "Oil in the Streets," 91.

46. *Los Angeles Times*, May 8, 1895; Franks and Lambert, *Early California Oil*, 75.

47. Nadeau, "When Doheny Struck Oil," 11.

48. Bertha H. Smith, "Emma A. Summers, Oil Operator," *Sunset* 2 (July 1912), 51; Lockwood, "In the Los Angeles Oil Boom," 196–197; Condas, "The Early Oil Boom," 13; and Buckley, "City Oil Field," 12.

49. Drummond Buckley, interview with Bruce Manley, April 29, 1988.

50. Rich Connell, "Clutter of Illegal Oil Wells of Little Interest in Barrio," *Los Angeles Times*, May 12, 1985, sec. 2, 1.

51. This section relies for background on Carolyn Patricia Flynn, "Pacific Ready-Cut Homes: Mass-Produced Bungalows in Los Angeles, 1908–1942" (M.A. thesis, UCLA, 1986). Also see *Pacific's Book of Homes: A Notable Exhibition of California Architecture* (Los Angeles: Pacific Ready-Cut Homes, Inc., 1925).

52. *Pacific's Book of Homes*, 1925. The firm used nonunion labor, to the ire of traditional building unions, and in some of its practices preceded the tactics of the Levitt firm after World War II.

53. For example, see Christine Frederick, *The New Housekeeping: Efficiency Studies in Home Management* (New York: Doubleday, Page and Company, 1914); and Lillian Gilbreth, *The Homemaker and Her Job* (New York, 1927).

54. Robert Winter, *The California Bungalow* (Los Angeles: Hennessey and Ingalls, Inc., 1980).

55. Carolyn Flynn, interview with Robert Butte, August 1985.

56. "A. J. Roberts Funeral Home Site," Historic Resources Inventory, State of California, 1980.

57. Arnett L. Heartsfield, Jr., *The Old Stentorians* (Santa Fe Springs, Calif.: Stockton Trade Press, 1974), 8–13. Rudolph Brown first called attention to all of Heartsfield's work in his unpublished 1983 paper, "The Stentorians and Stations No. 15 and 30." This section draws on his work and Hayden, Dubrow, and Flynn, *Los Angeles: The Power of Place.*

58. Several other Los Angeles fire stations have also been designated as landmarks. Fire Station No. 23 is advanced in its design of living and working quarters and is unique in its construction; No. 27 was the largest fire station west of the Mississippi when it was built in 1930; No. 1, which was built in 1940, is considered a sterling example of the streamline moderne; and the first fire station in Los Angeles is a part of the El Pueblo Historical Monument.

59. Also see Timothy Sales, "Blacks in Los Angeles: A Brief History of Central Avenue," Los Angeles *Conservancy* 11 (September–October 1989), 4–5; and Reginald Chapple, "Culture in the Midst," *L.A. Architect* (June 1992), 12. Both were students at UCLA who worked with The Power of Place.

60. Soja, *Postmodern Geographies,* is very good on this.

61. Michael Dear and Jennifer Wolch trace this in *Malign Neglect* (San Francisco: Jossey Bass, 1993).

62. Pierre Nora, "Between Memory and History: *Les Lieux de Mémoire,*" *Representations* 26 (Spring 1989), 7.

## 6 The View from Grandma Mason's Place

1. For a review of the black population in Los Angeles see J. Max Bond, "The Negro in Los Angeles" (Ph.D. dissertation, University of Southern California, 1936), 44; Emory J. Tolbert, *The UNIA and Black Los Angeles* (Los Angeles: UCLA Center for Afro-American Studies, 1980), 25–47; Lawrence B. de Graaf, "The City of Black Angels: Emergence of the Los Angeles Ghetto, 1890–1930," *Pacific Historical Review* 39 (August 1970), 323–352; Russell E. Belous, William M. Mason, and Burton A. Reiner, "Black Heritage at the Los Angeles County Museum of Natural History," Museum of Natural History, History Division *Bulletin* no. 5 (1969); William M. Mason and James Anderson, "Los Angeles' Black Heritage," Los Angeles County Museum of Natural History *Quarterly* 8 (Winter 1969–1970), 4–9; and Lonnie G. Bunch, *Black Angelenos: The Afro-American in Los Angeles, 1850–1950* (Los Angeles: California Afro-American Museum, 1988).

2. "Obituary," Los Angeles *Times,* January 16, 1891, and "Funeral Notice," Los Angeles *Times,* January 18, 1891; Kate Bradley Stovall, "The Negro Woman in Los Angeles," Los Angeles *Times,* February 12, 1909.

3. Elizabeth Jameson, "Toward a Multicultural History of Women in the Western United States (Review Essay)," *Signs: Journal of Women in Culture and Society* 13 (Summer 1988), 782. Jameson refers to Lenwood G. Davis, *The Black Woman*

in *American Society: A Selected Annotated Bibliography* (Boston: Hall, 1975), and, for an example of a well-known article, Lawrence B. de Graaf, "Race, Sex, and Region: Black Women in the American West, 1850–1920," *Pacific Historical Review* 49 (May 1980), 285–314. Also see Miriam Matthews, "The Negro in California from 1781 to 1910: An Annotated Bibliography," unpublished paper.

4. Stovall, "The Negro Woman"; Delilah L. Beasley, *The Negro Trail Blazers of California* (Los Angeles: no publisher, 1919); Barbara Jackson, "Biddy Mason: Pioneer (1818–1891)," unpublished paper delivered at a symposium, "The Life and Times of Biddy Mason," sponsored by The Power of Place, UCLA, November 21, 1987; Donna Mungen, *The Life and Times of Biddy Mason: From Slavery to Wealthy California Landowner* (Los Angeles: no publisher, 1976); Charlotta A. Bass, *Forty Years: Memoirs from the Pages of a Newspaper* (Los Angeles: Charlotta A. Bass, n.d. [1960?]); Susan M. Ruddick and Mary Beth Welch, "The Story of Biddy Mason," unpublished paper, 1984, UCLA Graduate School of Architecture and Urban Planning. Bunch, *Black Angelenos*, 14–18, follows the preceding ones in interpreting Mason while arguing that a wider look at her contemporaries is needed.

5. *Census of the City and County of Los Angeles, California, for the Year 1850* (Los Angeles: Times Mirror Press, 1929), analysis of Schedule 1. For a more general view, also see Barbara Laslett, "Household Structure on an American Frontier: Los Angeles, California, in 1850," *American Journal of Sociology* 81 (July 1975), 109.

6. Ward Ritchie, "Introduction," *The First Los Angeles City and County Directory*, 1872 (Los Angeles: Ward Ritchie Press, 1963), 9, 123; Belous, Mason, and Reiner, "Black Heritage," 46.

7. Robert M. Fogelson, *The Fragmented Metropolis: Los Angeles, 1850–1930* (Cambridge, Mass.: Harvard University Press, 1967); de Graaf, "City of Black Angels"; de Graaf, "Race, Sex, and Region"; Mason and Anderson, "Los Angeles' Black Heritage."

8. The place of Biddy Mason's birth is not known. The manuscript schedule of the 1860 census says Mississippi. The 1870 and 1880 schedules say Georgia. Population Schedules of the Eighth Census of the United States (1860), Reel 61; Ninth Census (1870), Reel 73; Tenth Census (1880), Reel 67 (Washington, D.C., National Archives and Records Service, General Services Administration, 1967). Beasley gave *both* Hancock County, Mississippi (on p. 90), and Hancock County, Georgia (on p. 106). Matthews and Mason say Georgia; Jackson and Bunch say Mississippi. (Bunch's suggestion that Mississippi was part of Georgia does not apply in 1818.) Biddy Mason's obituary gave her birthplace as Hancock County, Georgia (Los Angeles *Times*, January 16, 1891).

9. District Court, First Judicial District, Habeas Corpus, In the Matter of Hannah, Biddy and Others, Order, Certified Copy (Slave Papers, Biddy Mason and Children, 1856), photostat copy (from handwritten copy owned by Gladys Owens Smith, Los Angeles), Golden State Mutual Life Insurance collection, UCLA Special Collections. This collection also includes photostats of her deeds and her will and copies of photographs gathered by Miriam Matthews. On nursing, see Mungen, *Life and Times*, 1.

10. Jacqueline Jones, *Labor of Love, Labor of Sorrow: Black Women, Work and the Family from Slavery to the Present* (New York: Vintage, 1985), 11–43, emphasizes the importance of slaves' childbearing to their masters' wealth.

11. Dolores Hayden, *Seven American Utopias: The Architecture of Communitarian Socialism, 1790–1975* (Cambridge, Mass.: MIT Press, 1976), 141–143, gives details of the settlement of Deseret.

12. John Zimmerman Brown, ed., *Autobiography of Pioneer John Brown (1820–1896)* (Salt Lake City: privately printed, 1941), 88–102. For an exact count of the party, 96. For a popular, illustrated account of a parallel trail, see John G. Mitchell, "On the Seacoast of Nebraska," *Audubon* 91 (May 1989), 56–76.

13. Jackson, "Biddy Mason," refers to Hannah as Biddy's sister, but Mason's descendant, Linda Cox, in a personal communication to Hayden, March 1989, said the family is unclear about the relationship, but thinks Hannah was at most a half-sister.

14. Brown, *Autobiography*, 94, 99, 101.

15. Jackson, "Biddy Mason," 2.

16. Leonard J. Arrington and Davis Bitton, *The Mormon Experience: A History of the Latter-day Saints* (New York: Knopf, 1979), 199.

17. The Mormons outlined a prospective State of Deseret including not only Utah but large portions of Nevada, Arizona, New Mexico, and southern California. See Hayden, *Seven American Utopias*, 108; Warren A. Beck and Ynez D. Haase, "The Mormon Empire," *Historical Atlas of the American West* (Norman: University of Oklahoma Press, 1989), 39.

18. "Suit for Freedom," Los Angeles *Star*, February 2, 1856. In addition to Charles, Hannah's son born in Utah about 1850, Hannah gave birth to two girls in San Bernardino, Marion about 1852 and Martha about 1854. Hannah was pregnant again in 1855, and bore a boy in the first week of January 1856.

19. Stovall, "The Negro Woman." On free blacks in California towns, Rudolf M. Lapp, *Blacks in Gold Rush California* (New Haven: Yale University Press, 1977); Vivian B. Octavia, *The Story of the Negro in Los Angeles* (San Francisco: R. and E. Research, 1936). On the arrival date, Mason obituary in Los Angeles *Times*.

20. Richard R. Powell, *Compromises of Conflicting Claims: A Century of California Law, 1760–1860* (Dobbs Ferry, N.Y.: Oceana, 1977), 210.

21. In the Matter of Carter Perkins and Robert S. Perkins, *Reports of Cases, Supreme Court, State of California, 1852* (San Francisco: Bancroft-Whitney, 1906), 424–459; In the Matter of Archy, *Reports of Cases, Supreme Court, State of California, 1858* (San Francisco: Bancroft-Whitney, 1906), 148–171.

22. Quoted in Beasley, *Negro Trail Blazers*, 88.

23. Robert Curry Owens, "My Grandfather," typescript, 1930, UCLA Special Collections, 2.

24. Ibid., 1–3.

25. "Suit for Freedom," Los Angeles *Star*, February 2, 1856. This article (unsigned) is a full account of the case and the legal arguments supporting the decision by Judge Hayes.

26. Stovall, "The Negro Woman."

27. "Suit for Freedom," Los Angeles *Star*.

28. Ibid.

29. Ibid.

30. Ibid.

31. Ibid.

32. Ibid.

33. Ibid.

34. Jones, *Labor of Love*, 11–43.

35. Powell, *Compromises*, 210.

36. "Suit for Freedom," Los Angeles *Star*.

37. Ibid.

38. Ibid.

39. Ibid.

40. District Court, "In the matter of Hannah, Biddy and others."

41. In the Matter of Carter Perkins; In the Matter of Archy. Also see Howard Zinn, "Slavery without Submission," *A People's History of the United States* (New York: Harper and Row, 1980), 182.

42. "Suit for Freedom," Los Angeles *Star*.

43. Jackson, "Biddy Mason," 3. She says Lyman led them to San Bernardino. He was also with Biddy Mason's group going to Salt Lake. See Brown, *Autobiography*, 99–100. Lyman was in command of the first fifty; Biddy Mason was in the fourth ten, led by Brown, of the first fifty.

44. Laurel Thatcher Ulrich, *A Midwife's Tale: The Life of Martha Ballard, Based on Her Diary, 1785–1812*, (New York: Knopf, 1991), 62–64.

45. Los Angeles *Star*, May 14, 1859.

46. Jackson, "Biddy Mason," 3.

47. Ludwig Louis Salvator, *Los Angeles in the Sunny Seventies*, 1878, tr. M. E. Wilbur (Los Angeles: Zeitlin, 1929), 121. Harris Newmark also mentions her, according to de Graaf, "Race, Sex, and Region," 301, footnote 52.

48. Martia Graham Goodson, "Medical-Botanical Contributions of African Slave Women to American Medicine," *Western Journal of Black Studies* 11 (1987), 198–203.

49. Ibid., 198, 200–202.

50. Ibid., 200.

51. Linda Holmes, "Medical History: Alabama Granny Midwife," *Journal of the Medical Society of New Jersey* 81 (May 1984), 390.

52. Judy Barrett Litoff, *American Midwives: 1860 to the Present* (Westport, Conn.: Greenwood, 1978); Richard W. Wertz and Dorothy C. Wertz, *Lying-In: A History of Childbirth in America* (New York: Schocken, 1979); Debra Anne Susie, *In the Way of Our Grandmothers: A Cultural View of Twentieth-Century Midwifery in Florida* (Athens, Ga.: University of Georgia Press, 1988); Jacqueline Jones Royster, *Women as Healers: A Noble Tradition* (Atlanta, Ga.: Spelman College, 1983); Judith W. Leavitt, *Brought to Bed: Childbearing in America, 1750–1950* (New York: Oxford University Press, 1986).

53. Mungen, *Life and Times*, 4. On wages, see de Graaf, "Race, Sex, and Region," 299.

54. Holmes, "Medical History," 390.

55. Ibid.

56. Ibid. Barbara Ehrenreich and Deirdre English, *Witches, Midwives and Nurses: A History of Women Healers* (Old Westbury, N.Y.: Feminist Press, 1973), recount the midwives' professional struggles; Carolyn Conant Van Blarcom, "Rat Pie: Among the Black Midwives of the South," *Harper's* 160 (February 1930), 322–332, gives a condescending look at Virginia's "granny midwives."

57. Annie Mae Hunt, "It Wasn't No More Than Three Dollars to Catch a Baby," excerpt from Ruth Winegarten, ed., *I am Annie Mae* (Austin: Rosegarden Press, 1983), rpt. in Nancy Caldwell Sorel, ed., *Ever since Eve: Personal Reflections on Childbirth* (New York: Oxford University Press, 1984), 188–189. Also see Fran Leeper Buss, *La Partera: Story of a Midwife* (Ann Arbor, Mich.: University of Michigan Press, 1980), and Janice L. Reiff, Michael Dablin, and Daniel Smith, "Rural Push and Urban Pull: Work and Family Experiences of Older Black Women in Southern Cities, 1800–1900," *Journal of Social History* 15 (Summer 1983), 39–48.

58. Joan M. Jensen and Darlis A. Miller, "The Gentle Tamers Revisited: New Approaches to the History of Women in the American West," *Pacific Historical Review* 49 (May 1980), 198–199; also see Chris Rigby Arrington, "Pioneer Midwives," in Claudia L. Bushman, ed., *Mormon Sisters: Women in Early Utah* (Cambridge, Mass.: Harvard Univ. Press, 1976), 43–66.

59. Jensen and Miller, "Gentle Tamers Revisited," 201.

60. De Graaf, "Race, Sex, and Region," 303. The first black woman earned a medical degree in 1864, and the first earned a nursing degree in 1879, according to Royster, *Women as Healers*, 17.

61. Jensen and Miller, "Gentle Tamers Revisited," 184; also see Richard Griswold del Castillo, "La Familia Chicana: Social Changes in the Chicano Family of Los Angeles, 1850–1880," *Journal of Ethnic Studies* 3 (Spring 1975), 41–58.

62. De Graaf, "Race, Sex, and Region," 287–289.

63. Beasley, *Negro Trail Blazers*, 109.

64. Robert Curry Owens, "Robert C. Owens (Autobiography)," typescript, UCLA Special Collections, 1–3. Beasley *Negro Trail Blazers*, 110, dates the marriage October 16, 1856. Robert was born in 1860.

65. Ibid., 3; Beasley, *Negro Trail Blazers*, 109–110. Biddy's daughter Ann died in 1857; Harriet remained in Los Angeles.

66. This photograph is identified by Miriam Matthews's handwriting on the label. The fencing matches the Owens's house exactly and suggests it was close by. Census data and city directories also suggest this, though street numbers were not used consistently.

67. William L. Kahrl, *Water and Power: The Conflict over Los Angeles' Water Supply in the Owens Valley* (Berkeley: University of California Press, 1982), 9–17.

68. Deed, November 28, 1866, William M. Buffum and James F. Burns to Biddy Mason, copy at UCLA Special Collections.

69. Beasley, *Negro Trail Blazers*, 90.

70. The Pierce photo is in UCLA Special Collections; on the *zanjas* and fence, see Beasley, *Negro Trail Blazers*, 109. The city directories give the following residential addresses for Biddy Mason:

| | |
|---|---|
| 1872 (or 1873) | 1st Street Below Main |
| 1875 | no listing |
| 1878 | rear 155 Spring |
| 1879–80 | no listing |
| 1880–81 | no listing |
| 1883 | 108 Fort St. |
| 1884–5 | 237 S. Spring St. (later renumbered as 331–5; this is her homestead) |

| | |
|---|---|
| 1886–7 | no listing |
| 1887–8 | no listing |
| 1888 | no listing |
| 1890 | 235 S. Spring |
| 1891 | no listing |

71. Ritchie, "Introduction," *The First Los Angeles City and County Directory, 1872*, 9.

72. Ibid., 122.

73. Ibid.

74. Deed, Biddy Mason to J. H. Jones and Charles M. Wright, January 2, 1875, Los Angeles County Recorder's Office; Sanborn Map, Los Angeles, 1888, Map Library, California State University, Northridge.

75. Sanborn Map, 1888. A photo of her building in 1904 was published in *The Liberator* (Los Angeles) 5 (March 1904), 1.

76. Sanborn Map, Los Angeles, 1894, Map Library, California State University, Northridge.

77. Owens, "Robert C. Owens," 3; Deed, Biddy Mason to Robert C. Owens and Henry L. Owens, June 20, 1890, Los Angeles County Recorder's Office.

78. Owens, "Robert C. Owens," 3.

79. Beasley, *Negro Trail Blazers*, 109; Kathy Perkins, FAME Historical Committee, personal communication, June 1988, noted that Mason continued to attend the white Fort Street Methodist Church at times. Since California law began to segregate churches in this era, and required that blacks attend only churches founded by them (Powell, *Compromises*, 210), Mason's continued attendance at a white church could have been a political protest. For a general overview of early black churches, see Edward D. Smith, *Climbing Jacob's Ladder: The Rise of Black Churches in Eastern American Cities, 1740–1877* (Washington, D.C.: Smithsonian Institution Press, 1988).

80. Ruddick and Welch, "Story," 13.

81. Ibid., 17; Beasley, *Negro Trail Blazers*, 109.

82. Stovall, "The Negro Woman"; "Funeral Notice."

83. De Graaf, "Race, Sex, and Region," 301.

84. Bunch, *Black Angelenos.* Also see Mason and Anderson, "Los Angeles' Black Heritage".

85. "Negro Will Build Block," *Los Angeles Daily Times*, August 12, 1905.

86. Ibid. Robert C. Owens suffered financial reverses in the Depression and shot himself and other family members, according to Gladys Owens Smith, interview on "Black Angelenos," KCET, 1988.

87. Sue Bailey Thurman, *Pioneers of Negro Origin in California* (San Francisco: Acme, 1952), 47.

88. Jared Eliot, *The Blessings Bestowed on Them That Fear God* (New London: 1739), quoted in Ulrich, *A Midwife's Tale*, 97.

## 7 Rediscovering an African American Homestead

1. Marvin Brown, Robert Chattel, Dan Hoye, and Richard Rowe, *Palaces of Finance: A Walking Tour of the Spring Street Historic District* (Los Angeles: Los Angeles Conservancy, 1983).

2. Mark Irwin, John Miller, and Susan Richey, *Broadway Historic Theatre District* (Los Angeles: Los Angeles Conservancy, 1986).

3. Community Redevelopment Agency of the City of Los Angeles, *Status of Development Projects*, September 1986 (flyer).

4. Brown, Chattel, Hoye, and Rowe, *Palaces of Finance.*

5. See Timothy Sales, "Blacks in Los Angeles: A Brief History of Central Avenue," Los Angeles Conservancy *Newsletter* (1989), 4–5; and "Ode to Central Avenue: Resource Materials" (accompanying the film with the same title), Los Angeles History Project, KCET, 1989, which includes some of Sales's materials prepared for The Power of Place.

6. Prodded by Robert Chattel, the developers of the project (Robert Silberman of Allied Parking Ltd., Art Lumer of L&R Auto Parks, and Thomas Phillips of System Parking Investments, Inc.) agreed to include two installations by The Power of Place, in addition to other art they had planned for the building. The developers' art consultant, Michelle Isenberg, proved to be an enthusiastic promoter of our efforts as well as an experienced problem solver who worked well with huge public agencies, corporate developers, and individual artists.

7. Donna Graves and I had attended dozens if not hundreds of meetings with the members of our own team as well as with various city officials, city agencies, lawyers, developers' representatives, and contractors to ensure that the project was on track. Susan A. Grode volunteered her legal expertise to negotiate our final three-way contract. The CRA owned the land, the developers owned the buildings, and The Power of Place owned the art on site, so we essentially had to become noprofit developers ourselves to finish the on-site parts of our project.

8. Susan Ruddick and Mary Beth Welch, graduate students at UCLA, had researched some of the existing work on Biddy Mason in 1985. I began to make

a much more thorough examination of sources in 1987, helped by Drummond Buckley.

9. Lonnie G. Bunch, *Black Angelenos: The Afro-American in Los Angeles, 1850–1950,* exhibit catalogue (Los Angeles: California Afro-American Museum, 1988).

10. "The Life and Times of Biddy Mason," November 21, 1987, UCLA. This and all subsequent workshop quotations are transcribed from the audiotape.

11. Dolores Hayden, "Biddy Mason's Los Angeles, 1856–1891," *California History* 68 (Fall 1989), 86–98.

12. Poster text by Dolores Hayden.

13. The book included text by Susan King as well as passages from Hayden, "Biddy Mason's Los Angeles" and some additional research by Donna Graves. King's other collaborators included Wesley B. Tanner, a letterpress printer in Berkeley, and Klaus Rotzcher, a bookbinder in San Francisco, who executed the Japanese side stab binding and portfolio King designed.

14. I wrote the text for the wall; John Hogue, a concrete specialist, helped to construct the intricate web of metal letters, debossed images, slate, limestone, and granite panels de Bretteville designed; Chris Steinauer, a letter cutter, incised text on slate panels.

## 8 Reinterpreting Latina History at the Embassy Auditorium

1. The project was partly inspired by the work of the first historian recruited for the team, Vicki L. Ruiz, then professor of history at the University of California, Davis, and author of a moving account of the organization of UCAPAWA, including the roles played by Luisa Moreno and other organizers: *Cannery Women, Cannery Lives: Mexican Women, Unionization, and the California Food Processing Industry, 1930–1950* (Albuquerque: University of New Mexico Press, 1987).

2. Los Angeles, Cultural Heritage Board, "Historic-Cultural Monument Declaration: Embassy Hotel and Auditorium," submitted by Los Angeles Conservancy (June 1983); "Trinity Methodist Episcopal Church, South," Historic Resources Inventory, State of California, 1980.

3. The Embassy Auditorium was designed to generate cash flow for the Trinity Methodist Church while addressing the needs of Angelenos for an urban approach to salvation. "The world wants an electric-lighted, self-starting, eight-cylinder church," claimed pastor Charles C. Selecman, whose rhetoric jump-started its opening in 1914. "Trinity—An All-Around Church," *Independent* 84 (October 25, 1915), 154; Jennifer Schroeder, "Embassy Theater," unpublished paper, 1990, UCLA Graduate School of Architecture and Urban Planning.

According to the program of Trinity United Methodist Church of Los Angeles's *Trinity Jubilee Celebration*, June 10, 1973 (Los Angeles Central Library, California Collection), Selecman's congregation erected its first church in 1875 on First and Spring streets. They moved south twice to escape the growth of the commercial center. To launch this million-dollar high-rise cathedral to "everyday Christianity," Selecman's predecessor, Reverend R. P. Howell, demolished the existing church at Ninth and Grand in 1912 and arranged for the congregation to worship at the Temple B'nai B'rith while new construction proceeded. But Selecman's group couldn't make it financially and moved to other quarters.

4. "Trinity Auditorium," advertisement, *Los Angeles City Directory*, 1916, 34.

5. Rodolfo Acuña, *Occupied America: A History of Chicanos* (New York: Harper and Row, 1981), 317; Leobardo Arroyo, "Industrial Unionism and the Los Angeles Furniture Industry, 1818–1954," Ph.D. dissertation, UCLA, Department of History, 1979, 290; Ronald Brooks, "Embasssy Theater," unpublished paper, UCLA, 1983, cites the Embassy Auditorium Log Books, 1947–1949, which he found in the building but are now lost.

6. On Moreno, in addition to Ruiz, *Cannery Workers*, see Mario T. García, *Mexican Americans: Leadership, Ideology and Identity, 1930–1960* (New Haven: Yale University Press, 1989). García also discusses Fierro de Bright. For a contemporary's view of their leadership, see Mario T. García's oral history, *Memories of Chicano History: The Life and Narrative of Bert Corona* (Berkeley: University of California Press, 1993). On Pesotta, see Elaine Leeder, *The Gentle General: Rose Pesotta, Anarchist and Labor Organizer* (Ithaca: SUNY Press, 1993); John H. M. Laslett, "Gender, Class, or Ethno-Cultural Struggle? The Problematic Relationship between Rose Pesotta and the ILGWU," *California History* 72 (Spring 1993), 20–39.

7. "Garment Workers' Strike—1933," Historic Resources Inventory, State of California, 1980; George Sánchez, "'An Injury to One Is an Injury to All': Labor Organizing and Mexican Women Workers in Los Angeles, 1930–1950," unpublished paper commissioned by The Power of Place, 1991.

8. Rose Pesotta, *Bread upon the Waters* (New York: Dodd Mead, 1944); manuscript letter to David Dubinsky, September 30, 1933, ILGWU Archives.

9. Laslett, "Gender, Class, or Ethno-Cultural Struggle?," 31.

10. Leeder, *The Gentle General*, xi–xii.

11. García, *Memories of Chicano History*, 108–128.

12. Ibid., 109. Variations of this organization's name exist.

13. Ibid., 120–123.

14. Ruiz and Sánchez think Moreno was deported; García and Bert Corona think she left during attempts to deport her. See Luisa Moreno Bemis, "Address" to the Twelfth Annual Convention, California CIO Council, October 15, 1949.

15. "La fuerza de unión," audiotape, The Power of Place. All subsequent quotations from the workshop are from this tape.

16. Much of the published work on these three women has come out since the workshop, including George J. Sánchez, *Becoming Mexican American: Ethnicity, Culture, and Identity in Chicano Los Angeles, 1900–1945* (New York: Oxford University Press, 1993), 227–252; Laslett, "Gender, Class, or Ethno-Cultural Struggle?,"; García, *Memories of Chicano History*; Leeder, *The Gentle General*.

17. Donna Graves resigned as project director right after the workshop in the spring of 1991. As the person who had spent two years planning and administering the project, she was irreplaceable. As the organization's president, I had to take over her job and try to wrap the project up with the help of Nancy Stillger. Funding for the showcases was raised from the Rockefeller Foundation and the Warhol Foundation in New York. The National Endowment for the Arts, the California Council on the Arts, and the Los Angeles Cultural Affairs Department had already committed funds to the poster and the book. The California Council for the Humanities supported the workshop.

**9 Remembering Little Tokyo on First Street**

1. Ichiro Mike Murase, *Little Tokyo: One Hundred Years in Pictures* (Los Angeles: Visual Communications, 1983), 11. This has an excellent introductory essay and a detailed bibliography in both English and Japanese. On the Japanese in Los Angeles also see Don and Nadine Hata, "The Far East Meets the Far West," *California History*, 60 (Spring 1981), 90; William M. Mason and John A. McKinstry, *The Japanese of Los Angeles, 1869–1920* (Los Angeles: County of Los Angeles, Museum of Natural History, 1969); Carey McWilliams, *Southern California: An Island on the Land* (Salt Lake City: Peregrine Smith Books, 1983); John Modell, *The Economics and Politics of Racial Accommodation: The Japanese of Los Angeles, 1900–1942* (Urbana: University of Illinois Press, 1977).

   On the first-generation immigrants (Issei) see Yuji Ichioka, *The Issei: The World of the First Generation Japanese Immigrants, 1885–1924* (New York: Free Press, 1988). Second-generation are Nisei; third-generation, Sansei. All people of Japanese descent are Nikkei. Little Tokyo is also called Japanese Town and J-Town (Murase, *Little Tokyo*, 23–24).

2. H. Cooke Sunoo, quoted in David Holley, "Old Temple, Church Symbolize Efforts to Preserve Little Tokyo," *Los Angeles Times*, September 4, 1985, II, 1.

3. Murase, *Little Tokyo*, 16. Also see Roger Daniels, *Asian America: Chinese and Japanese in the United States Since 1850* (Seattle: University of Washington Press, 1988); Ronald Takaki, *Strangers from a Different Shore: A History of Asian Americans* (New York: Penguin, 1990); Sucheng Chan, *Asian Americans: An Interpretive History* (Boston: Twayne Publishers, 1991).

4. See Maisie and Richard Conrat, *Executive Order 1066*, photographs by Dor-

othea Lange and others (Los Angeles: UCLA Asian American Studies Center, 1990). On the effects of the landscapes on the internees, and their impact on the surrounding environments, see Patricia Nelson Limerick, "Disorientation and Reorientation: The American Landscape Discovered from the West," *The Journal of American History* (December 1992), 1021–1049.

5. Itabari Njeri, "The Turning Point: Now That the Redress Issue Is Settled, Japanese Americans Are Confronting Questions on Their Culture's Future," *Los Angeles Times*, January 1, 1989, VI, 1.

6. Christopher Doi, Tom Fujita, Lewis Kawahara, Brian Nuva, and Karen Umemoto, "Little Tokyo Redevelopment: The North Side of First Street," unpublished paper for Asian-American Studies 200C, UCLA, June 20, 1986, 31.

7. "Japanese Americans in the Flower Fields and the Flower Market," tape from public history workshop, The Power of Place, February 23, 1985.

8. A brief account of his life is Teresa Austin, "Kuwahara Grew Up with Little Tokyo," Los Angeles *Downtown News*, March 20, 1989, 1.

9. Donna Graves et al., "City Market," application for Los Angeles Historic Cultural Landmark, from the files of The Power of Place. We were persuaded not to pursue this.

10. As an individual, I had served on the jury for the architectural competition run by MOCA and the CRA and become aware of the dangers of bypassing Japanese American community organizations' own desires for the area, and the need for Japanese American architects and artists to participate in decision making. For a critical review of the CRA's real estate development activities, see Mike Davis, "The Infinite Game: Redeveloping Downtown L.A.," in Diane Ghirardo, ed., *Out of Site: A Social Criticism of Architecture* (Seattle: Bay Press, 1991), 77–113.

11. There are four noncontributing buildings out of thirteen. "Little Tokyo Historic District," National Register of Historic Places Inventory-Nomination Form, prepared by Los Angeles Conservancy volunteers and Little Tokyo Advisory Committee, October 1986.

12. Michael Tanji, "Union Church of Los Angeles," Historic Resources Inventory, Department of Parks and Recreation, State of California, March 1980.

13. Susan Sztaray, "A Proposal for Public Art: Little Tokyo's Historic District," unpublished paper, March 12, 1989, UCLA Graduate School of Architecture and Urban Planning. She is also the author of *Little Tokyo: A Walking Tour Sponsored by the Los Angeles Conservancy* (Los Angeles: Los Angeles Conservancy, 1992).

14. National Register Inventory-Nomination Form; National Landmark nomination, Gloria H. L. Uchida, letter to the author, May 1, 1993.

15. John J. Miyauchi, "We're Here," brochure of the Japanese American National

Museum, quoted in *Cultural and Ethnic Diversity in Historic Preservation*, Information series No. 65 (Washington D.C.: National Trust for Historic Preservation, 1992), 19; "Things That Make Us Unique and Yet So American," *L.A. Architect* (June 1992), 11.

## 10 Storytelling with the Shapes of Time

1. Jeremy Brecher, *History from Below: How to Uncover and Tell the Story of Your Community, Association, or Union* (New Haven: Commonwork Pamphlets/ Advocate Press, 1986), is a valuable guide to this process. Dolores Root, *Special Places* (South Hadley, Mass.: Massachusetts Foundation for the Humanities), suggests many ways to develop grant proposals and projects that engage people in discovering their local places. Randolph Hester, *Community Design Primer* (Mendocino, Calif.: Ridge Time, 1990) may be helpful to designers and planners learning about process.

2. Rosalyn Driscoll, "The Place of Imagination," *Places* 7 (Winter 1990), 87–91, discusses mapping in a Vermont town. For a British example of a project that used artists to create local maps, see "Knowing Your Place: An exhibition of Artists' Parish Maps," poster by David Holmes (London: Common Ground, 1985). An urban atlas for St. Paul on GIS is under way by Roger Miller.

3. These projects are discussed in Chapter 3 of this book; for citations, see notes 7 and 13 of that chapter.

## Epilogue: Los Angeles after April 29, 1992

1. Staff of the Los Angeles *Times*, *Understanding the Riots: Los Angeles before and after the Rodney King Case* (Los Angeles: Times Mirror, 1992); R. Gooding-Williams, ed., *Reading Rodney King, Reading Urban Uprising* (New York: Routledge, 1993); Maria Rosario Jackson, James H. Johnson, Jr., Walter C. Farrell, Jr., "After the Smoke Has Cleared: An Analysis of Selected Responses to the Los Angeles Civil Unrest of 1992," *Contention* 3 (Spring 1994), 3–21; Allen J. Scott and E. Richard Brown, eds., *South Central Los Angeles: Anatomy of an Urban Crisis* (Los Angeles: Lewis Center for Regional Policy Studies, UCLA, 1993).

2. Jackson, Johnson, and Farrell, "After the Smoke Has Cleared," 5.

3. "The Dialog Begins," *L.A. Architect* (June 1992), 6–7.

4. The Labor/Community Strategy Center, *Reconstructing Los Angeles from the Bottom Up: A Long Term Strategy for Workers, Low-Income People, and People of Color to Create an Alternative Vision of Urban Development* (Los Angeles: The Labor/Community Strategy Center, n.d.); Paul Feldman, "Another RLA Co-Chair to Step Down," Los Angeles *Times*, January 13, 1994, B-1. Ueberroth and co-chair Barry Sanders were replaced by Bernard Kinsey, who stepped down in

January 1994. Linda Griego took over; see Calvin Sims, "Who Said Los Angeles Could Be Rebuilt in a Day?," New York *Times*, May 22, 1994, sec. 3, 5.

5. Bernard Kinsey, "We've Got to Make This City Work," Los Angeles *Times*, January 12, 1994, B-7.

6. Henry G. Cisneros, ed., *Interwoven Destinies: Cities and the Nation* (New York: Norton, 1993), 38–39; Mike Davis, "Who Killed L.A.? The War against the Cities," *Crossroads* (June 1993), 2–19.

7. Scott and Brown, *South Central*, 5, estimate that Latinos will comprise 44 percent of Los Angeles in 2000, ahead of Anglos at 31 percent.

8. Keith H. Basso, "Stalking with Stories: Names, Places, and Moral Narratives among the Western Apache," in Daniel Halperin, ed., *On Nature: Nature, Landscape, and Natural History* (San Francisco: North Point Press, 1987), 99–102, 112, 115.

9. T. H. Breen, *Imagining the Past: East Hampton Histories* (Reading, Mass.: Addison Wesley, 1989), xiii.

10. Susan Porter Benson, Stephen Brier, and Roy Rosenzweig, eds., introduction to *Presenting the Past: Essays on History and the Public* (Philadelphia: Temple University Press, 1986), xxiii–xxiv; Michael Frisch, "The Memory of History," ibid., 17.

# Index